ECDL

EUROPEAN COMPUTER DRIVING LICENCE

Module AM4 Spreadsheets (Advanced Level)

Matthew Strawbridge

www.payne-gallway.co.uk

Published by Payne-Gallway Publishers
Payne-Gallway is an imprint of Harcourt Education Ltd., Halley Court, Jordan Hill,
Oxford, OX2 8EJ
Tel: 01865 888070
Fax: 01865 314029
E-mail: orders@payne-gallway.co.uk
Web: www.payne-gallway.co.uk

First published 2006

10 09 08 07 06 05
10 9 8 7 6 5 4 3 2 1

British Library Cataloguing in Publication Data is available from the British Library on request

10-digit ISBN: 1 904467 89 X
13-digit ISBN: 97 1 904467 89 X

Copyright notice

Design and Typesetting by Direction Marketing and Communications Ltd.

Printed by Printer Trento S.r.l

With thanks to Dr Cristopher Sheasby for his help with testing the exercises.

Ordering Information

You can order from:
Payne-Gallway
FREEPOST (OF1771),
PO Box 381, Oxford OX2 8BR

Tel: 01865 888070
Fax: 01865 314029
E-mail: orders@payne-gallway.co.uk
Web: www.payne-gallway.co.uk

Contents

Preface

Who is this book for?

This book is suitable for anyone studying for **ECDL Advanced Syllabus v1.0 Module 4: Spreadsheets**, whether at school, in an adult class, or at home. Students are expected to have a level of knowledge of Microsoft Excel equivalent to the basic-level ECDL Spreadsheets module.

The approach

The approach is very much one of learning by doing. Students are guided step by step through creating real spreadsheets, with numerous screenshots showing exactly what should appear on the screen at each stage.

Chapter 1 covers topics that are not explicitly in the ECDL syllabus, but which are either important foundation topics or useful productivity tips.

In subsequent chapters, syllabus topics are introduced naturally whenever they are needed in the current document. This helps to demonstrate **why**, as well as **how**, to use these advanced features. Each of these chapters ends with a **Test Yourself** section, which contains exercises that consolidate the skills learned in that chapter.

Software used

For this module you will be using **Microsoft Excel**, one of many spreadsheet packages. **Excel 2003** has been used in this book, but you should still be able to follow the book (with a little common sense) if you are using a different version of Excel.

Chapter 15 (Linking) also requires **Microsoft Word**, since it covers how to link data created in Excel into a Word document.

Extra resources

The exercises have been designed so that you do not need to load documents from CD or the Internet – you create the documents as you go along. The one exception to this is the large worksheet **videoshop.xls**, which is used throughout the book: it would be impractical to ask you to create this from scratch, so instead you should download it from the publisher's website: www.payne-gallway.co.uk/ecdl. This also contains lots of other useful supporting material.

1 Basic Concepts

Introduction

This introductory chapter follows a slightly different format from those that follow: there is much more information, and there are fewer practical steps for you to perform.

However, this chapter provides a solid foundation for the more advanced topics. I think you will find that it is well worth the effort you make to carefully read and remember the information presented here. Although you won't be tested directly on most of the tools and techniques in this chapter, a thorough knowledge of them will make you a more productive user of Excel.

In this chapter you will

- learn what is meant by some of the **terms** that will be referred to throughout this book
- learn the use of each of the commands on the basic toolbars: the **Menu** bar, the **Standard** toolbar, and the **Formatting** toolbar
- learn about the information displayed on the **status bar**
- get a useful list of **keyboard shortcuts**
- learn some **time-saving tips**.

Common terms

Names of keys

This book assumes that you are familiar with the names of the keys on the computer keyboard. Where it is necessary to press a combination of keys to run a particular command, a plus sign is used in the text; for example, you can copy text by pressing **Ctrl+C** (meaning you must hold down the **Ctrl** key while you tap **C**).

Workbooks and worksheets

A **workbook** is the actual spreadsheet file. A workbook can contain one or more **worksheets** – independent pages that can be named. By default, when you create a new blank **workbook** it will contain three **worksheets**: **Sheet1**, **Sheet2** and **Sheet3**.

Graphical user interface

Figure 1.1 gives the names of some of the **graphical user interface** (**GUI**) elements that will be referred to throughout the rest of this book. It is well worth getting used to calling these things by their correct names, so that you will be able to better communicate with other people when asking for or providing help.

There is an important distinction between the **mouse pointer** (which moves around the screen as you move your mouse) and the **text insertion point** (which is the marker for the location at which any text you type will appear, and is set by clicking the mouse or using the arrow keys on your keyboard).

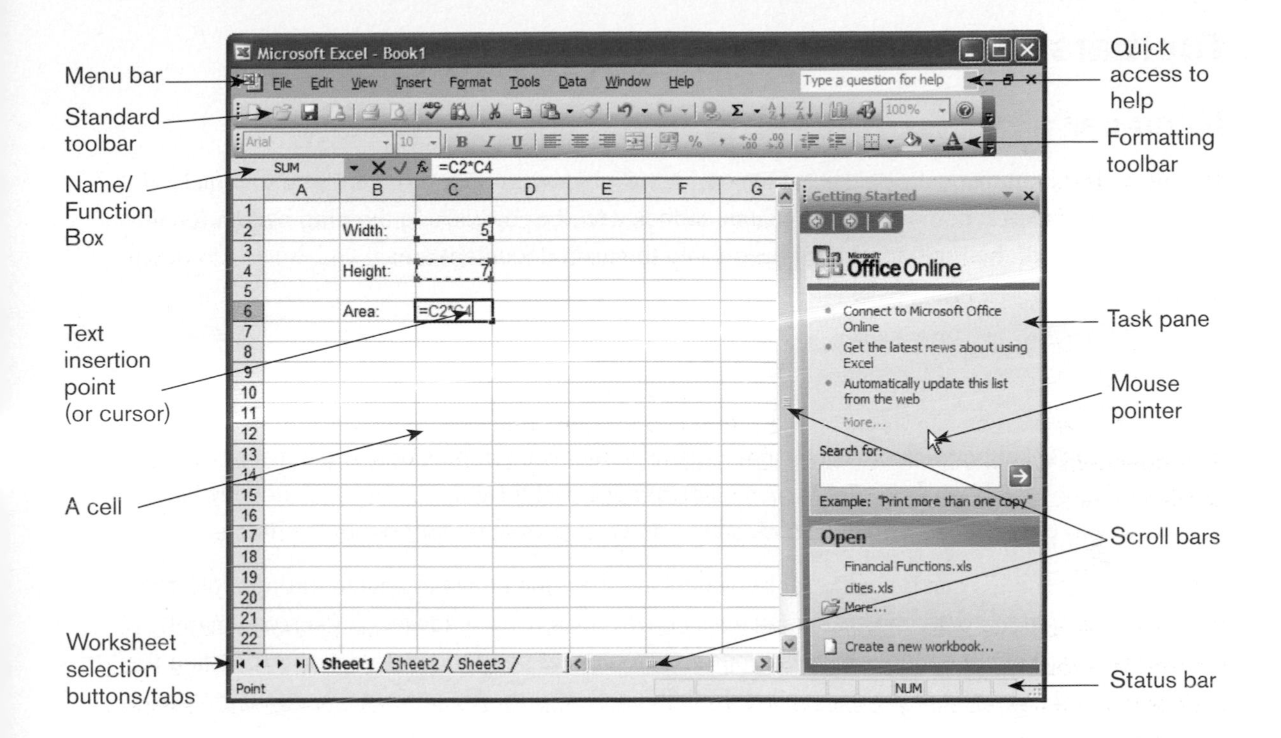

Figure 1.1: Names for parts of Microsoft Excel

Cell references

There are two types of cell reference – relative and absolute.

A **relative reference** is the default, and it takes the form **B6**, where **B** is the column and **6** is the row. Suppose you enter the formula **=B6+1** into cell **A6**. If you then copy the formula and paste it into cell **A7** then Excel will change the formula to **=B7+1** for you – it translates the relative position of the cells you have referred to.

In an **absolute reference**, you fix the column or the row by preceding it with a dollar symbol (**$**). You can fix just the column, just the row or both. For instance, using the example given in the previous paragraph, if the formula had been **=B$6+1** then the pasted formula would still be **=B$6+1**. Similarly **=$B$6** would be preserved as **=$B$6**. However **=$B6** would become **=$B7**, since only the column would be locked.

If you need to use an absolute reference to a single cell then you should consider naming the cell and using the name instead of the reference in your formula. Chapter 4 explains how to name cells and ranges of cells (see page 50).

Toolbars

Menu bar

The **Menu bar** is traditionally docked at the top of the window, although you are free to move it if you wish (this is not recommended). You can undock a toolbar by clicking the drag handle (vertical dots) on the left of the toolbar and dragging it into the main document area.

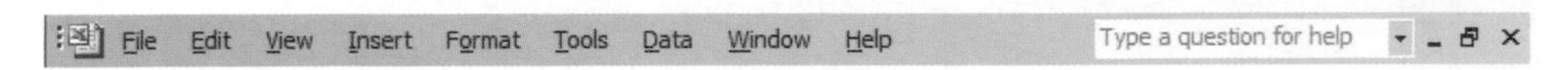

Figure 1.2: Menu bar

By default, Excel keeps track of which menu options you use most often and customises the menus to match. Figure 1.3(a) shows a **Tools** menu with options that have not been used recently hidden from view – to get to these, you must click on the down arrows at the bottom of the menu.

These dynamic menus can be useful for beginners, so they don't have to search through lots of commands to find the ones they use frequently. However, as a more advanced user, you might find it simpler to have the menus always expanded. You never need to waste a click expanding the menus, and the positions of the commands don't keep changing. You can set this up as follows:

 Start Excel, if you haven't already done so.

 Right-click anywhere in the **Menu bar**, then select **Customize**. The **Customize** dialogue appears, as shown in Figure 1.4.

 Click on the **Options** tab to display it, then make sure that **Always show full menus** is ticked.

 While you've got this dialogue open, you will probably find it useful to make sure that **Show Standard and Formatting toolbars on two rows** is also ticked. By default, the **Standard** and **Formatting** toolbars are displayed next to each other with some of their buttons hidden so that both toolbars fit on a single row; setting this option displays both toolbars in full.

 Press **Close** to confirm the change.

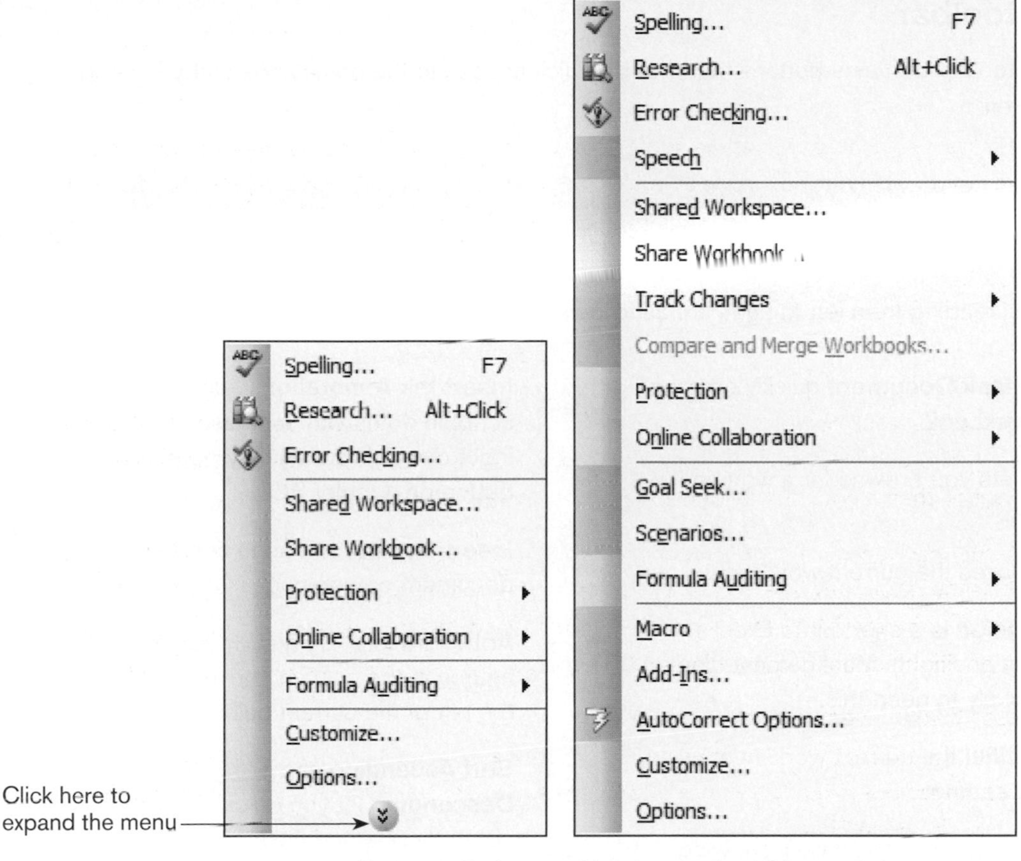

Figure 1.3: Tools menu (a) compressed and (b) expanded

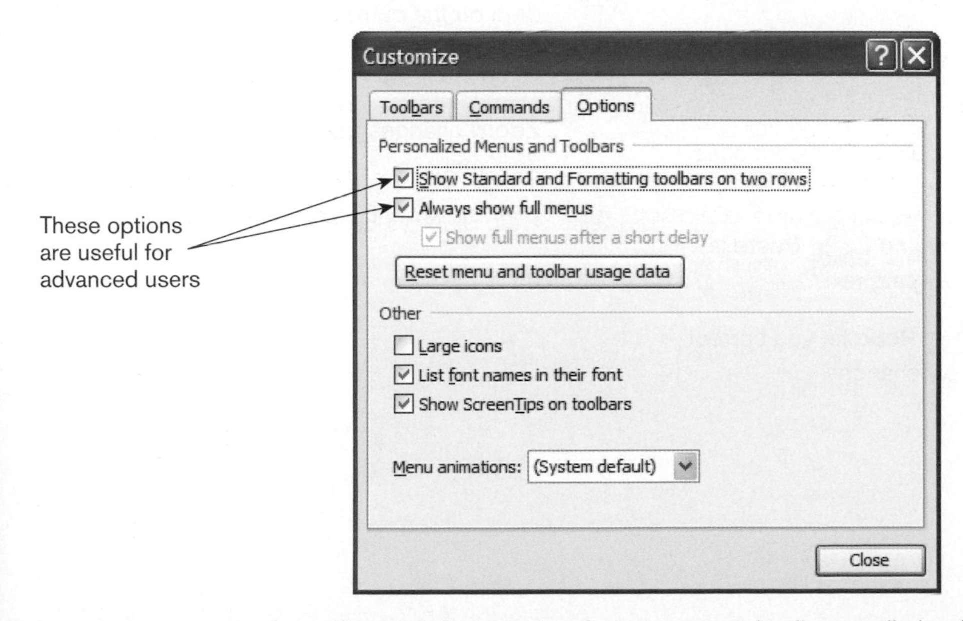

Figure 1.4: Setting options for how menus and toolbars are displayed

Standard toolbar

The **Standard** toolbar contains buttons that provide quick access to the commands that you need to use most often.

Figure 1.5: Standard toolbar

The commands, reading from left to right, are as follows.

New Blank Document quickly opens a new workbook.

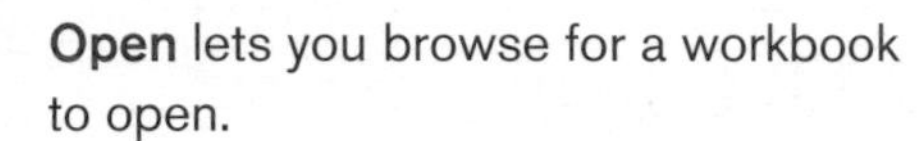

Open lets you browse for a workbook to open.

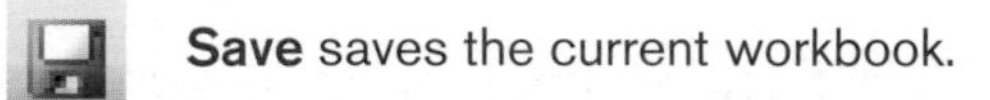

Save saves the current workbook.

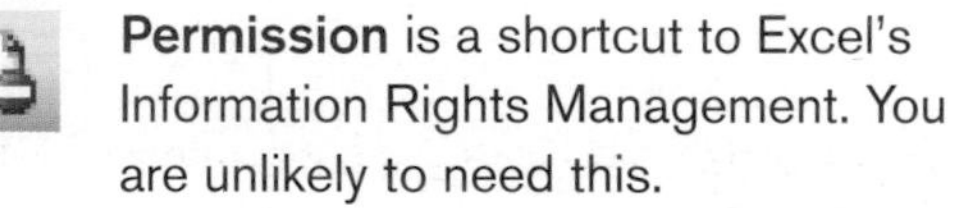

Permission is a shortcut to Excel's Information Rights Management. You are unlikely to need this.

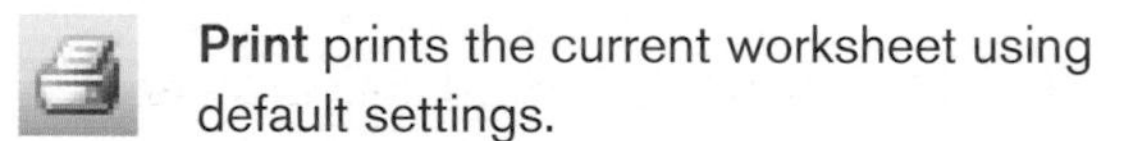

Print prints the current worksheet using default settings.

Print Preview opens a view showing how the current worksheet will look when you print it.

Spelling finds spelling mistakes in the current worksheet.

Research lets you search dictionaries, thesauri, etc.

Cut, **Copy** and **Paste** let you move or duplicate text.

Undo and **Redo** let you correct mistakes/reapply changes.

Insert Ink Annotations lets you scribble notes with a mouse or other input device. You will only get this button on a tablet PC.

Insert Hyperlink links to another document or web page.

AutoSum lets you quickly add the figures in the column above or row to the left of the current cell.

Sort Ascending and **Sort Descending** let you quickly sort the currently selected cells.

Chart Wizard creates a chart from the data on the current worksheet.

Drawing toggles this toolbar on/off.

Zoom changes the magnification of the document.

Help displays Excel's Help task pane.

Formatting toolbar

The **Formatting** toolbar provides quick access to commands that let you change the format of the currently selected cells.

Figure 1.6: Formatting toolbar

The commands, reading from left to right, are as follows.

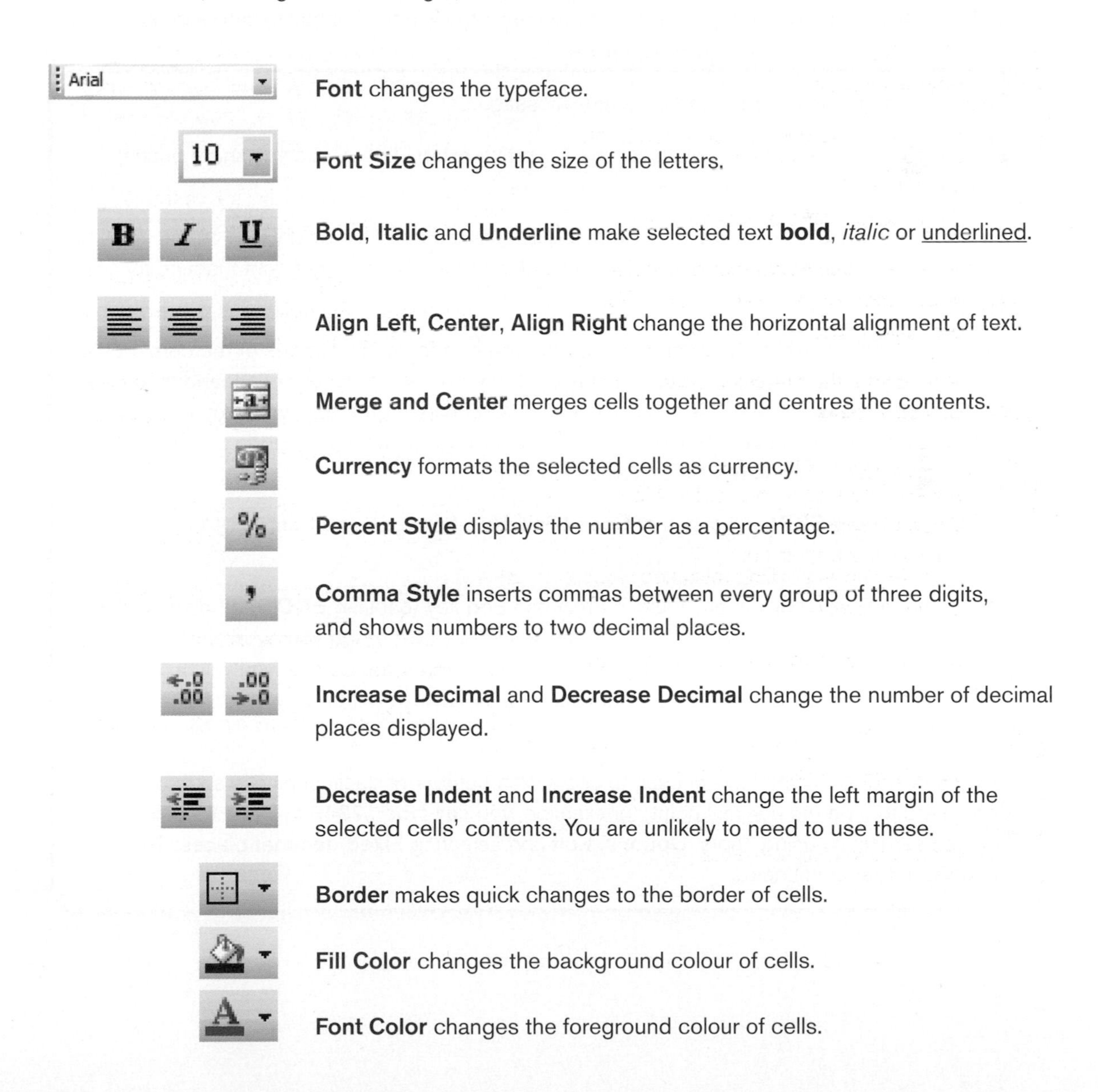

Font changes the typeface.

Font Size changes the size of the letters.

Bold, **Italic** and **Underline** make selected text **bold**, *italic* or underlined.

Align Left, **Center**, **Align Right** change the horizontal alignment of text.

Merge and Center merges cells together and centres the contents.

Currency formats the selected cells as currency.

Percent Style displays the number as a percentage.

Comma Style inserts commas between every group of three digits, and shows numbers to two decimal places.

Increase Decimal and **Decrease Decimal** change the number of decimal places displayed.

Decrease Indent and **Increase Indent** change the left margin of the selected cells' contents. You are unlikely to need to use these.

Border makes quick changes to the border of cells.

Fill Color changes the background colour of cells.

Font Color changes the foreground colour of cells.

Status bar

This isn't strictly a toolbar (since it is fixed at the bottom of the page). However, you can turn it on and off (**Tools**, **Options**, **View**, **Show: Status Bar**), and it is worth examining the information that it gives you.

Ready	Sum=11	EXT	CAPS	NUM	SCRL	END	FIX

Figure 1.7: Status bar

Using the status bar shown in Figure 1.7 as an example, the various things indicated are as follows.

Ready – this area is used for general status messages.

– the world icon appears when you are importing external data, such as share prices, from the Internet.

Sum=11 – this area allows you to perform a quick calculation (sum by default) on the contents of the selected cells. Right-click the status bar to choose a different function to apply.

EXT – this appears when the extend selection mode is in force. Select one of the corner cells for the area you want to select, press the **F8** key to turn on extended selection, and then click on the opposite corner cell. This can be useful for selecting large areas when you need to scroll around the worksheet. Note that you cannot turn extend selection mode on and off by double-clicking Excel's status bar as you can in Word.

CAPS, **NUM**, and **SCRL** indicate that **Caps Lock**, **Number Lock** and **Scroll Lock**, respectively, are turned on.

END – when **Scroll Lock** is off, you can press the **End** key (causing **END** to be displayed in the status bar) followed by an arrow key to move a long way through your worksheet. If you are inside the area of your worksheet containing values when you do this, you will be moved to the extremity of this area; if you are outside, then these keys will move you to the very edge of the worksheet.

FIX – this appears if you have chosen to use a fixed number of decimal places so that you don't need to type the decimal point; for example, you can type **12345** to input **123.45**. You can set this by using **Tools**, **Options**, **Edit** and selecting **Fixed decimal places**. This option is not recommended.

Commands

Keyboard commands

It is well worth taking the trouble to learn some of the shortcut keys that Excel assigns to its commands. Rather than having to hunt through the toolbars and menus, it is often quicker to use the keyboard shortcut.

The following list gives some of the most useful shortcut keys; you can find more by searching Excel's help.

Command	Keyboard shortcut
Undo	Ctrl+Z
Redo/Repeat	Ctrl+Y
Save	Ctrl+S
Select All	Ctrl+A
Copy	Ctrl+C
Cut	Ctrl+X
Paste	Ctrl+V
Edit cell's contents	F2
Cancel edit	Esc
Fill selected cell range with value	Ctrl+Enter
Start a new line in the same cell	Alt+Enter
Move to edge of current data region	Ctrl+arrow
Jump to beginning of worksheet	Ctrl+Home
Jump to bottom-right non-blank cell	Ctrl+End
Change between worksheets	Ctrl+PgUp/PgDn
Next Window	Ctrl+F6
Find & Replace	Ctrl+F
Go To	Ctrl+G
Bold	Ctrl+B
Italic	Ctrl+I
Underline	Ctrl+U
Insert current date	Ctrl+;
Insert current time	Ctrl+:

Paste special

> **Syllabus Ref: AM4.1.1.5**
> Use paste special options.

By default, when you paste from the clipboard into a worksheet, Excel tries to preserve as much of the information from the original as possible. If you are pasting cells (rather than, say, a picture) Excel will try to preserve the original formulas, cell number formats, borders and other formatting, and so on.

Sometimes you need finer control over what you are pasting – for example, stripping out all of the formatting. This is when you need **Edit**, **Paste Special**.

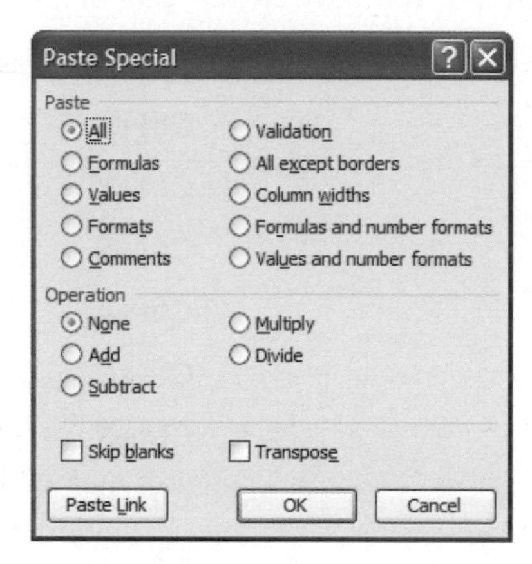

Figure 1.8: The Paste Special dialogue

Figure 1.8 shows the options available when pasting spreadsheet cells. The **Paste** options are self-explanatory – most commonly you would select **Formulas**, which will remove any formatting.

The **Operation** options let you paste cells over the top of other cells that already have values, so that each cell's final value is the result of applying the selected operation to the original and pasted cell contents. For example, if you copy cells with values **{1,2,3}** and do a **Paste Special** using the **Add Operation** on to cells with values **{3,6,10}**, the result would be **{4,8,13}**.

The **Skip blanks** option prevents copied blank cells from overwriting information in the area you are pasting into.

The **Transpose** option changes the copied cells so that rows become columns and columns become rows. Figure 1.9 shows an example.

	A	B	C	D	E	F	G	H	I
1		Original data				Transposed data			
2									
3		1	2	3		1	4	7	10
4		4	5	6		2	5	8	11
5		7	8	9		3	6	9	12
6		10	11	12					
7									

Figure 1.9: Example of transposing data with Paste Special

Time savers

Office Clipboard

When you copy text from any program, it is placed in the **Windows Clipboard** so that you can paste it somewhere else. Because all programs work with this central clipboard, it is easy to share information among different programs.

The disadvantage of the **Windows Clipboard** is that it can hold only one thing at a time: each time you cut or copy something, it replaces the previous contents of the clipboard.

The **Microsoft Office** suite has its own, more advanced, clipboard, which can contain up to 24 items. When you display the **Office Clipboard** in Excel, it overrides the **Windows Clipboard** so that you can copy multiple snippets from whichever programs you like, and then paste these items into a spreadsheet or other Office document.

 From the menu, select **Edit**, **Office Clipboard**. The **Clipboard** task pane appears.

Figure 1.10 shows an **Office Clipboard** after three items have been copied to it (earliest at the bottom): the number 42 copied from Excel, a sentence copied from Word and a picture copied from a graphics program. Notice how each copied item has an icon to its left to represent its associated program, and how you get a thumbnail representation for any graphics you copy.

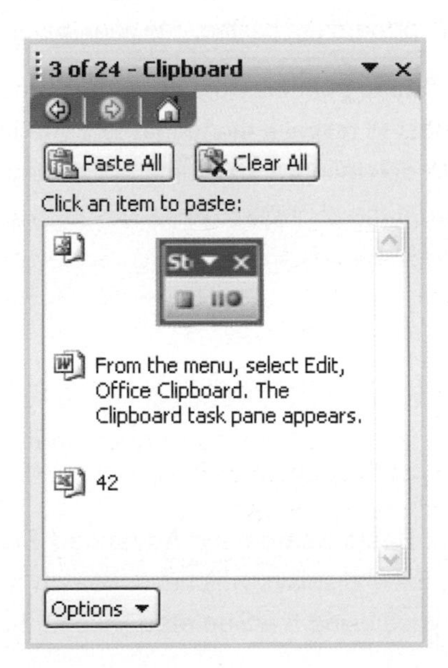

Figure 1.10: The Office Clipboard, showing three types of copied item

Although you can copy to the **Office Clipboard** from any program, only **Microsoft Office** programs work with its paste. Because of this, whenever you copy something, it is placed into both the **Office Clipboard** and the **Windows Clipboard** (replacing whatever was already in the **Windows Clipboard**, but allowing you to paste it into any program).

- Press the **Clear All** button to empty the **Office Clipboard**.
- In a blank worksheet, type the values **A**, **B**, **C** and **D** in cells **A1:D1**.
- Repeat this with **E**, **F**, **G**, **H** and **I**, **J**, **K**, **L** in the next two rows.
- Select cells **A1:D1** and copy them as you normally would (for example, by pressing **Ctrl+C**). Notice that the copied information appears in the **Clipboard** task pane.
- Copy cells **A3:C2**. This information also appears in the **Clipboard**.
- Click in cell **A5**, then press the **Paste All** button on the **Clipboard** task pane.

Both sets of data from the **Office Clipboard** are pasted, one after the other in the order they were copied.

Notice also that if you hover the mouse pointer over any of the items in the **Clipboard** task pane, an arrow appears. You can click this to reveal a menu that lets you individually paste or delete the items. This is useful if you need to delete individual items because you are nearing the 24-item limit; however, to paste a single item from the clipboard, you can simply click that item, which is quicker than using the menu.

File Search

Unless you are incredibly well organised, you will occasionally forget where you have saved a file. Office has a built-in tool that you can use to track down documents when you know what they are called or some of the information they contain.

There are two types of file search: **Basic Search** and **Advanced Search**. When you select **File**, **File Search** from the menu, Excel displays whichever search type you used last. You can switch between the two search types using the **See also** links at the bottom of each.

Save and close the file you have been working on as **chapter1.xls**, and then use the **Basic File Search** to find it again by searching for some of the text it contains (see Figure 1.11(a)).

Use the **Advanced File Search** to find all the Excel documents that have been modified in the last month (see Figure 1.11(b)). Set **Property** to **Last modified**, **Condition** to **This month** and then press **Add.** Untick everything apart from **Excel Files** in the **Selected file types** list, then press **Go**

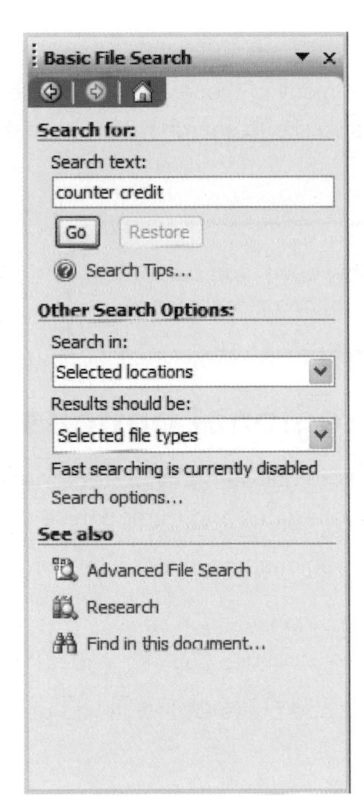

Figure 1.11: (a) Basic File Search and (b) Advanced File Search

The **Basic File Search** will find any document that contains all of the words in the search term, whether in the document text or its properties – it does not treat the search term as a phrase.

Online help

Don't forget that one of the quickest and easiest ways to find out how to do something in Excel is to consult its online help.

From the menu, select **Help**, **Microsoft Excel Help**. The **Excel Help** task pane appears.

In the **Search for** box, type **About** and press **Enter**.

A list of help topics with the word **About** in appears – many of these are introductions to complex topics, so click on any that catch your eye. You may also like to search for **Troubleshoot**.

Whenever you have a dialogue window open, you can press the **F1** key to display help about the options it provides.

Important information about regional options

The instructions in this book assume that your PC is correctly set up with **Regional Options** set to **United Kingdom**. Excel uses these settings to work with dates and to recognise currency values.

You can use a blank Excel worksheet to test that your regional options are set correctly.

Type **1/2/3** in cell **A1** and **5** in cell **A2**.

Select cell **A1** and press **Ctrl+#**. Select cell **A2** and press **Ctrl+$**. If you get **01-Feb-03** and **£5.00** then your settings are correct.

If you get different results then you should open the **Control Panel** via the Windows **Start** menu and change the **Regional Options** to **United Kingdom**. If these settings have been locked by an administrator and you cannot get them changed then you will have to adapt the exercises as you work through them (using the date and currency formats your PC expects instead of those given in the instructions – for example **12/1/2003** instead of **1/12/2003** and **$5** instead of **£5**.

2 Navigation & Auditing

Introduction

This chapter introduces some general techniques that you will find useful when dealing with large worksheets. In the first part, we look at ways to navigate around tall, wide worksheets, so that the information you need is available on the screen. In the second part, we use formula auditing to show and hide formulas and to trace dependencies between cells.

In this chapter you will

- learn how to **split windows**, **freeze panes** and open **multiple windows** on the same document
- learn how to **hide columns and rows** in a worksheet
- learn how to **hide a worksheet** so that its tab doesn't appear in its workbook
- learn how to **switch between viewing formulas and their values**
- examine how **formula auditing** can be used to trace the dependencies between cells on a worksheet.

Loading the sample workbook

Throughout this book, we will be using a video shop as an example. This shop rents out and sells videos, DVDs and video games, and it stores information about its business in an Excel workbook.

Figure 2.1 shows the **Members** worksheet of the **videoshop.xls** workbook. As you can see, there's a lot of information on there. Don't worry though – you don't have to type it all in for yourself.

Download the file **videoshop.xls** from the publisher's website: www.payne-gallway.co.uk/ecdl

	A	B	C	D	E	F	G	H	I	J	K	L	M	N
1	Member	Title	Initial	Surname	Date of birth	Address1	Address2	Village	Town/City	Post Code	Daytime Telephone	Evening Telephone	Date Joined	Total Spend
2	1	Mr	T	Henderson	21/04/1976	The Barn	Mill Road	Blakely	Middlington	MI2 2UC	(01211) 963156	(01211) 226585	23/01/2001	£93.09
3	2	Mr	M	Thompson	04/12/1976	2 Cooper Ave			Middlington	MI1 4DL	(01211) 885049	(01211) 728021	16/07/2003	£140.21
4	3	Mrs	N	Smith	21/07/1975	6, The Cuttings	Hampton Street		Middlington	MI1 5BE	(01211) 596380	(01211) 483232	09/05/2002	£0.00
5	4	Ms	A	Brown	01/02/1982	64 Broad Street			Middlington	MI1 1RT	(01211) 467059	(01211) 467059	02/06/2004	£7.03
6	5	Mr	G	Jones	06/02/1980	8 St. John's Road			Middlington	MI1 6QS	(01211) 153798	(01211) 380438	07/06/2000	£267.76
7	6	Ms	E	Patel	05/11/1981	7 Compton Drive			Middlington	MI1 5SI	(01211) 661890	(01211) 174892	12/07/2001	£88.37
8	7	Ms	T	Kendal	13/03/1979	The Forge	Mill Road	Blakely	Middlington	MI2 7AC	(01211) 763804	(01211) 302378	10/06/2000	£154.36
9	8	Dr	A	Hooper	08/04/1968	3 Parson's Close			Middlington	MI1 5RB	(01211) 530500	(01211) 567363	13/04/2001	£87.94
10	9	Mr	E	McBride	30/03/1980	11 Elmer St			Middlington	MI1 5QK	(01211) 574553	(01211) 546985	25/12/2004	£3.02
11	10	Mr	O	Trapp	12/10/1979	19 Chapel Street			Middlington	MI1 4UX	(01211) 704444	(01211) 306897	15/04/2003	£107.79
12	11	Mrs	S	Honeywell	15/05/1971	211 St. John's Road			Middlington	MI1 9OR	(01211) 110504	(01211) 973145	07/06/2004	£167.66
13	12	Ms	J	Stroud	05/10/1983	14 North Lane			Middlington	MI1 9VN	(01211) 383584	(01211) 485313	28/04/2001	£20.78
14	13	Mr	J	Levington	28/07/1977	The Lodgings	Baker Street		Middlington	MI1 9PG	(01211) 576957	(01211) 485816	06/08/2001	£9.31
15	14	Ms	T	Stewart	05/01/1987	6 Little Row		Pickerington	Middlington	MI3 9JH	(01211) 857128	(01211) 857128	07/04/2004	£46.82
16	15	Ms	B	Taylor	17/11/1981	5 West Way			Middlington	MI1 1UU	(01211) 497373	(01211) 497373	18/03/2000	£236.98
17	16	Ms	K	Bennett	29/05/1973	13 Broad Street			Middlington	MI1 6UO	(01211) 840184	(01211) 896503	06/03/2002	£135.46
18	17	Mr	A	White	18/01/1982	16 Parson's Close			Middlington	MI1 9QU	(01211) 104271	(01211) 685885	16/10/2003	£23.31
19	18	Ms	E	King	24/03/1979	1 Tebbit Rd			Middlington	MI1 9KM	(01211) 170625	(01211) 234989	07/07/2000	£199.24
20	19	Mr	N	Wright	06/07/1975	Greenacres	Baker Street		Middlington	MI1 8EL	(01211) 297132	(01211) 297132	03/12/2003	£350.23
21	20	Mr	M	Carter	09/12/1968	2 King's Road			Middlington	MI1 3NU	(01211) 813189	(01211) 323840	25/02/2004	£128.95
22	21	Ms	C	Foster	17/11/1974	54 Elmer St			Middlington	MI1 6CN	(01211) 344968	(01211) 166158	22/08/2001	£0.00
23	22	Mrs	O	Mitchell	05/10/1978	The Bungalow	Poplar Drive		Middlington	MI1 8NF	(01211) 261548	(01211) 104371	05/07/2003	£73.35
24	23	Ms	W	Miller	17/07/1969	1 London Road		Pickerington	Middlington	MI3 1LN	(01211) 710278	(01211) 284965	18/10/2003	£18.47
25	24	Mr	R	Collins	21/01/1983	2 Hobart Place			Middlington	MI1 8ZZ	(01211) 843841	(01211) 459132	30/10/2003	£97.66
26	25	Mr	T	Russell	27/05/1970	The Old Rectory	Mill Road	Blakely	Middlington	MI2 6VW	(01211) 460476	(01211) 883911	04/04/2000	£97.22
27	26	Ms	V	Wilson	17/05/1968	2 Bridge Row			Middlington	MI1 2SC	(01211) 611159	(01211) 204658	24/01/2002	£226.21
28	27	Mr	L	Clark	23/05/1986	51 St. John's Road			Middlington	MI1 6GO	(01211) 685980	(01211) 103789	21/03/2002	£184.69
29	28	Mrs	R	Rogers	21/06/1972	7 Tebbit Rd			Middlington	MI1 6TA	(01211) 982690	(01211) 876663	08/08/2003	£30.33
30	29	Mr	W	Lee	08/11/1975	Sunnyside	Poplar Drive		Middlington	MI1 6IC	(01211) 620784	(01211) 481943	01/11/2004	£103.31
31	30	Mrs	J	Barber	11/06/1979	1 Long Ridge			Middlington	MI1 6NL	(01211) 564707	(01211) 463676	15/06/2003	£2.65
32	31	Mr	J	Perez	15/09/1973	3 Chester Way			Middlington	MI1 4YY	(01211) 548412	(01211) 913897	29/05/2002	£192.65
33	32	Ms	J	Roberts	12/03/1983	5 Bridge Row			Middlington	MI1 4PN	(01211) 472253	(01211) 328414	31/01/2002	£56.14
34	33	Ms	K	Salmon	29/10/1976	The Croft	Lester Street		Middlington	MI1 3IJ	(01211) 642830	(01211) 264562	02/12/2001	£1.35
35	34	Mr	B	Reed	29/01/1985	4 Parson's Close			Middlington	MI1 1IC	(01211) 483436	(01211) 483436	07/08/2001	£30.36
36	35	Ms	C	Moore	13/03/1979	Bluebirds	Granger Street		Middlington	MI1 9SG	(01211) 896488	(01211) 456389	27/05/2002	£64.83
37	36	Mr	E	Reed	13/02/1979	8 Chapel Street			Middlington	MI1 5RH	(01211) 196940	(01211) 957055	12/09/2000	£210.48
38	37	Mr	L	Smith	09/02/1981	5 Chester Way			Middlington	MI1 5JM	(01211) 223891	(01211) 338320	15/02/2003	£0.00
39	38	Rev	I	Priestly	21/06/1986	The Vicarage	Church Lane	Hamshaw	Middlington	MI4 5TW	(01211) 781826	(01211) 200594	23/05/2001	£129.92
40	39	Mr	H	Barker	05/10/1975	6 Market Road			Middlington	MI1 8MN	(01211) 174325	(01211) 393908	05/01/2001	£178.67
41	40	Mr	J	Jones	17/07/1986	12 Shepherd's Pass			Middlington	MI1 3AR	(01211) 518739	(01211) 247507	16/01/2001	£28.08
42	41	Mrs	V	Carter	20/01/1981	12 Tennant Street			Middlington	MI1 6IH	(01211) 775069	(01211) 430957	28/06/2001	£75.81
43	42	Ms	K	Garcia	05/05/1986	2 Elmer St			Middlington	MI1 3XE	(01211) 143707	(01211) 362090	09/09/2003	£60.90
44	43	Mr	F	Sanderson	19/02/1981	The Firs	Lester Street		Middlington	MI1 2YC	(01211) 919798	(01211) 237810	23/07/2000	£102.98
45	44	Ms	H	Lewis	11/09/1984	9 Shepherd's Pass			Middlington	MI1 4XA	(01211) 513505	(01211) 123815	20/05/2004	£6.74
46	45	Ms	L	Green	04/11/1970	9 Chapel Street			Middlington	MI1 9AN	(01211) 793160	(01211) 350604	09/03/2000	£45.72
47	46	Ms	A	Thompson	04/12/1983	Dunroamin	Pepperpot Ave		Middlington	MI1 9UE	(01211) 560884	(01211) 237385	10/04/2000	£166.65
48	47	Mr	S	Cook	01/05/1957	1 Compton Drive			Middlington	MI1 2UX	(01211) 303526	(01211) 249023	02/10/2004	£321.80
49	48	Ms	M	Cook	26/06/1980	3 Compton Drive			Middlington	MI1 2UZ	(01211) 536964	(01211) 194767	17/12/2004	£107.10
50	49	Mrs	S	Cook	14/03/1959	1 Compton Drive			Middlington	MI1 2UX	(01211) 652289	(01211) 249023	29/08/2000	£21.08
51	50	Ms	T	Smith	12/06/1971	14 Pulman Drive			Middlington	MI1 7EE	(01211) 388350	(01211) 869854	17/07/2003	£5.32
52	51	Mr	L	Collins	13/03/1968	The Old Post Office	High Street	Blakely	Middlington	MI2 3XP	(01211) 662654	(01211) 128059	19/09/2004	£11.90
53	52	Ms	C	Thomas	06/11/1973	8 Parson's Close			Middlington	MI1 7BS	(01211) 390293	(01211) 966162	20/03/2004	£182.24
54	53	Mr	V	Clark	30/07/1979	7 Broad Street			Middlington	MI1 6EF	(01211) 673904	(01211) 244053	14/02/2003	£16.96
55	54	Mr	T	Green	23/11/1978	30 St. John's Road			Middlington	MI1 1NW	(01211) 502605	(01211) 502605	16/09/2004	£2.58
56	55	Ms	J	Chen	20/09/1972	4 Tebbitt Rd			Middlington	MI1 2IO	(01211) 166852	(01211) 981085	18/10/2002	£6.45
57	56	Mr	E	Martin	31/08/1974	Ivy Cottage	Crooked Street		Middlington	MI1 8ZW	(01211) 300733	(01211) 351775	27/09/2002	£214.52
58	57	Mr	J	Baker	27/10/1970	3 Little Row		Pickerington	Middlington	MI3 2SV	(01211) 636265	(01211) 245895	29/09/2001	£122.82
59	58	Ms	A	Miller	30/03/1975	13 Lucky Lane			Middlington	MI1 4PL	(01211) 259715	(01211) 795880	13/05/2003	£262.18
60	59	Ms	C	Nelson	19/06/1973	2 West Way			Middlington	MI1 1ED	(01211) 424296	(01211) 829791	05/03/2003	£3.06
61	60	Mrs	V	Edwards	26/01/1973	1 King's Road			Middlington	MI1 9ND	(01211) 838049	(01211) 740837	26/10/2003	£7.20
62	61	Mr	M	Allen	25/06/1986	Oaklands	Lester Street		Middlington	MI1 9HX	(01211) 554173	(01211) 546323	27/07/2004	£13.41
63	62	Mrs	R	Bailey	06/11/1986	18 Hobart Place			Middlington	MI1 4GF	(01211) 410310	(01211) 462960	08/10/2002	£69.52
64	63	Ms	P	Nasa	19/11/1974	5 Long Lane			Middlington	MI1 6LF	(01211) 886799	(01211) 545549	01/09/2003	£194.99
65	64	Mr	K	Brown	08/02/1987	The White House	Poplar Drive		Middlington	MI1 8UW	(01211) 908656	(01211) 245647	30/07/2003	£98.21
66	65	Ms	L	Rodriguez	28/05/1969	2 Shepherd's Pass			Middlington	MI1 2IK	(01211) 272168	(01211) 272168	19/10/2001	£113.75
67	66	Mr	S	Richardson	18/09/1972	1 Chester Way			Middlington	MI1 5PQ	(01211) 201897	(01211) 667264	03/02/2004	£277.14
68	67	Mr	B	Tropshaw	30/11/1970	101 Elmer St			Middlington	MI1 1LF	(01211) 118886	(01211) 118886	03/10/2004	£330.31
69	68	Ms	C	Turner	21/05/1983	1 Pellow Place			Middlington	MI1 8PD	(01211) 221017	(01211) 181838	22/02/2002	£214.81
70	69	Mr	F	Riggs	21/01/1980	Honeysuckle Cottage	Crooked Street		Middlington	MI1 5LE	(01211) 828170	(01211) 130732	21/09/2002	£17.17
71	70	Ms	J	Maple	21/04/1986	12 Chapel Street			Middlington	MI1 3NX	(01211) 922796	(01211) 340294	02/02/2003	£65.17
72	71	Mr	L	Bennett	11/04/1970	18 Pulman Drive			Middlington	MI1 5YE	(01211) 701174	(01211) 978128	01/08/2004	£257.65
73	72	Ms	K	MacDonald	24/09/1982	6 Shepherd's Pass			Middlington	MI1 9LU	(01211) 400487	(01211) 640633	23/01/2003	£103.64
74	73	Mrs	E	Chang	01/10/1976	14 London Road		Pickerington	Middlington	MI3 2WM	(01211) 169357	(01211) 462454	12/08/2004	£4.56
75	74	Ms	A	Addison	08/07/1986	3 Bridge Row			Middlington	MI1 4MB	(01211) 634343	(01211) 861648	04/08/2001	£80.60
76	75	Mr	C	Thomas	26/09/1978	3 Richmond Ave			Middlington	MI1 4HB	(01211) 968703	(01211) 968703	19/05/2001	£62.42
77	76	Mr	J	Singh	04/08/1976	The Willows	Moon Crescent		Middlington	MI1 9BD	(01211) 332612	(01211) 695306	25/08/2003	£125.42
78	77	Ms	S	Little	10/06/1973	The Swallows	Granger Street		Middlington	MI1 5PS	(01211) 364951	(01211) 205707	03/11/2004	£136.49
79	78	Mr	E	Thomas	19/09/1986	45 St. John's Road			Middlington	MI1 5QQ	(01211) 735278	(01211) 402979	09/05/2003	£46.63
80	79	Mrs	D	Martinez	27/07/1982	Tippington Court	Logan's Cross	Hamshaw	Middlington	MI4 3UU	(01211) 384155	(01211) 674429	14/05/2002	£39.83
81	80	Mr	S	Straw	10/02/1973	14 Compton Drive			Middlington	MI1 7HW	(01211) 287385	(01211) 556367	19/07/2004	£39.38
82	81	Ms	J	Bridge	27/01/1973	5 King's Road			Middlington	MI1 3DY	(01211) 291168	(01211) 957823	22/04/2000	£131.09
83	82	Ms	S	Jones	22/11/1980	17 Little Row		Pickerington	Middlington	MI3 5VT	(01211) 218812	(01211) 250373	12/10/2004	£138.70
84	83	Ms	C	Foster	21/07/1972	The Beeches	Lester Street		Middlington	MI1 4FQ	(01211) 352322	(01211) 310895	16/01/2004	£31.06
85	84	Mrs	T	Taylor	22/06/1979	19 Market Road			Middlington	MI1 4VL	(01211) 597040	(01211) 293424	25/10/2004	£198.99
86	85	Ms	A	Richards	08/04/1986	Highfield	Logan's Cross	Hamshaw	Middlington	MI4 4SA	(01211) 510559	(01211) 251943	23/08/2003	£17.10
87	86	Mr	E	Anderson	27/01/1987	4 Milber Rise			Middlington	MI1 9LO	(01211) 796740	(01211) 137578	24/02/2002	£60.45
88	87	Ms	E	Jackson	27/03/1965	11 Tebbit Rd			Middlington	MI1 2TQ	(01211) 343461	(01211) 591422	15/07/2002	£100.70
89	88	Mr	T	Russell	18/07/1973	31 Broad Street			Middlington	MI1 3GH	(01211) 977876	(01211) 741819	20/02/2000	£60.78
90	89	Mr	M	Lee	08/12/1972	9 Hobart Place			Middlington	MI1 6VB	(01211) 178835	(01211) 445957	28/02/2003	£188.42
91	90	Mr	S	Adams	21/12/1968	The Granary	St Mark's Square		Middlington	MI1 7KB	(01211) 898307	(01211) 467784	25/04/2001	£305.04
92	91	Ms	N	Harris	14/02/1984	23 Regent Street		Pickerington	Middlington	MI3 2ZG	(01211) 152606	(01211) 648634	11/01/2002	£18.50
93	92	Mr	E	Oberman	13/09/1976	5 North Lane			Middlington	MI1 7GK	(01211) 416478	(01211) 849310	10/01/2004	£206.75
94	93	Mrs	S	Bagnal	08/05/1980	Treetops	Lester Street		Middlington	MI1 3FG	(01211) 613219	(01211) 112312	01/02/2003	£39.66
95	94	Mr	A	Turner	09/10/1977	11 Parson's Close			Middlington	MI1 5NA	(01211) 431569	(01211) 309451	04/02/2003	£198.15
96	95	Ms	E	Evans	16/12/1978	3 West Way			Middlington	MI1 3NI	(01211) 455846	(01211) 766595	14/03/2001	£2.00
97	96	Mrs	J	Clark	30/11/1971	22 London Road		Pickerington	Middlington	MI3 5JY	(01211) 628568	(01211) 374166	30/10/2004	£137.67
98	97	Mr	E	Hall	09/07/1980	4 St Mark's Drive		Hamshaw	Middlington	MI4 8MS	(01211) 422084	(01211) 637577	16/02/2001	£79.96
99	98	Mr	T	Phillips	02/12/1967	Rose Cottage	Crooked Street		Middlington	MI1 1GP	(01211) 322673	(01211) 322673	01/10/2003	£159.57
100	99	Mr	S	Walker	01/05/1978	6 Milber Rise			Middlington	MI1 4ZR	(01211) 856124	(01211) 255010	29/02/2000	£79.67

Figure 2.1: The video shop's customer information

Changing the display

The maximum size of a worksheet in Excel is 65,536 rows by 256 columns: almost 16.5 million cells in total. Although you are unlikely to ever need to use every cell, you will inevitably find yourself working on some very large worksheets from time to time. We'll look at some ways to navigate around such large worksheets.

These apparently strange maximums are actually powers of two: $2^8 = 256$ and $2^{16} = 65{,}536$. The columns are usually referenced by letter not number. The first 26 columns are named **A** to **Z**, then come **AA** to **AZ** and so on up to **IV**.

Splitting windows

Sometimes you need to view information on different parts of a worksheet at the same time, perhaps to view sales figures for two different years.

Open the file **videoshop.xls** in Excel (you can download it from www.payne-gallway.co.uk/ecdl if you haven't already done so).

Switch to display the **Members** worksheet by clicking on the **Members** tab at the bottom of the workbook.

This worksheet holds information about the 99 members of the video shop's rental club. Unless your display is set to use a very high resolution, you should find that the worksheet is too wide and too long to fit on the screen.

Let's look at some ways to handle such large worksheets, starting with splitting windows.

Select **Window**, **Split** from the main menu.

Two **split boundaries** appear, one running horizontally and the other vertically, as shown in Figure 2.2. The exact initial position of these boundaries will depend on how large your Excel window is.

Notice that there are now four scroll bars, instead of the usual two. Each scroll bar controls scrolling in one direction for two of the split areas. For example, the top vertical scrollbar allows you to scroll up and down both of the top two split areas at the same time.

Scroll the bottom vertical scrollbar and the right-hand horizontal scrollbar to view column **K** and row **90**, as shown in Figure 2.2.

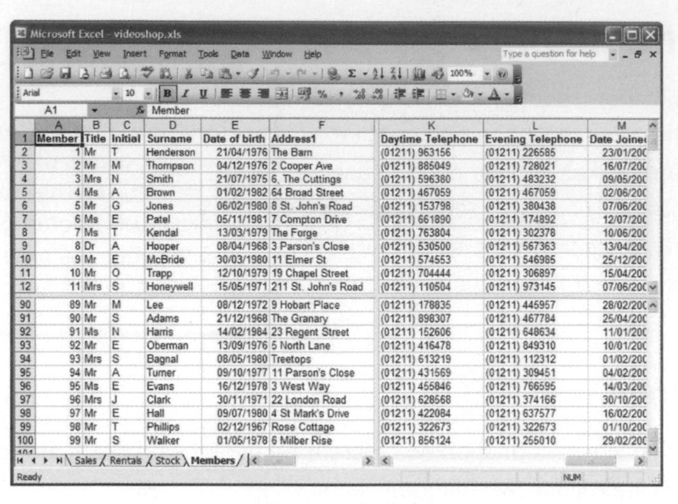

	A	B	C	D	E	F	K	L	M
1	Member	Title	Initial	Surname	Date of birth	Address1	Daytime Telephone	Evening Telephone	Date Joine
2	1	Mr	T	Henderson	21/04/1976	The Barn	(01211) 963156	(01211) 226585	23/01/200
3	2	Mr	M	Thompson	04/12/1976	2 Cooper Ave	(01211) 885049	(01211) 728021	16/07/200
4	3	Mrs	N	Smith	21/07/1975	6, The Cuttings	(01211) 596380	(01211) 483232	09/05/200
5	4	Ms	A	Brown	01/02/1982	64 Broad Street	(01211) 467059	(01211) 467059	02/06/200
6	5	Mr	G	Jones	06/02/1980	8 St. John's Road	(01211) 153798	(01211) 380438	07/06/200
7	6	Ms	E	Patel	05/11/1981	7 Compton Drive	(01211) 661890	(01211) 174892	12/07/200
8	7	Ms	T	Kendal	13/03/1979	The Forge	(01211) 763804	(01211) 302378	10/06/200
9	8	Dr	A	Hooper	08/04/1968	3 Parson's Close	(01211) 530500	(01211) 567363	13/04/200
10	9	Mr	E	McBride	30/03/1980	11 Elmer St	(01211) 574553	(01211) 546985	25/12/200
11	10	Mr	O	Trapp	12/10/1979	19 Chapel Street	(01211) 704444	(01211) 306897	15/04/200
12	11	Mrs	S	Honeywell	15/05/1971	211 St. John's Road	(01211) 110504	(01211) 973145	07/06/200
90	89	Mr	M	Lee	08/12/1972	9 Hobart Place	(01211) 178835	(01211) 445957	28/02/200
91	90	Mr	S	Adams	21/12/1968	The Granary	(01211) 898307	(01211) 467784	25/04/200
92	91	Ms	N	Harris	14/02/1984	23 Regent Street	(01211) 152606	(01211) 648634	11/01/200
93	92	Mr	E	Oberman	13/09/1976	5 North Lane	(01211) 416478	(01211) 849310	10/01/200
94	93	Mrs	S	Bagnal	08/05/1980	Treetops	(01211) 613219	(01211) 112312	01/02/200
95	94	Mr	A	Turner	09/10/1977	11 Parson's Close	(01211) 431569	(01211) 309451	04/02/200
96	95	Ms	E	Evans	16/12/1978	3 West Way	(01211) 455846	(01211) 766595	14/03/200
97	96	Mrs	J	Clark	30/11/1971	22 London Road	(01211) 628568	(01211) 374166	30/10/200
98	97	Mr	E	Hall	09/07/1980	4 St Mark's Drive	(01211) 422084	(01211) 637577	16/02/200
99	98	Mr	T	Phillips	02/12/1967	Rose Cottage	(01211) 322673	(01211) 322673	01/10/200
100	99	Mr	S	Walker	01/05/1978	6 Milber Rise	(01211) 856124	(01211) 255010	29/02/200

Figure 2.2: A split window

Try clicking and dragging the split boundaries. This lets you change the proportion of space allocated to each of the split areas.

If you drag a split boundary to the very edge and drop it there, it will disappear. This is useful if you only need a split in one direction. You can bring it back again by dragging the mini **split boundary indicator**, which appears next to the scroll bar (see Figure 2.3), back into the worksheet.

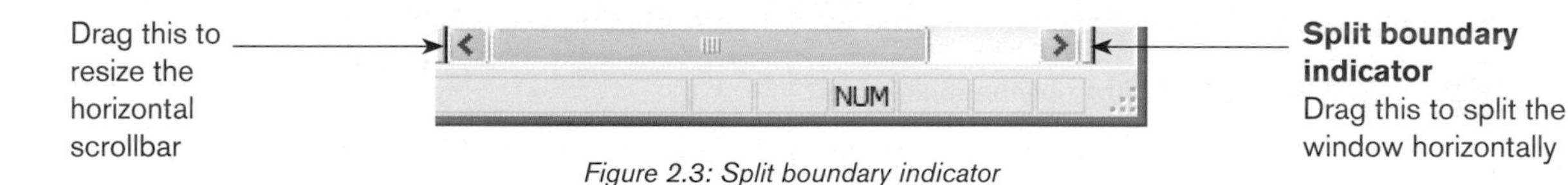

Figure 2.3: Split boundary indicator

Multiple windows

You can also have more than one window open, providing multiple views of the same document. These windows can be split independently.

From the menu, select **Window, New Window.**

You will notice very little difference, apart from the disappearance of any splits you had. However, the text in the title bar now ends with **:2**, indicating that this is the second window open for the same workbook.

You can use the **Window** menu to switch between these two different views.

From the menu, select **Window, videoshop.xls:1.**

The original window is displayed again, complete with any splits you added.

From the menu, select **Window, Arrange**. The **Arrange Windows** dialogue appears.

Select the **Vertical** option, as shown in Figure 2.4, and press **OK**.

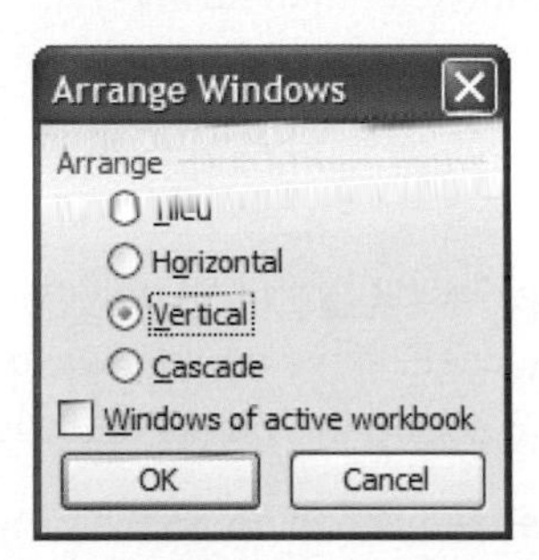

Figure 2.4: Arranging windows vertically

Your Excel window should now look something like Figure 2.5.

Microsoft Excel
File Edit View Insert Format Tools Data Window Help
Type a question for help
100%
Arial 10
A1 Member

videoshop.xls:1

	A	B	C	D	E	
1	Member	Title	Initial	Surname	Date of birth	Address1
2	1	Mr	T	Henderson	21/04/1976	The Barn
3	2	Mr	M	Thompson	04/12/1976	2 Cooper
4	3	Mrs	N	Smith	21/07/1975	6, The Cu
5	4	Ms	A	Brown	01/02/1982	64 Broad
6	5	Mr	G	Jones	06/02/1980	8 St. Johı
7	6	Ms	E	Patel	05/11/1981	7 Compto
8	7	Ms	T	Kendal	13/03/1979	The Forge
9	8	Dr	A	Hooper	08/04/1968	3 Parson'
10	9	Mr	E	McBride	30/03/1980	11 Elmer
11	10	Mr	O	Trapp	12/10/1979	19 Chape
12	11	Mrs	S	Honeywell	15/05/1971	211 St. J
90	89	Mr	M	Lee	08/12/1972	9 Hobart I
91	90	Mr	S	Adams	21/12/1968	The Gran:
92	91	Ms	N	Harris	14/02/1984	23 Regen
93	92	Mr	E	Oberman	13/09/1976	5 North L:
94	93	Mrs	S	Bagnal	08/05/1980	Treetops
95	94	Mr	A	Turner	09/10/1977	11 Parsoı
96	95	Ms	E	Evans	16/12/1978	3 West W
97	96	Mrs	J	Clark	30/11/1971	22 Londoı
98	97	Mr	E	Hall	09/07/1980	4 St Mark

Sales / Rentals / Stock / Members

videoshop.xls:2

	A	B	C	D	E	F
1	Member	Title	Initial	Surname	Date of birth	Address1
2	1	Mr	T	Henderson	21/04/1976	The Barn
3	2	Mr	M	Thompson	04/12/1976	2 Cooper Ave
4	3	Mrs	N	Smith	21/07/1975	6, The Cuttin
5	4	Ms	A	Brown	01/02/1982	64 Broad Str
6	5	Mr	G	Jones	06/02/1980	8 St. John's I
7	6	Ms	E	Patel	05/11/1981	7 Compton C
8	7	Ms	T	Kendal	13/03/1979	The Forge
9	8	Dr	A	Hooper	08/04/1968	3 Parson's C
10	9	Mr	E	McBride	30/03/1980	11 Elmer St
11	10	Mr	O	Trapp	12/10/1979	19 Chapel St
12	11	Mrs	S	Honeywell	15/06/1971	211 St. John'
13	12	Ms	J	Stroud	05/10/1983	14 North Lan
14	13	Mr	J	Levington	28/07/1977	The Lodgings
15	14	Ms	T	Stewart	05/01/1987	6 Little Row
16	15	Ms	B	Taylor	17/11/1981	5 West Way
17	16	Ms	K	Bennett	29/05/1973	13 Broad Str
18	17	Mr	A	White	18/01/1982	16 Parson's
19	18	Ms	E	King	24/03/1979	1 Tebbit Rd
20	19	Mr	N	Wright	06/07/1975	Greenacres
21	20	Mr	M	Carter	09/12/1968	2 King's Roa
22	21	Ms	C	Foster	17/11/1974	54 Elmer St

Sales / Rentals / Stock / Members

Ready NUM

Figure 2.5: Two windows, both with views of the same document, arranged vertically

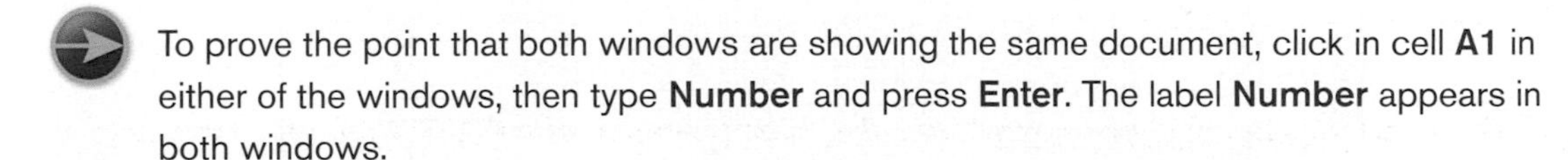

To prove the point that both windows are showing the same document, click in cell **A1** in either of the windows, then type **Number** and press **Enter**. The label **Number** appears in both windows.

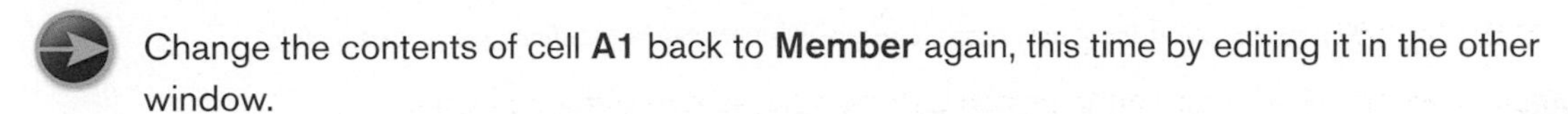

Change the contents of cell **A1** back to **Member** again, this time by editing it in the other window.

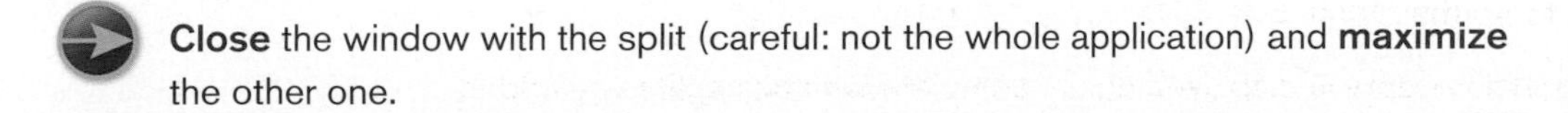

Close the window with the split (careful: not the whole application) and **maximize** the other one.

Freezing panes

Syllabus Ref: AM4.1.2.5
Freeze row and/or column titles.

Spreadsheets often contain long lists of information, and you need to keep the headings in view to help with data entry. In this situation, freezing panes is more useful than splitting them.

 Press **Ctrl+End**. This is a quick way of jumping to the last data cell in the worksheet.

The headings from row **1** are no longer visible: you can only tell what each bit of information represents by guesswork. It would be useful if we could always see the headings in row **1**, as well as the member number in column **A**. Freezing the panes allows us to do this.

 Select cell **B2**. We want to **freeze** everything above or to the left of it.

 From the menu, select **Window, Freeze Panes.** Notice that solid black lines have appeared to the left of column **B** and above row **2** to indicate the position of the freeze.

 Use the arrow keys to scroll around the worksheet. Notice that column **A** and row **1** are always visible, however far into the worksheet you scroll.

Microsoft Excel - videoshop.xls

File Edit View Insert Format Tools Data Window Help

N72 257.65

	A	H	I	J	K	L	M	N
1	Member	Village	Town/City	Post Code	Daytime Telephone	Evening Telephone	Date Joined	Total Spend
51	50		Middlington	MI1 7EE	(01211) 388350	(01211) 869854	17/07/2003	£5.32
52	51	Blakely	Middlington	MI2 3XP	(01211) 662654	(01211) 128059	19/09/2004	£11.90
53	52		Middlington	MI1 7BS	(01211) 390293	(01211) 966162	20/03/2004	£182.24
54	53		Middlington	MI1 6EF	(01211) 673904	(01211) 244053	14/02/2003	£16.96
55	54		Middlington	MI1 1NW	(01211) 502605	(01211) 502605	16/09/2004	£2.58
56	55		Middlington	MI1 2IO	(01211) 166852	(01211) 981085	18/10/2002	£6.45
57	56		Middlington	MI1 8ZW	(01211) 300733	(01211) 351775	27/09/2002	£214.52
58	57	Pickerington	Middlington	MI3 2SV	(01211) 636265	(01211) 245895	29/09/2001	£122.82
59	58		Middlington	MI1 4PL	(01211) 259715	(01211) 795880	13/05/2003	£262.18
60	59		Middlington	MI1 1ED	(01211) 424296	(01211) 829791	05/03/2003	£3.06
61	60		Middlington	MI1 9ND	(01211) 838049	(01211) 740837	26/10/2003	£7.20
62	61		Middlington	MI1 9HX	(01211) 554173	(01211) 546323	27/07/2004	£13.41
63	62		Middlington	MI1 4GF	(01211) 410310	(01211) 462960	08/10/2002	£69.52
64	63		Middlington	MI1 6LF	(01211) 886799	(01211) 545549	01/09/2003	£194.99
65	64		Middlington	MI1 8UW	(01211) 908656	(01211) 245647	30/07/2003	£98.21
66	65		Middlington	MI1 2IK	(01211) 272168	(01211) 272168	19/10/2001	£113.75
67	66		Middlington	MI1 5PQ	(01211) 201897	(01211) 667264	03/02/2004	£277.14
68	67		Middlington	MI1 1LF	(01211) 118886	(01211) 118886	03/10/2004	£330.31
69	68		Middlington	MI1 8PD	(01211) 221017	(01211) 181838	22/02/2002	£214.81
70	69		Middlington	MI1 5LE	(01211) 828170	(01211) 130732	21/09/2002	£17.17
71	70		Middlington	MI1 3NX	(01211) 922796	(01211) 340294	02/02/2003	£65.17
72	71		Middlington	MI1 5YE	(01211) 701174	(01211) 978128	01/08/2004	£257.65
73	72		Middlington	MI1 9LU	(01211) 400487	(01211) 640633	23/01/2003	£103.64

Sales / Rentals / Stock / Members

Ready NUM

Figure 2.6: Worksheet with frozen panes – the first row and column are always visible

 From the menu, select **Window, Unfreeze Panes**. This command returns the scrolling to normal.

Hiding information

Sometimes you may want to have information in your workbook that is not on display. A typical example of this would be intermediate calculations that you need to make, but which are of little interest in themselves. Excel lets you hide rows and columns, and even entire worksheets.

You may also choose to hide columns temporarily when you have very wide worksheets. This lets you see all of the columns that you are interested in on screen at the same time.

Hiding rows and columns

Syllabus Ref: AM4.1.2.6
Hide/unhide rows or columns.

First, let's hide the **Total Spend** column (column **N**).

Right-click the column heading for column **N**. This selects the whole column and displays a context-sensitive menu. Choose **Hide** from this menu, as shown in Figure 2.7.

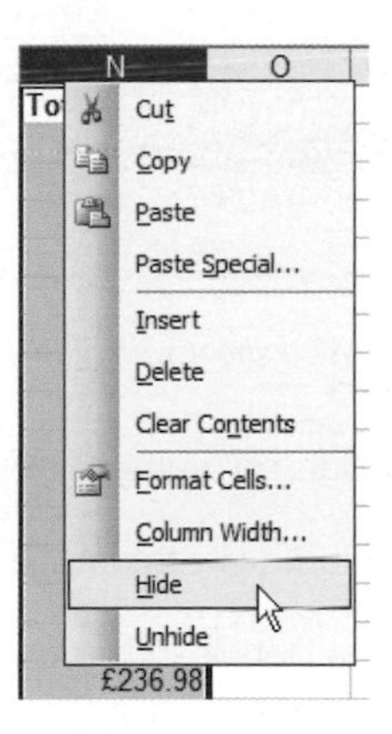

Figure 2.7: Hiding a column in a worksheet

Column **N** disappears! If you look along the column headings, they jump straight form **M** to **O**. Of course, the column is still there, it just isn't being displayed. You can think of it as having zero width (in fact, resizing a column to have zero width produces exactly the same effect).

You can hide more than one column at once. Let's try hiding all of the address columns so that the columns to the right of the addresses fit on the screen.

Click and drag the mouse pointer across the column headings (above row **1**) for columns **F** to **J** to select the address columns.

Right-click and select **Hide** from the menu, as before.

Your worksheet should now look like Figure 2.8. Suppose you had a list of membership numbers for those people with long-overdue rentals, and you needed to phone them all to remind them. Hiding the address details could save you a lot of scrolling!

Microsoft Excel - videoshop.xls

	A	B	C	D	E	K	L	M	O	P
1	**Member**	**Title**	**Initial**	**Surname**	**Date of birth**	**Daytime Telephone**	**Evening Telephone**	**Date Joined**		
2	1	Mr	T	Henderson	21/04/1976	(01211) 963156	(01211) 226585	23/01/2001		
3	2	Mr	M	Thompson	04/12/1976	(01211) 885049	(01211) 728021	16/07/2003		
4	3	Mrs	N	Smith	21/07/1975	(01211) 596380	(01211) 483232	09/05/2002		
5	4	Ms	A	Brown	01/02/1982	(01211) 467059	(01211) 467059	02/06/2004		
6	5	Mr	G	Jones	06/02/1980	(01211) 153798	(01211) 380438	07/06/2000		
7	6	Ms	E	Patel	05/11/1981	(01211) 661890	(01211) 174892	12/07/2001		
8	7	Ms	T	Kendal	13/03/1979	(01211) 763804	(01211) 302378	10/06/2000		
9	8	Dr	A	Hooper	08/04/1968	(01211) 530500	(01211) 567363	13/04/2001		
10	9	Mr	E	McBride	30/03/1980	(01211) 574553	(01211) 546985	25/12/2004		
11	10	Mr	O	Trapp	12/10/1979	(01211) 704444	(01211) 306897	15/04/2003		
12	11	Mrs	S	Honeywell	15/05/1971	(01211) 110504	(01211) 973145	07/06/2004		
13	12	Ms	J	Stroud	05/10/1983	(01211) 383584	(01211) 485313	28/04/2001		
14	13	Mr	J	Levington	28/07/1977	(01211) 576957	(01211) 485816	06/08/2001		
15	14	Ms	T	Stewart	05/01/1987	(01211) 857128	(01211) 857128	07/04/2004		
16	15	Ms	B	Taylor	17/11/1981	(01211) 497373	(01211) 497373	18/03/2000		
17	16	Ms	K	Bennett	29/05/1973	(01211) 840184	(01211) 896503	06/03/2002		
18	17	Mr	A	White	18/01/1982	(01211) 104271	(01211) 685885	16/10/2003		
19	18	Ms	E	King	24/03/1979	(01211) 170625	(01211) 234989	07/07/2000		
20	19	Mr	N	Wright	06/07/1975	(01211) 297132	(01211) 297132	03/12/2003		
21	20	Mr	M	Carter	09/12/1968	(01211) 813189	(01211) 323840	25/02/2004		
22	21	Ms	C	Foster	17/11/1974	(01211) 344968	(01211) 166158	22/08/2001		
23	22	Mrs	O	Mitchell	05/10/1978	(01211) 261548	(01211) 104371	05/07/2003		
24	23	Ms	W	Miller	17/07/1969	(01211) 710278	(01211) 284965	18/10/2003		

Sales / Rentals / Stock / **Members**

Ready

Figure 2.8: Worksheet with hidden columns

There are a couple of ways to restore hidden columns. Since they are quick, we'll cover both here.

The first technique is similar to resizing column widths.

Hover the mouse pointer in the area between the column headings for columns **M** and **O**. If you hover on the right of the border, the pointer will change to show two vertical bars instead of one – see the difference between parts (a) and (b) of Figure 2.9. When the pointer shows a double vertical bar, click and drag it to the right to restore column **N**.

M	O
Date Joined	
23/01/2001	
16/07/2003	
09/05/2002	
02/06/2004	

M	O
Date Joined	
23/01/2001	
16/07/2003	
09/05/2002	
02/06/2004	

Figure 2.9: The mouse pointer shape for (a) resizing column M and (b) restoring column N

We'll use a different technique to unhide the address columns.

Click and drag the mouse pointer over the column headings for columns **E** and **K** to select both columns. Right-click and select **Unhide** from the menu that appears, as shown in Figure 2.10.

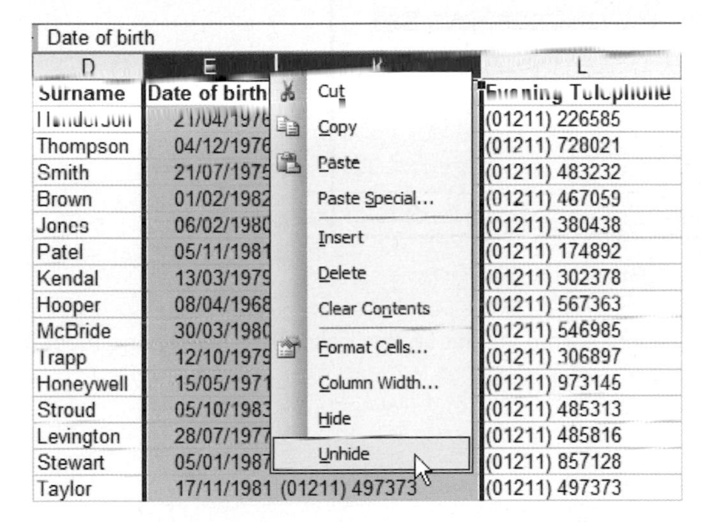

Figure 2.10: Unhiding multiple hidden columns using the right-click menu

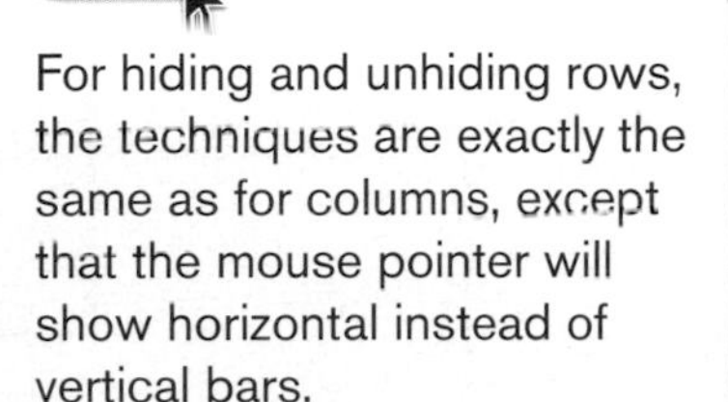

For hiding and unhiding rows, the techniques are exactly the same as for columns, except that the mouse pointer will show horizontal instead of vertical bars.

The address columns reappear. If you look across the column headings, all of the letters should be there again.

Hiding worksheets

Syllabus Ref: AM4.1.2.7
Hide/unhide worksheets.

Sometimes you might need to hide an entire worksheet. This is also straightforward.

Look at the tabs at the bottom of your Excel window. Each tab represents a worksheet in the workbook. Let's hide the **Stock** worksheet.

With **Stock** on display, select **Format**, **Sheet**, **Hide** from the menu. **Stock** disappears.

Hiding worksheets can be particularly useful in combination with **protection** (preventing changes and adding passwords), which we will cover in Chapter 9.

To unhide a hidden worksheet, the method is similar.

From the menu, select **Format**, **Sheet**, **Unhide**. The **Unhide** dialogue box appears, as shown in Figure 2.11.

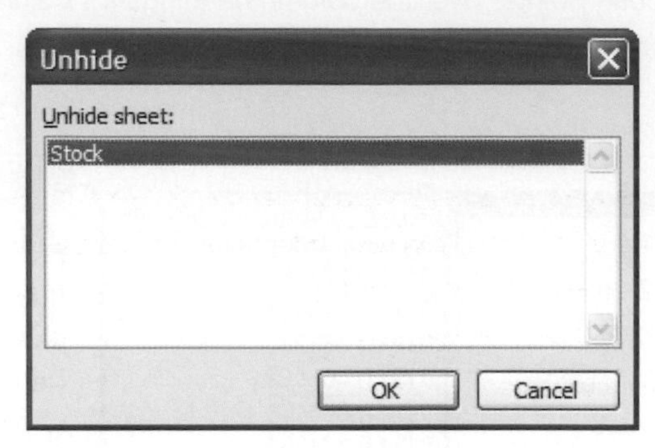

Figure 2.11: Unhiding the Stock worksheet

To unhide a particular worksheet, select it from the list (in this case there is only one hidden worksheet, which is already selected) and press **OK**.

Formula auditing

Finally, we'll have a look at a couple of techniques for working with worksheets that contain formulas.

Switch to the **Sales** worksheet.

This is a summary of the shop's sales of ex-rental products over a two-year period. The sales are split up by category – video, DVD and game – and then formulas are used to generate the quarterly sales figure and a running total.

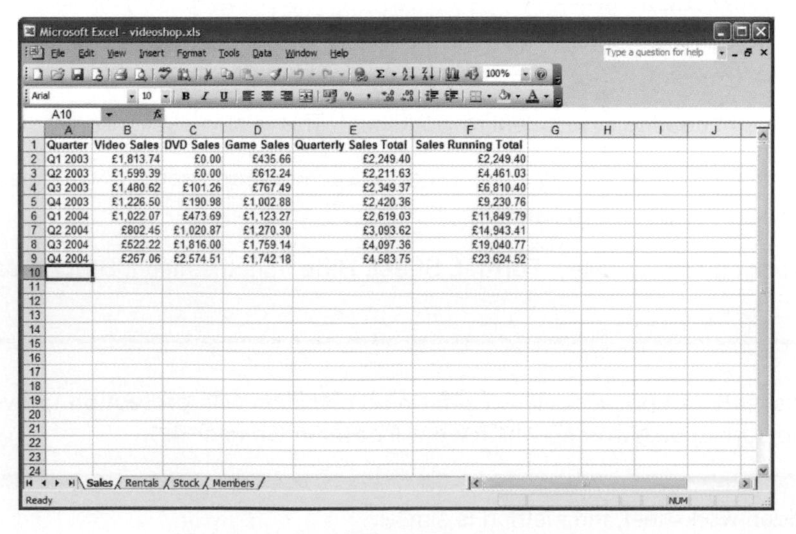

Quarter	Video Sales	DVD Sales	Game Sales	Quarterly Sales Total	Sales Running Total
Q1 2003	£1,813.74	£0.00	£435.66	£2,249.40	£2,249.40
Q2 2003	£1,599.39	£0.00	£612.24	£2,211.63	£4,461.03
Q3 2003	£1,480.62	£101.26	£767.49	£2,349.37	£6,810.40
Q4 2003	£1,226.50	£190.98	£1,002.88	£2,420.36	£9,230.76
Q1 2004	£1,022.07	£473.69	£1,123.27	£2,619.03	£11,849.79
Q2 2004	£802.45	£1,020.87	£1,270.30	£3,093.62	£14,943.41
Q3 2004	£522.22	£1,816.00	£1,759.14	£4,097.36	£19,040.77
Q4 2004	£267.06	£2,574.51	£1,742.18	£4,583.75	£23,624.52

Figure 2.12: A worksheet that contains formulas

We will use this worksheet to learn some useful techniques for managing formulas. Remember that, although this is a simple worksheet, you will be able to use the same methods whenever you need to untangle a complicated worksheet in the future.

Displaying formulas

If you're trying to understand someone else's worksheet, or one you created yourself some time ago, it can be useful to display all of the formulas instead of their results. In fact, it's not always obvious which cells contain formulas, and which are just values, so first we'll look at a method of highlighting all of the formulas on the current worksheet.

Syllabus Ref: AM4.4.3.3
Display all formulas or view location of all formulas in a worksheet.

From the menu, select **Edit**, **Go To** (or press the shortcut key **Ctrl+G**). The **Go To** dialogue appears.

We will use this dialogue to select all of the cells that contain formulas.

Press the **Special** button. The **Go To Special** dialogue appears.

Select the **Formulas** option and leave all of the sub-options ticked, as shown in Figure 2.13. Press **OK**.

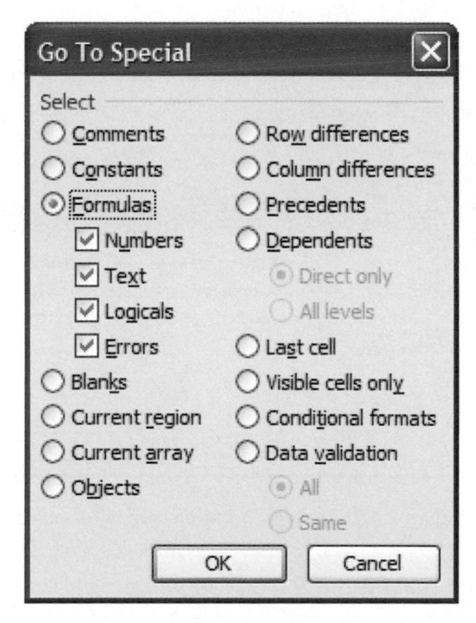

Figure 2.13: Selecting all of the formulas in a worksheet

The 16 cells that contain formulas (**E2:F9**) have been selected, as shown in Figure 2.14. You could, for example, change the background colour of these cells to indicate that they contain formulas, or you could protect them if you don't want them to be changed accidentally.

	A	B	C	D	E	F
1	Quarter	Video Sales	DVD Sales	Game Sales	Quarterly Sales Total	Sales Running Total
2	Q1 2003	£1,813.74	£0.00	£435.66	£2,249.40	£2,249.40
3	Q2 2003	£1,599.39	£0.00	£612.24	£2,211.63	£4,461.03
4	Q3 2003	£1,480.62	£101.26	£767.49	£2,349.37	£6,810.40
5	Q4 2003	£1,226.50	£190.98	£1,002.88	£2,420.36	£9,230.76
6	Q1 2004	£1,022.07	£473.69	£1,123.27	£2,619.03	£11,849.79
7	Q2 2004	£802.45	£1,020.87	£1,270.30	£3,093.62	£14,943.41
8	Q3 2004	£522.22	£1,816.00	£1,759.14	£4,097.36	£19,040.77
9	Q4 2004	£267.06	£2,574.51	£1,742.18	£4,583.75	£23,624.52

Figure 2.14: The cells that contain formulas have been selected

If you actually need to be able to see the formulas themselves then you can change the view settings to display the formulas instead of their values.

From the menu, select **Tools**, **Options**. The **Options** dialogue box appears. On the **View** tab, tick **Formulas** in the **Window options** section, as shown in Figure 2.15. Press **OK**.

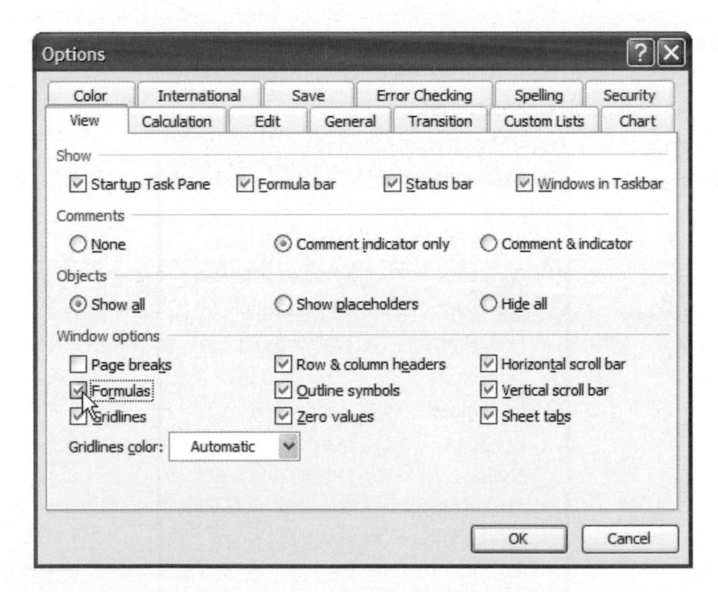

Figure 2.15: Turning on the display of formulas

The formulas will appear as shown in Figure 2.16. You will probably need to resize the columns to fit them all on the screen.

	A	B	C	D	E	F
1	Quarter	Video Sales	DVD Sales	Game Sales	Quarterly Sales Total	Sales Running Total
2	Q1 2003	1813.74	0	435.66	=SUM(B2:D2)	=E2
3	Q2 2003	1599.39	0	612.24	=SUM(B3:D3)	=F2+E3
4	Q3 2003	1480.62	101.26	767.49	=SUM(B4:D4)	=F3+E4
5	Q4 2003	1226.5	190.98	1002.88	=SUM(B5:D5)	=F4+E5
6	Q1 2004	1022.07	473.69	1123.27	=SUM(B6:D6)	=F5+E6
7	Q2 2004	802.45	1020.87	1270.3	=SUM(B7:D7)	=F6+E7
8	Q3 2004	522.22	1816	1759.14	=SUM(B8:D8)	=F7+E8
9	Q4 2004	267.06	2574.51	1742.18	=SUM(B9:D9)	=F8+E9

Figure 2.16: Displaying the formulas

Press **Ctrl+`** (where ` is the opening single quote character – not the apostrophe – probably located just below the **Esc** key).

The formulas are replaced by their values again. This is simply the shortcut key for toggling on and off the formula view. It's much quicker but more difficult to remember.

Resize the columns to fit their values.

Precedent cells

Formula auditing lets you see which cells refer to which other cells. Excel presents this information using arrows.

Suppose we want to know which cells are used by the formula in cell **F5**. (Remember, it could be a much more complicated formula than the one we have.)

Syllabus Ref: AM4.4.3.1
Trace precedent cells in a worksheet.

Select cell **F5**. From the menu, choose **Tools**, **Formula Auditing**, **Trace Precedents**. Two blue arrows appear, coming from cells **F4** and **E5**; this indicates that these cells **precede** ('are used by') cell **F5**.

	A	B	C	D	E	F
1	Quarter	Video Sales	DVD Sales	Game Sales	Quarterly Sales Total	Sales Running Total
2	Q1 2003	£1,813.74	£0.00	£435.66	£2,249.40	£2,249.40
3	Q2 2003	£1,599.39	£0.00	£612.24	£2,211.63	£4,461.03
4	Q3 2003	£1,480.62	£101.26	£767.49	£2,349.37	£6,810.40
5	Q4 2003	£1,226.50	£190.98	£1,002.88	£2,420.36	£9,230.76
6	Q1 2004	£1,022.07	£473.69	£1,123.27	£2,619.03	£11,849.79
7	Q2 2004	£802.45	£1,020.87	£1,270.30	£3,093.62	£14,943.41
8	Q3 2004	£522.22	£1,816.00	£1,759.14	£4,097.36	£19,040.77
9	Q4 2004	£267.06	£2,574.51	£1,742.18	£4,583.75	£23,624.52

Figure 2.17: Cells F4 and E5 are precedents of cell F5

Dependent cells

Syllabus Ref: AM4.4.3.2
Trace dependent cells in a worksheet.

In a similar way, we can find out which cells are **dependent on** ('use') a particular cell. Let's try this for cell **C8**.

Select cell **C8**, and choose **Tools**, **Formula Auditing**, **Trace Dependents** from the menu.

An arrow appears leading to cell **E8**, as shown in Figure 2.18. This indicates that the value in cell **C8** is used in the calculation for cell **E8**. This is correct, since **E8** holds the sum of the three cells **B8**, **C8** and **D8**.

	A	B	C	D	E	F
1	Quarter	Video Sales	DVD Sales	Game Sales	Quarterly Sales Total	Sales Running Total
2	Q1 2003	£1,813.74	£0.00	£435.66	£2,249.40	£2,249.40
3	Q2 2003	£1,599.39	£0.00	£612.24	£2,211.63	£4,461.03
4	Q3 2003	£1,480.62	£101.26	£767.49	£2,349.37	£6,810.40
5	Q4 2003	£1,226.50	£190.98	£1,002.88	£2,420.36	£9,230.76
6	Q1 2004	£1,022.07	£473.69	£1,123.27	£2,619.03	£11,849.79
7	Q2 2004	£802.45	£1,020.87	£1,270.30	£3,093.62	£14,943.41
8	Q3 2004	£522.22	£1,816.00	£1,759.14	£4,097.36	£19,040.77
9	Q4 2004	£267.06	£2,574.51	£1,742.18	£4,583.75	£23,624.52

Figure 2.18: Tracing dependent cells

Clear all the arrows by selecting **Tools**, **Formula Auditing**, **Remove All Arrows** from the menu.

Test yourself

1. Hide columns **B** to **E** in the **Sales** worksheet to leave just a list of quarters and their running totals. Now hide the four rows containing the 2003 sales. Unhide everything again when you have finished.

2. In the **Members** worksheet, hide the **Title** and **Initial** columns. Freeze the panes so that the **Member** and **Surname** columns and the first row are always visible. Test this by scrolling through the worksheet, then unhide the hidden columns and unfreeze the panes.

3. In the **Sales** worksheet, select cell **B2**. Use **Trace Dependents** repeatedly to follow the path of cells that depend on the value in cell **B2**. You may find it easier to use the **Formula Auditing toolbar** – which you can open using **View, Toolbars**, **Formula Auditing** – instead of the menu. Clear the arrows when you have finished.

3 Importing Data

Introduction

This chapter shows how you can create a spreadsheet from an external source of information, and how to use Excel to quickly format and manipulate that information.

In this chapter you will

- obtain some raw weather information in plain text format (you can download this from the Internet or type it in yourself)
- import this external information into a spreadsheet and use **AutoFormat** to quickly tidy it up
- create a **custom number format** to change the way temperature values are presented
- use **conditional formatting** to colour-code the temperatures so that cold ones are blue, hot ones are red and so on
- use Excel's **text functions** to manipulate imported text – concatenating text strings and converting their case
- learn how to add, edit and remove **comments**.

Holiday weather

This chapter is all about importing raw (unprocessed) information and using Excel to present it in a more interesting and useful way. The first step is to get hold of the raw information.

Imagine you are planning a holiday for next year, but you have not yet decided where or when you want to go. Your local travel agent has emailed you some details of what kind of weather you can expect in various different cities – see Figure 3.1 – but you're finding it difficult to get your head around what it all means.

cities.txt - Notepad

File Edit Format View Help

```
City,Month,Ave.Sunlight (hours),Min. Ave. Temp.,Max. Ave. Temp.,Min. Temp.,Max. Temp.,Rainfall (mm)
Prague,Jan,2,-5,0,-23,13,18
Prague,Jul,8,13,23,6,38,68
Stockholm,Jan,1,-5,-1,-28,10,43
Stockholm,Jul,10,14,22,8,35,61
Copenhagen,Jan,1,-2,2,-24,10,49
Copenhagen,Jul,8,14,22,8,31,71
Sydney,Jan,7,18,26,11,46,89
Sydney,Jul,6,8,16,2,26,117
Cairo,Jan,7,8,18,2,31,5
Cairo,Jul,12,21,36,16,43,0
London,Jan,1,2,6,-10,14,54
London,Jul,6,14,22,7,34,57
New York,Jan,5,-4,3,-21,20,94
New York,Jul,10,19,28,12,39,107
Mexico City,Jan,7,6,19,-3,23,13
Mexico City,Jul,6,12,23,8,28,170
Zurich,Jan,2,-3,2,-17,17,74
Zurich,Jul,8,14,25,7,38,136
```

Figure 3.1: Raw weather information for popular holiday destinations

First, we'll type in this file (and pretend that the travel agent did it!). Then we'll look at how to use Excel to format it nicely.

If you prefer, you can download the file **cities.txt** from the publisher's website at www.payne-gallway.co.uk/ecdl.

From the **Start** menu, select **All Programs**, **Accessories**, **Notepad**.

Notepad is a simple editing application that comes with Windows. **Notepad** is used for creating and editing **plain text files**: documents that don't have any formatting information embedded in them.

Type the text from Figure 3.1 into your **Notepad** window. Every line should have eight things on it, separated by commas (making this a **comma-delimited** file). Press **Enter** at the end of each line (it is OK to have a blank line at the bottom)

Press **Ctrl+S** and save the file as **cities.txt**.

That's the boring bit done. Now that you've got your impenetrable list of numbers and commas, we can get on to the fun stuff, in Excel itself.

Start Excel if it isn't already running.

From the menu, select **File**, **Open**. The **Open** dialogue appears, as shown in Figure 3.2.

Syllabus Ref: AM4.1.1.6

Import/Export data in different formats (e.g. csv, txt, xml) to a specified location on a drive.

You can use **File**, **Save As** to export data. Any file type except **xls** is likely to strip out formatting or other information.

Change the **Files of type** drop-down to **Text Files (*.prn; *.txt; *.csv)**. Navigate to the folder in which you saved **cities.txt** and double-click it to open it.

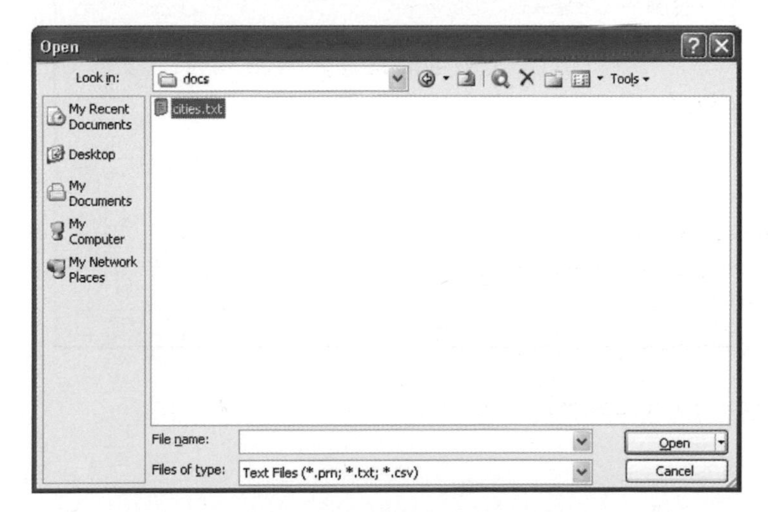

Figure 3.2: Importing a text file

The **Text Import Wizard** appears, showing **Step 1 of 3**. Make sure that the **Original data type** is set to **Delimited** and then press **Next**.

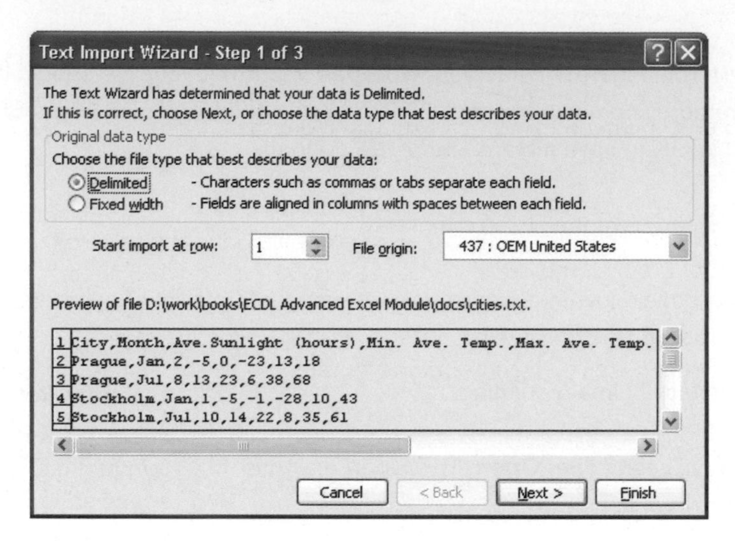

Figure 3.3: Starting to import a plain text file

In **Step 2**, change the **Delimiters** so that only **Comma** is ticked. The **Data preview** area shows the effect the chosen delimiters have on how Excel breaks the information into columns (for example, if you tick **Space** too, you get too many columns, because some of the headings contain spaces).

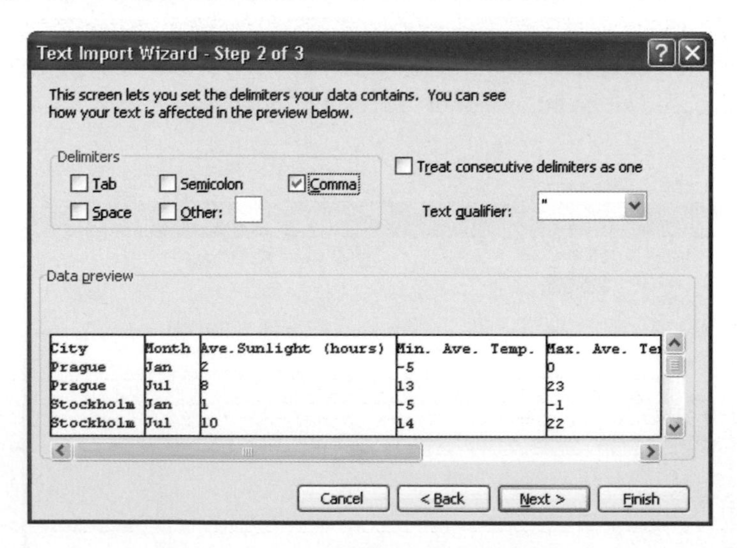

Figure 3.4: Setting delimiters for imported text

Press **Next**.

You need a good understanding of the options from this step of the import process, so that you can choose settings to match the layout of any raw data you need to import.

The various **Delimiters** represent the characters that are most commonly used for separating fields (such as **City** and **Month**) in a text file, and you can use **Other** to give a specific different delimiter character if you need to. You can specify more than one delimiter; each time Excel encounters any of them, it will treat the data that follows as a separate field.

The **Treat consecutive delimiters as one** option can be used in the special case where there are no blank fields, and where more than a single delimiter character has been used between fields. For example, if **Tab** characters have been used to line up the columns in a text file, then there may be several **Tab** characters between one field and the next (depending how long the contents of the fields are). In this case, two consecutive **Tab** characters should be treated as a single delimiter (because they haven't got a blank value between them), so this option should be ticked.

The **Text qualifier** drop-down has three options: " (double quotes), ' (single quotes) and **{none}**. If a text field is **qualified** (that is, wrapped in quotes), then any delimiter characters it contains are taken to be part of the text field itself.

The final step lets you specify formats for the information being imported. It is generally OK to leave everything as the **General** type, since you can change the format of cells afterwards if you need to. Just press **Finish**.

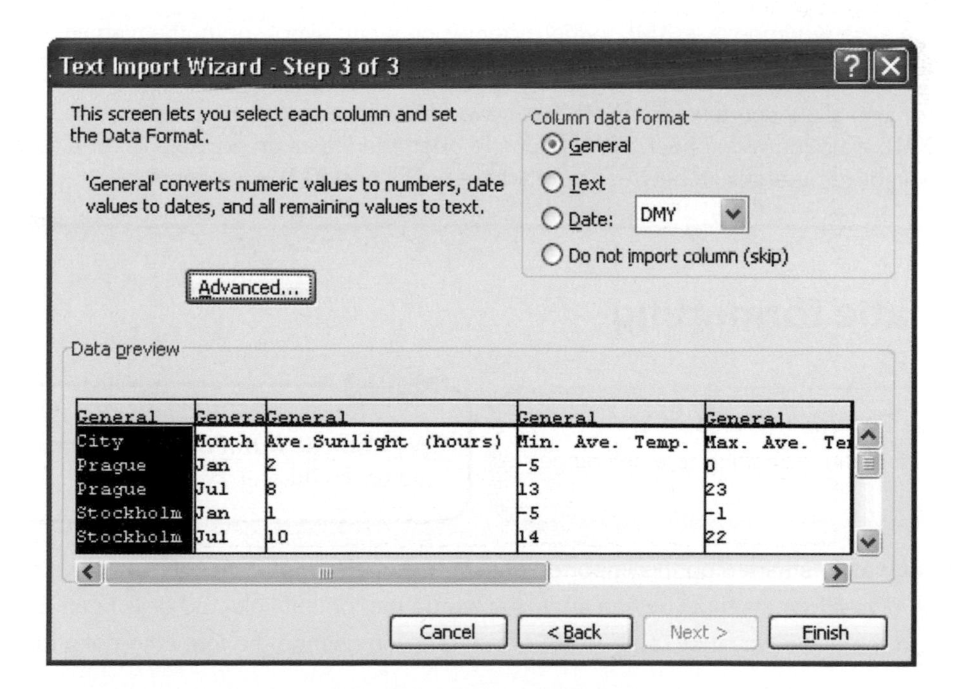

Figure 3.5: Column data formats

The initial imported file doesn't look very good (see Figure 3.6), but at least the figures should line up in their columns.

	A	B	C	D	E	F	G	H
1	City	Month	Ave.Sunlig	Min. Ave.	Max. Ave.	Min. Temp	Max. Tem	Rainfall (mm)
2	Prague	Jan	2	-5	0	-23	13	18
3	Prague	Jul	8	13	23	6	38	68
4	Stockholm	Jan	1	-5	-1	-28	10	43
5	Stockholm	Jul	10	14	22	8	35	61
6	Copenhag	Jan	1	-2	2	-24	10	49
7	Copenhag	Jul	8	14	22	8	31	71
8	Sydney	Jan	7	18	26	11	46	89
9	Sydney	Jul	6	8	16	2	26	117
10	Cairo	Jan	7	8	18	2	31	5
11	Cairo	Jul	12	21	36	16	43	0
12	London	Jan	1	2	6	-10	14	54
13	London	Jul	6	14	22	7	34	57
14	New York	Jan	5	-4	3	-21	20	94
15	New York	Jul	10	19	28	12	39	107
16	Mexico Cit	Jan	7	6	19	-3	23	13
17	Mexico Cit	Jul	6	12	23	8	28	170
18	Zurich	Jan	2	-3	2	-17	17	74
19	Zurich	Jul	8	14	25	7	38	136
20								

Figure 3.6: Raw weather data – how it looks immediately after import

XML stands for **eXtensible Markup Language**. This is a popular language for exchanging data betweeen applications.

Excel can save workbooks in **XML** format, after which it can simply open them again – there is no import process to go through.

Excel will also allow you to import **XML** files saved from other programs. In this case, the **Open XML** dialogue will appear, with options to open the file as an editable list or a read-only workbook, or to create links between spreadsheet cells and **XML** data items.

Automatic formatting

Syllabus Ref: AM4.1.1.2 (1 of 2)
Apply automatic formatting to a cell range.

We also use **AutoFormat** to format pivot tables in Chapter 16.

The quickest way to smarten up this imported data is to **AutoFormat** it. **AutoFormat** is a built-in collection of cell formats that you can apply to change the look of selected cells in an Excel worksheet, in the same way that **Table AutoFormat** lets you change the formatting of a table in Word.

Click and drag the mouse pointer over cells **A1:H19** to select them (this should be all of the information in the worksheet).

From the menu, select **Format**, **AutoFormat**. The **AutoFormat** dialogue appears.

Scroll down the list and select **Colorful 2**. Notice how you can use the **Options** button to toggle on and off the detailed display of which **Formats to apply**; make sure all the boxes are ticked. Press **OK**.

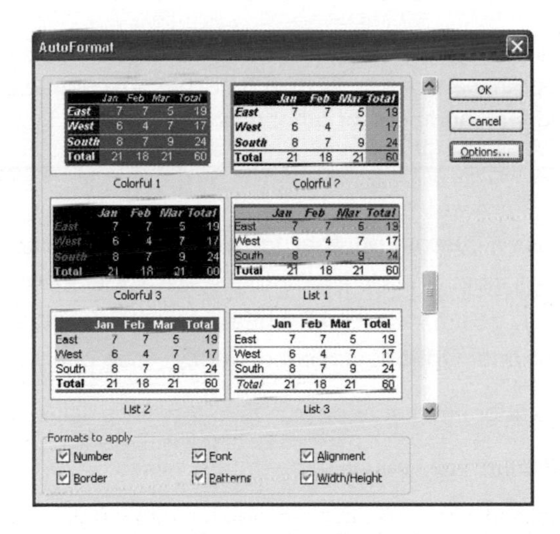

Figure 3.7: Applying AutoFormat to selected cells in a worksheet

If you now click in some other cell to clear the selection, you should see that your worksheet looks like Figure 3.8. Notice how, despite the preview in the **AutoFormat** dialogue, neither the bottom row nor the right-hand column have received any special formatting – **AutoFormat** is smart enough to know that these do not contain totals, so they are formatted in the same way as the other body cells.

	A	B	C	D	E	F	G	H
1	City	Month	Ave.Sunlight (hours)	Min. Ave. Temp.	Max. Ave. Temp.	Min. Temp.	Max. Temp.	Rainfall (mm)
2	Prague	Jan	2	-5	0	-23	13	18
3	Prague	Jul	8	13	23	6	38	68
4	Stockholm	Jan	1	-5	-1	-28	10	43
5	Stockholm	Jul	10	14	22	8	35	61
6	Copenhagen	Jan	1	-2	2	-24	10	49
7	Copenhagen	Jul	8	14	22	8	31	71
8	Sydney	Jan	7	18	26	11	46	89
9	Sydney	Jul	6	8	16	2	26	117
10	Cairo	Jan	7	8	18	2	31	5
11	Cairo	Jul	12	21	36	16	43	0
12	London	Jan	1	2	6	-10	14	54
13	London	Jul	6	14	22	7	34	57
14	New York	Jan	5	-4	3	-21	20	94
15	New York	Jul	10	19	28	12	39	107
16	Mexico City	Jan	7	6	19	-3	23	13
17	Mexico City	Jul	6	12	23	8	28	170
18	Zurich	Jan	2	-3	2	-17	17	74
19	Zurich	Jul	8	14	25	7	38	136
20								

Figure 3.8: Imported data after AutoFormat has been applied

Custom number formats

Syllabus Ref: AM4.1.1.3
Create custom number formats.

It would be nice if we could display the temperatures with their units in the table, for example showing **18°C** instead of just **18**. We could type these in, but this would replace all of the numbers with strings, so we would lose the ability to perform calculations on them.

The word **string** in this sense simply means **text**. Excel's help file also refers to strings. This is the term that programmers use for textual data, because it can be thought of as a string (or chain) of individual letters, numbers, or other characters.

A better approach is to create a **custom number format** that just changes the way these cells are displayed, leaving their values intact. This is similar to the way Excel treats currency values: if you type **£15** into a cell, it actually gets a value of **15**, but a currency format is applied to it so that it is displayed as **£15** (if the **Regional Options** are set correctly – see page 14).

Let's create a custom number format that appends **°C** to the cell's value when it is displayed.

 Select cells **D2:G19**, which all contain temperature values.

 From the menu, select **Format**, **Cells**. The **Format Cells** dialogue appears (see Figure 3.9).

 With the **Number** tab selected, choose **Custom** as the **Category**. Click in the edit box beneath the label **Type** on the right-hand side and delete its contents.

 In the edit box, type the three characters **0°C**. (The first character is a **zero**. To get the degrees sign, make sure the **Number Lock** light is on and hold down **Alt** while typing the four digits **0176** on the numeric keypad. You don't need to remember how to do this for the exam). Press **OK** to apply the change.

You can use the **Alt+number** trick to enter symbols that may not appear directly on your keyboard. You will need to know the **ASCII code** (1–255) for the symbol you want. Note that this will work in any Windows program, not just Excel.

If the menu command **Insert**, **Symbol** is available then this is usually easier. You can also use the dialogue box that appears to find the ASCII codes for symbols you use often (change the **from** drop-down to **ASCII(decimal)** to see the correct code).

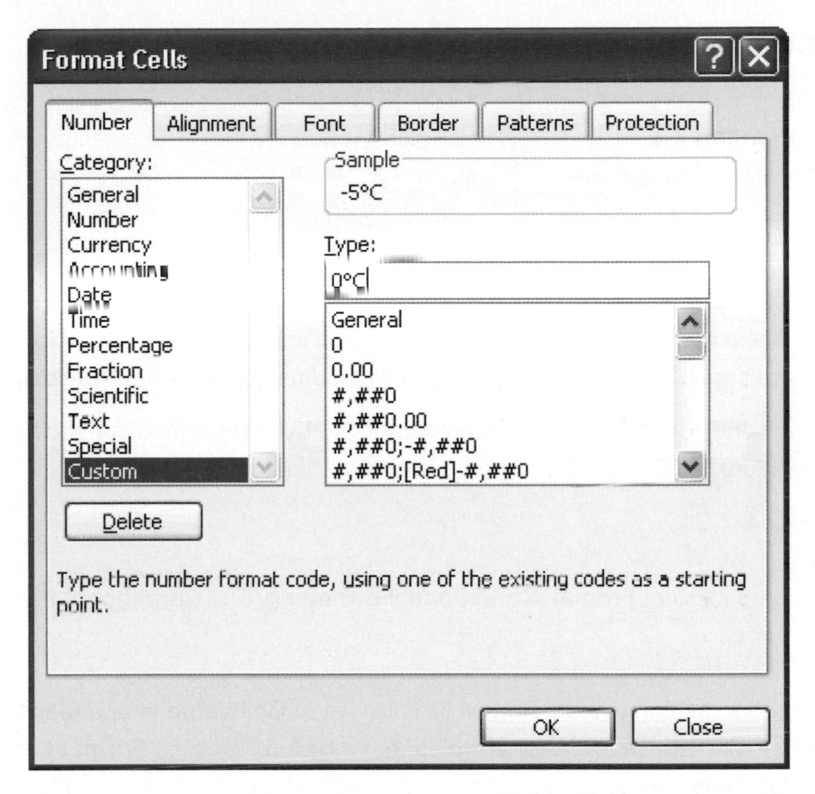

Figure 3.9: Creating a custom number format for degrees Celsius

The **zero** you added at the beginning of the format is a **format code** that tells Excel to display a number at that location. Excel provides lots of format codes, such as

0 display digit, even if not significant

display only significant digits

' display thousands separator

. display decimal point

So, for example:

#,### displays **1234** as **1,234**

00.000 displays **1.2** as **01.200**, and **1.2345** as **01.235**

There are many more options than this, and you should familiarise yourself with them – search for the article **Create or delete a custom number format** in the online help.

Conditional formatting

Syllabus Ref: AM4.1.1.4
Use conditional formatting options.

Sometimes it can be useful to apply formatting to cells based on the values they contain. A typical example of this is highlighting all of the negative values by displaying them in red. For this simple case, you could use a **custom number format**, which lets you specify the colour for negative numbers. For more sophisticated control, you must instead use **conditional formatting**.

Let's set up conditional formatting for the temperatures so that they are colour-coded: less than 5°C as blue, 25°C to 35°C as orange and more than 35°C as red.

Select cells **D2:G19**.

From the menu, select **Format**, **Conditional Formatting**. The **Conditional Formatting** dialogue appears.

Make sure that the first two drop-down lists are set to **Cell Value Is** and **less than** respectively. Click in the text area to the right and type **5**. Click the **Format** button. The **Format Cells** dialogue appears. With the **Font** tab selected, choose blue as the **Color** (see Figure 3.10) and press **OK**.

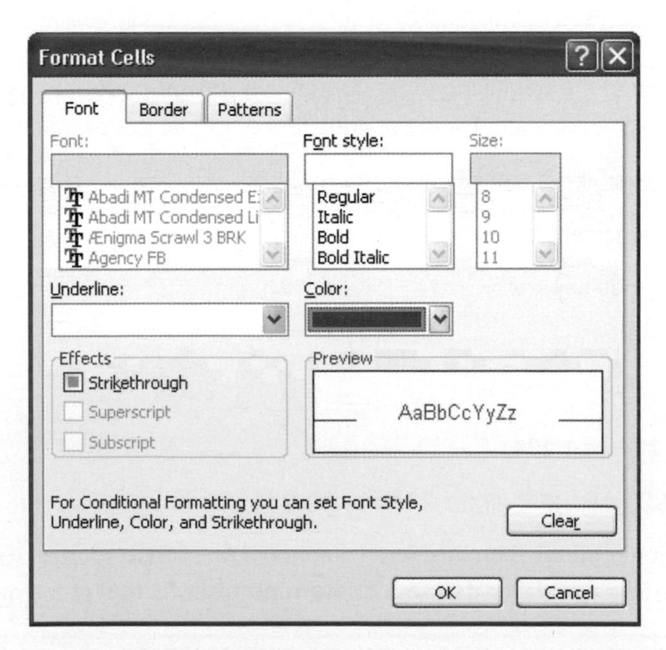

Figure 3.10: Setting cell formats – changing font colour to blue

The **Conditional Formatting** dialogue should now look like Figure 3.11. This instructs Excel that if the cell value is less than 5, the cell should be displayed with a blue font.

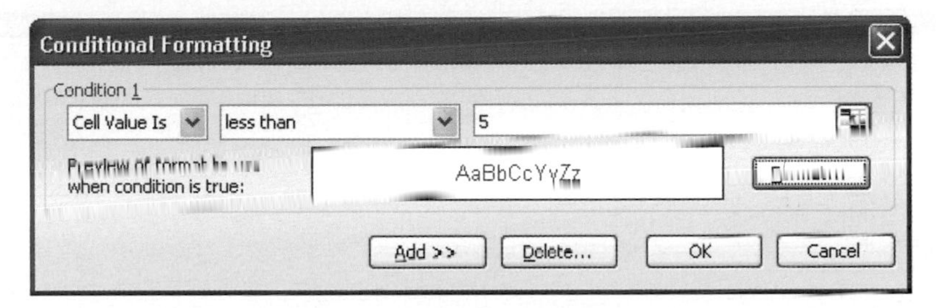

Figure 3.11: Setting the conditional format for cold temperatures

We have used a constant value (**5**) for the comparison, but we could have used a cell reference instead.

Instead of **Cell Value Is**, you could choose **Formula Is**. This is useful when you want to set the formatting of a row (or column) of cells based on values in another row (or column); for example, making the city name bold if the rainfall is above 50 mm.

Click **Add >>** on the **Conditional Formatting** dialogue; this allows us to add a second condition that can be formatted differently from the first one. This time, set the condition so that if the cell value is between 25 and 35 then it will use an orange font.

Add a third condition so that if the cell value is greater than 35 then it will be displayed in red. The **Conditional Formatting** dialogue should now look like Figure 3.12. Press **OK** to apply the formatting.

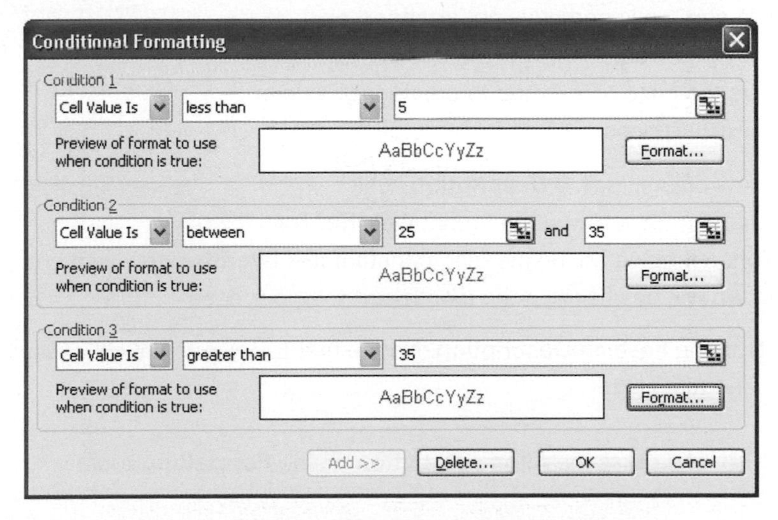

Figure 3.12: Conditional formats for three temperature ranges

The temperatures are now colour-coded and the spreadsheet should look like Figure 3.13.

	A	B	C	D	E	F	G	H
1	City	Month	Ave.Sunlight (hours)	Min. Ave. Temp.	Max. Ave. Temp.	Min. Temp.	Max. Temp.	Rainfall (mm)
2	Prague	Jan	2	-5°C	0°C	-23°C	13°C	18
3	Prague	Jul	8	13°C	23°C	6°C	38°C	68
4	Stockholm	Jan	1	-5°C	-1°C	-28°C	10°C	43
5	Stockholm	Jul	10	14°C	22°C	8°C	35°C	61
6	Copenhagen	Jan	1	-2°C	2°C	-24°C	10°C	49
7	Copenhagen	Jul	8	14°C	22°C	8°C	31°C	71
8	Sydney	Jan	7	18°C	26°C	11°C	46°C	89
9	Sydney	Jul	6	8°C	16°C	2°C	26°C	117
10	Cairo	Jan	7	8°C	18°C	2°C	31°C	5
11	Cairo	Jul	12	21°C	36°C	16°C	43°C	0
12	London	Jan	1	2°C	6°C	-10°C	14°C	54
13	London	Jul	6	14°C	22°C	7°C	34°C	57
14	New York	Jan	5	-4°C	3°C	-21°C	20°C	94
15	New York	Jul	10	19°C	28°C	12°C	39°C	107
16	Mexico City	Jan	7	6°C	19°C	-3°C	23°C	13
17	Mexico City	Jul	6	12°C	23°C	8°C	28°C	170
18	Zurich	Jan	2	-3°C	2°C	-17°C	17°C	74
19	Zurich	Jul	8	14°C	25°C	7°C	38°C	136

Figure 3.13: Temperatures with a custom number format and conditional formatting

It is important to understand that conditional formatting changes the format to reflect the data held in the spreadsheet – it is dynamic and will change as the values change.

The Minimum Average Temperature for Zurich in July is 14°C; this does not have any special formatting applied since it doesn't fall into the temperature bands we specified. Change the cell's value to **-1**, and check that the colour changes to **blue**. Change it to **30**, and check that the colour becomes **orange**. Change it to **36**, and check that it becomes **red**. Finally, change the value back to **14**.

Transforming text

Sometimes the text you are importing is not arranged or formatted in the way you would like. You can use Excel's text functions to change the case of text, and to create new values by concatenating existing ones.

> **Syllabus Ref: AM4.3.1.4**
> Use text functions: PROPER; UPPER; LOWER; CONCATENATE.

We will create a new column called **Description**, which will contain a description for each row in the format **Weather for Prague (JAN)**. Notice that we will be merging constant text (**Weather for**) with cell values (**Prague** from cell **A2**), and we will be changing the month part to upper case.

In cell **I1**, type the heading **Description**. Notice that Excel automatically formats this cell to match the one to its left.

Align Left

Click in cell **I1** and press the **Align Left** button on the **Formatting** toolbar.

We want cell **I2** to contain a formula that builds the description in the correct format. First, we'll use the **CONCATENATE** function to add together the fixed text and cell values; once this is working, we can capitalise the month part.

In cell **I2**, type the formula **=CONCATENATE("Weather for ", A2)**. Notice that there is a space before the second quote.

This should give the result **Weather for Prague** in cell **I2**. We can add as many parameters as we like to the **CONCATENATE** function, so let's add the rest of the description text.

Change the formula in cell I2 to **=CONCATENATE("Weather for ", A2, " (", B2, ")")**.

This should result in **Weather for Prague (Jan)**, which is close to what we want. The only thing that remains is for us to convert the month part to upper case. For this we can use the **UPPER** function.

Change the formula in cell **I2** by changing the reference to **B2** to **UPPER(B2)**, so that the whole formula becomes **=CONCATENATE("Weather for ", A2, "(", UPPER(B2), ")")**.

You should now have the result you wanted – **Weather for Prague (JAN)**.

Notice that when you select a cell or a group of cells, there is a small black rectangle in the bottom-right of the selected area. This is called the **fill handle**. Your mouse pointer changes into a black cross when you hover it over the fill handle. You can then click and drag the fill handle to fill adjacent cells with new values based on those in the selected cells. If you don't get a fill handle, check that **Tools**, **Options**, **Edit**, **Allow cell drag and drop** is ticked.

Use the **fill handle** to copy the formula down the column to cell **I19**.

Select cell **A2** and press the **Format Painter** button on the **Standard** toolbar. Click and drag the mouse pointer down cells **I2:I19** to give them a yellow background to match the other cells in the table.

Format Painter

Double-click the vertical line between the column headings for columns **I** and **J**. This resizes column **I** to fit its contents. Column **I** should now look like Figure 3.14.

I
Description
Weather for Prague (JAN)
Weather for Prague (JUL)
Weather for Stockholm (JAN)
Weather for Stockholm (JUL)
Weather for Copenhagen (JAN)
Weather for Copenhagen (JUL)
Weather for Sydney (JAN)
Weather for Sydney (JUL)
Weather for Cairo (JAN)
Weather for Cairo (JUL)
Weather for London (JAN)
Weather for London (JUL)
Weather for New York (JAN)
Weather for New York (JUL)
Weather for Mexico City (JAN)
Weather for Mexico City (JUL)
Weather for Zurich (JAN)
Weather for Zurich (JUL)

Figure 3.14: List of descriptions created using Excel's text functions

Instead of using the **CONCATENATE** function directly, you can put an **&** character between each of the parameters. For example, an equivalent to the final version of our formula would be **="Weather for "&A2&" ("&UPPER(B2)&")"**. In your work you should use whichever version seems clearest to you, but you should stick with the **CONCATENATE** function in the exam itself, since this is the one mentioned in the syllabus.

In addition to **UPPER**, there are two other functions for changing the case of text.

The **LOWER** function, as you would expect, converts text to lower case. For example, **LOWER("SHOUT!")** results in **shout!**.

The **PROPER** function capitalises the first letter of each word, changing the rest to lower case. It is often used with people's names; for example, **PROPER("matthew STRAWBRIDGE")** results in **Matthew Strawbridge**. Take care, however, because this rule may be too simple for some names (think about Paul McCartney and Chris de Burgh).

Comments

Syllabus Ref: AM4.4.3.4
Add or remove worksheet comments.

If you need to explain a value, or to highlight something that you need to investigate later, then you can use a comment. Excel uses comments that look like the sticky yellow paper notes (you know the ones) used in offices.

We'll add a note to the cell with the maximum rainfall.

 Select cell **H17**, which shows the 170 mm rainfall for Mexico City in July.

 Right-click, then select **Insert Comment** from the menu that appears.

 Your user name should appear at the top of the comment. Type the text **Far too dry**, as shown in Figure 3.15, and then click in any other cell to stop editing.

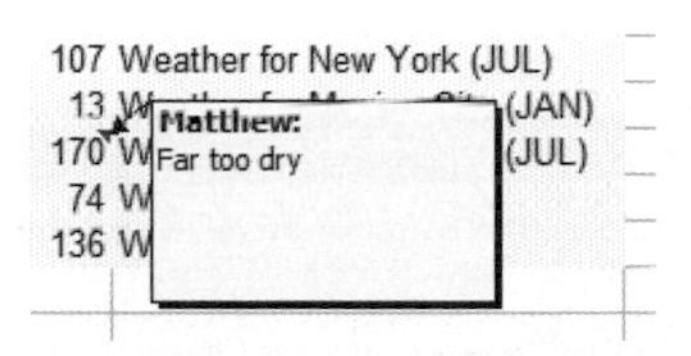

Figure 3.15: Adding a comment

The comment disappears, but a red triangle in the top-right of cell **H17** indicates that there is a comment attached to the cell.

 Hover your mouse pointer over cell **H17**. The comment is displayed but is hidden again as soon as you move your mouse away.

We've made a mistake – the comment should, of course, be **Far too wet** not **Far too dry**. Let's edit it.

Syllabus Ref: AM4.4.3.5
Edit worksheet comments.

 Right-click cell **H17** and select **Edit Comment** from the menu that appears.

 Change the text **dry** to **wet**, then click away again.

Now when you hover over cell **H17** it displays the revised text **Far too wet**.

It's just as easy to delete a comment completely.

 Right-click cell **H17** and select **Delete Comment** from the menu that appears. The comment and its red triangle disappear.

Let's save the changes we've made to the spreadsheet.

From the menu, select **File**, **Save**. Because we imported a plain text file but have since added formatting to it, Excel displays the warning message shown in Figure 3.16. If we were to save the spreadsheet over the top of **cities.txt**, we would lose all of the colours and other formatting we have added. Instead, we want to save it as an **Excel workbook**. Press **No**. The **Save As** dialogue appears. The default name of **cities.xls** is fine, so just press **Save**.

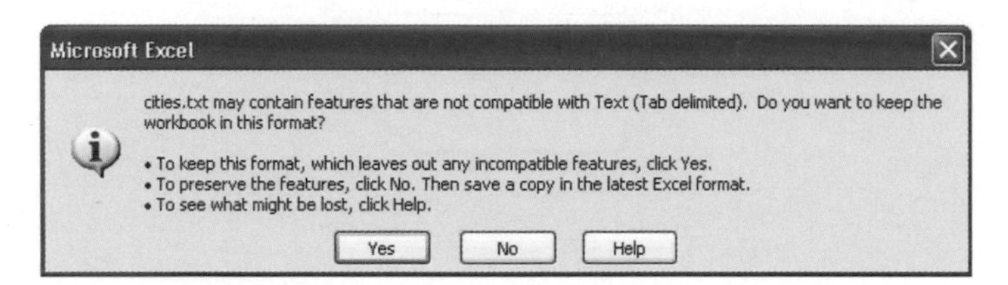

Figure 3.16: Warning – we are trying to save a formatted spreadsheet as a plain text file

Test yourself

1. If you haven't already done so, find the article entitled **Create or delete a custom number format** in Excel's online help, then print it.

2. Use conditional formatting to display in bold any 'average sunlight' values greater than 7 hours.

3. In a blank worksheet, create a function that will take a name and transform it into the form '**FAMILY NAME, Given name**' in a single cell. For example, a given name '**matthew**' and family name '**strawbridge**' would become '**STRAWBRIDGE, Matthew**', as shown in Figure 3.17. (Tip: remember that you can use **&** to concatenate strings. For example **="hello "&"world"** results in '**hello world**'.)

	A	B	C
1	**Name:**	matthew	strawbridge
2			
3	**Transformed name:**	STRAWBRIDGE, Matthew	
4			

Figure 3.17: Transforming a name

4 Financial Functions

Introduction

This chapter is all about money: borrowing it, saving it and spending it! Excel has some functions that help you to work with compound interest; we'll go through these in detail.

In this chapter you will

- use the **RATE** function to work out the interest rate of a loan from its payment schedule
- use the **NPV** function to calculate **net present value** and see what this means in practice
- use the **PV** function to calculate the **present value** of a fixed payment schedule
- use the **FV** function to work out the **future value** of a loan or investment
- use the **PMT** function to calculate the fixed payment required to save or pay a given amount in a given time.

Before starting this chapter, make sure that your **Regional Options** are set correctly, as explained on page 14.

Excel's built-in financial functions

Syllabus Ref: AM4.3.1.5
Use financial functions: FV; NPV; PMT; PV; RATE.

Unless you're an accountant, terms such as **future value** and **net present value** probably don't mean much to you. However, the five Excel financial functions you need to know – **FV**, **NPV**, **PMT**, **PV** and **RATE** – are all concerned with calculating loans and fixed-interest investments, and they are quite straightforward once you understand what each one is for.

We'll work through these functions one by one, explaining the parameters that each function takes and what the calculation tells you.

Interest rate: RATE()

We'll start with the **RATE** function, which works out the interest rate for a loan from details about the number and size of payments made.

Suppose you want to buy a sofa for **£799**. The shop is offering three different credit deals: you can pay **£27.50** a month for **four** years, **£23.00** a month for **five** years, or **£20.00** a month for **six** years. You're interested to find out what interest rates the furniture shop is offering, but these are buried in the small print, so you decide to create a quick Excel spreadsheet to find out.

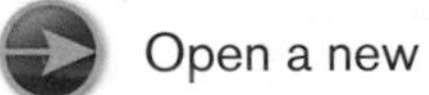 Open a new blank Excel workbook.

 In cell **A1**, type the label **Sofa Cost:**, then in cell **B1**, type **£799**.

 In cell **A3**, type **Years**. In the column below this, type the other headings: **Months**, **Monthly Fee**, **Total Repaid** and **Rate**.

 Some of these headings are too wide for column **A**, so double-click the vertical line between the column headings **A** and **B**, which will resize column **A** to fit its contents.

Now we're ready to enter the details of the first credit deal and work out the rate.

 In cell **B3**, type **4**. This column will have the details for the four-year credit deal.

 In cell **B4**, type **=B3*12**. This calculates the number of months in four years (**48**).

 The four-year credit deal costs £27.50 a month, so type **£27.50** in cell **B5**.

 In cell **B6**, type **=B4*B5**, since there will be 48 payments of £27.50.

That's the framework in place; now we need to use the **RATE** function to work out what interest rate is being charged.

Each piece of information that you pass into a function in Excel is called a **parameter**. When you start to type a function, Excel pops up a yellow box, called a **tooltip**, to remind you what parameters the function needs (see Figure 4.1). The parameters for the financial functions are quite complicated, so we'll go through them in detail.

DGET ▾ X ✓ fx =RATE(

	A	B	C	D	E
1	Sofa Cost:	£799			
2					
3	Years	4			
4	Months	48			
5	Monthly Fee	£27.50			
6	Total Repaid	£1,320.00			
7	Rate	=RATE(			
8		RATE(**nper**, pmt, pv, [fv], [type], [guess])			
9					

Figure 4.1: Tooltip showing parameters for the RATE function

RATE(nper, pmt, pv, [fv], [type], [guess])

nper is the **n**umber of payment **per**iods. For example, a five-year loan with monthly payments will have **nper = 5 * 12 = 60**.

pmt is the **p**ay**m**en**t** made for each period, and it must be a fixed value. You can exclude **pmt** if there is a value for **fv**.

pv is the **p**resent **v**alue. We'll cover this in more detail later; for now, just think of it as the outstanding balance on a loan.

fv is the **f**uture **v**alue: what the balance will be after the last payment is made. You can omit this parameter (which is why it is in square brackets), in which case it will default to **0**.

type lets you specify when payments are made: **0** (the default) is used when payments occur at the end of each period; **1** is used for payments at the beginning of each period.

guess allows you to give a starting point for Excel to work out the rate. The **RATE** function works by iteration – making successive guesses that get closer and closer to the solution. If **RATE** doesn't get close enough after 20 iterations, it will give up and return a **#NUM!** error value; if you know roughly what the rate is going to be, then supplying a guess can make it more likely for Excel to get to an answer. The default **guess** is **10%**.

 In cell **B7**, type the formula **=RATE(B4, -B5, $B$1)*12**. Format this cell as a percentage.

This deserves some explanation. The first parameter is the number of payment periods (**48**), which is held in cell **B4**. The second parameter is the payment size, held in cell **B5**; the only tricky thing about this is that it must be made negative: in all of these financial functions, if you are paying money out then you should use negative values. The third parameter is the value of the loan, which is **£799**; the dollar signs are used in **$B$1** so that copies of the formula will still refer to cell **B1**. Finally, it is important to know that the **RATE** formula returns the rate per period – we are using monthly payments, so we must multiply the monthly rate by **12** to get the (non-compound) annual rate.

> **Reminder:** Use negative values for payments you are making; use positive values for money being paid to you.

You should find that the result of the **RATE** function in this case comes out as **27%**. That seems expensive – no wonder it was hidden away in the small print! Perhaps the longer-term loans will be more competitive.

 Type **5** and **6** in cells **C3** and **D3** respectively.

 Type **£23.00** and **£20.00** in cells **C5** and **D5** respectively.

 Select cell **B4** and click and drag the **fill handle** to the right to copy the formula into cells **C4** and **D4** (see Figure 4.2).

B4 =B3*12

	A	B	C	D	E
1	Sofa Cost:	£799			
2					
3	Years	4	5	6	
4	Months	48			
5	Monthly Fee	£27.50	£23.00	£20.00	
6	Total Repaid	£1,320.00			
7	Rate	27%			
8					

B4 =B3*12

	A	B	C	D	E
1	Sofa Cost:	£799			
2					
3	Years	4	5	6	
4	Months	48	60	72	
5	Monthly Fee	£27.50	£23.00	£20.00	
6	Total Repaid	£1,320.00			
7	Rate	27%			
8					

Figure 4.2: Copying a formula using the fill handle

 Select cells **B6** and **B7** and drag the fill handle over columns **C** and **D**.

The final values are shown in Figure 4.3. This shows that the interest rate goes down as the loan period goes up, but the total amount you pay increases.

	A	B	C	D	E
1	Sofa Cost:	£799			
2					
3	Years	4	5	6	
4	Months	48	60	72	
5	Monthly Fee	£27.50	£23.00	£20.00	
6	Total Repaid	£1,320.00	£1,380.00	£1,440.00	
7	Rate	27%	24%	22%	
8					
9					

Figure 4.3: Calculated interest rates for the three loan periods

Net present value: NPV()

We can extend the example of buying a sofa to look at a more complicated financial function: **NPV**. This is one of two Excel financial functions that deal with the concept of **present value**, so it's important that you understand how this works.

Suppose you have £10,000 to invest and that two people (let's call them Sam and Robin) ask you to lend it to them. Sam promises to pay back £13,000 after one year; Robin promises to pay you £1000 every month for a year. So, whom do you lend to? Sam would pay you £13,000 in total, whereas Robin would pay you only £12,000, but you would start to get your money back more quickly. The missing piece of the puzzle is what else you could be doing with the money; if you can get a good rate of interest by putting the money in a bank or building society then there is value associated with getting your money back as quickly as possible – this is called **opportunity cost**.

The present value of an investment is arrived at by looking at all future payments and rolling back the interest to see what they are worth today. Let's look at an example to make this clearer.

So, back to the sofa shop. For customers who are willing to pay for their purchases more quickly than in four years' time, the shop is advertising the following offer: 'Nothing to pay for a year, and then two years' interest-free credit.'

Suppose you're still interested in the £799 sofa, and you have the money in your bank account. You think the store manager might give you a discount if you pay in full instead of taking their free credit offer, but you're not sure how much to ask for. So again you turn to Excel for inspiration.

Click on the **Sheet2** tab at the bottom of your workbook. We'll use this new blank sheet to look at the 'interest free' offer.

In cell **A1**, type **Sofa Cost**, then in cell **B1**, type **£799**.

It is often convenient to give a name to a cell or range of cells, so that you can refer to the name instead of the cell reference in your formulas. We'll assign the name **SOFA_COST** to cell **B1**.

Syllabus Ref: AM4.1.1.1
Name cell range(s) in a worksheet.

Syllabus Ref: AM4.1.2.3 (1 of 2)
Understand how referencing can improve efficiency (e.g. using hyperlinks, naming of cells and ranges).

Select cell **B1** and type **SOFA_COST** into the name area, as shown in Figure 4.4. Press **Enter** to confirm the name change.

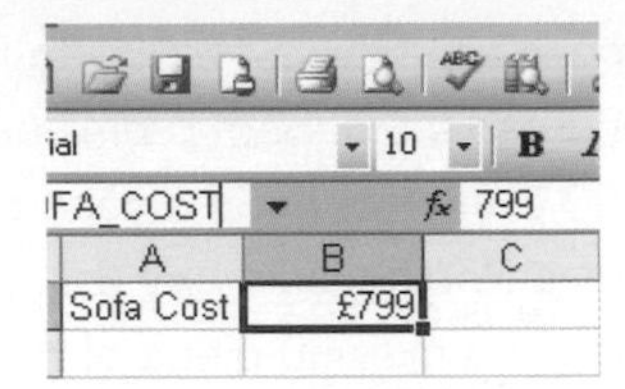

Figure 4.4: Naming a cell

You can assign a name to any range of cells that you have selected. You can even select several ranges (by holding down the **Ctrl** key while you click and drag your mouse pointer over each range in turn) and then give them a single name. To remove a name from a range of cells, select **Insert**, **Name**, **Define** from the menu. You can then use the **Delete** button in the **Define** dialogue box that appears.

Using names for cells and ranges of cells improves efficiency – your workbooks will become easier to navigate, easier to understand and easier to maintain, all of which saves time for the people using them.

In cell **A3**, type the label **Month 1**.

Select cell **A3** and drag the fill handle downwards. Even though the cell's value is text, because it ends with a number, Excel guesses that we want the copied cells to have the values **Month 2**, **Month 3** and so on. Drag down until the tooltip says **Month 36**, as shown in Figure 4.5, and then release the mouse.

Figure 4.5: Using the fill handle to copy text labels

Enter the label **Bank Rate** in cell **A40** and the label **NPV** in cell **A42**.

The credit deal says that there is nothing to pay for the first year, so let's enter a value of **£0.00** (Make sure you type the **.00** because it affects the formatting) against each of the labels for **Month 1** to **Month 12**.

Select cells **B3:B14** (months 1–12). Type **£0.00** and then press **Ctrl+Enter**. This tells Excel to set the same value for all of the cells in the selection and is a useful tip to remember.

Select cells **B15:B38** (months 13–36). Type **= -SOFA_COST/24** and press **Ctrl+Enter**. Notice that these are negative values, because they represent payments you are making.

Excel doesn't realise that these are currency values, so let's tidy them up by applying the same formatting as the values above them.

Select cell **B14** (any of the cells **B3:B14** would do), and then click the **Format Painter** button on the **Standard** toolbar.

Format Painter

Click and drag the mouse pointer over cells **B15:B38**. They are reformatted to each show **-£33.29** (in red, because they are negative values).

Suppose your bank account pays 4.75% interest. Type **4.75%** into cell **B40** and give it the name **BANK_RATE**.

Now we are ready to calculate the **net present value** of the credit agreement using the **NPV** function.

NPV(rate, value1, [value2], ...)

rate is the discount over one period. For example, when calculating the net present value of a series of future weekly payments, given that you could instead invest your money in a bank and earn 3% interest on it, you would use a **rate** of **3%/52**.

value1, **value2**, ... are the equally spaced payments that occur at the end of each period. The payments can be positive (money received) or negative (money paid).

Businesses like using net present value when appraising potential investments because it gives an absolute answer in a clear 'yes' or 'no' form: if the NPV is negative, the yield of the investment will be less than the chosen discount rate and so the investment is probably not worthwhile; if the value is positive then the yield exceeds the discount rate, indicating a good investment; an NPV of zero suggests that the investment exactly matches the discount rate. The important thing to remember is that an NPV is a comparison against zero, not against an initial investment. Most investments have an up-front cost, but because the NPV function concerns itself with only payments made at the end of each period, such up-front costs must be dealt with manually by subtracting them from the value returned by the NPV function.

In cell **B42**, type **=NPV(BANK_RATE/12, B3:B38)+SOFA_COST**.

The NPV should come out as **£73.44**, meaning that taking the interest-free credit represents a saving of £73.44 over paying the full £799 up front; in other words, by leaving the money in the bank until each payment is due, you would earn over £73 in interest.

Now you know that if you haggle with the store manager but only manage to get a £50 discount for paying up front, you would be better off paying the full £799 but accepting their interest-free credit offer.

Present value: PV()

The **NPV** function is useful when the payment amounts vary. If the amount of the payment is fixed then you can use the **PV** function to calculate the present value of a loan or investment.

Imagine that there's a competition on your cornflakes box, where you have to complete the slogan 'I love super crispy crunchy flakes because…' You're convinced that your entry – '… they put the crunch in brunch' – is a sure-fire winner. First prize is a choice between a £15,000 lump sum or £1000 a year for life, but you're not sure which option to go for.

Let's use Excel to look at the two alternatives:

 Switch to the **Sheet3** tab in your workbook.

PV(rate, nper, pmt, [fv], [type])

rate is the interest **rate** per period.

nper is the **n**umber of payment **per**iods.

pmt is the **paym**en**t** made in each period.

fv is the **f**uture **v**alue; the value after all of the payments have been made. You must include a value for one of **pmt** or **fv**.

type specifies when the payments are made: **0** (default) for the end of the period, or **1** for the beginning of the period. This contrasts with the **NPV** function, which will accept payments only at the end of the period.

Two important factors that will affect which prize you should take are the interest rate (currently 5%) and the number of years you expect to live for.

 In cell **A1**, type the label **Interest Rate.** In cell **B1**, type **5%**.

 In cell **A2**, type the label **Life Expectancy (years)**. Resize column **A** so that the labels fit. For this example, suppose you are in your late forties or early fifties, and so estimate your life expectancy as 30 years: in cell **B2**, type **30**.

 Give cell **B1** the name **INTEREST_RATE** and cell **B2** the name **LIFE_EXPECTANCY**.

 In cell **A3**, type the label **PV of £1000/year**.

 In cell **B3**, type the formula **=PV(INTEREST_RATE, LIFE_EXPECTANCY, 1000)**.

This gives a present value of **-£15,372.45**, as shown in Figure 4.6. Note that this is a negative number, meaning that you should consider **paying** up to £15,372.45 in order to join such a scheme (membership of which you will be getting for free as your prize). In other words, assuming that the interest rate and life expectancy estimates are sound, the £1000-a-year prize represents slightly better value for money than the £15,000 lump sum.

B3 | fx =PV(INTEREST_RATE,LIFE_EXPECTANCY,1000)

	A	B	C	D	E
1	Interest Rate	5%			
2	Life Expectancy (years)	30			
3	PV of £1000/year	-£15,372.45			
4					

Figure 4.6: Calculating the present value of receiving £1000 a year for the next 30 years, given a savings rate of 5%

Future value: FV()

Suppose you decide not to spend any of the money. How much will you (or your heirs) have after 30 years? We can use the FV function to calculate the future value of the £1000-a-year prize:

Type the following formula into cell **A4**:
="FV of £1000/year after "&LIFE_EXPECTANCY&" years".
Make sure you include the spaces – they are important.

Remember that you can use the **&** operator to concatenate strings. This is an alternative to the **CONCATENATE** function, which we covered in Chapter 3.

The value of cell **A4** becomes **FV of £1000/year after 30 years**, and the label will update if you change the value for the life expectancy (try it, but set it back to **30** again when you've finished).

Resize column **A** so that it is big enough to fit the new label.

Now we're ready to use the FV function to calculate the future value of investing £1000 a year over 30 years with an interest rate of 5%.

FV(rate, nper, pmt, [pv], [type])

rate is the interest **rate** per period.

nper is the **n**umber of payment **per**iods.

pmt is the **p**ay**m**en**t** made in each period.

pv is the **p**resent **v**alue of the loan or investment.

type specifies when the payments are made: **0** (default) for the end of the period, or **1** for the beginning of the period.

 In cell **B4**, type the formula **=FV(INTEREST_RATE, LIFE_EXPECTANCY, -1000)**.

The value of cell **B4** becomes **£66,438.85** – this is the nest egg you would get by investing £1000 a year over 30 years, assuming that the interest rate remained constant at 5%.

Remember that the other prize offered was a £15,000 lump sum. How much would that be worth after 30 years if it was just invested and left to gather interest?

 Give cell **B4** the name **FV_OF_ANNUAL_PAYMENTS**.

 In cell **A5**, type the label **="FV of £15,000 after "&LIFE_EXPECTANCY&" years"**

We don't need any of the built-in financial functions to work this out; just a bit of logic. After the first year, there will be 105% of £15,000 in the account: the lump sum, plus 5% interest. After the second year, there will be 105% of 105% of £15,000: interest is earned on the total in the account, including any previous interest. This means that the total after 30 years will be **£15,000 * (105% ^ 30)**, where * represents multiplication and ^ represents raising to a power (in this case, 30 lots of 105% multiplied together).

 In cell **B5**, enter the formula **=15000*(100%+INTEREST_RATE)^LIFE_EXPECTANCY**.

This formula has a couple of interesting features worth discussing. First, notice how you can work directly with percentages – you don't have to convert them into decimals. Second, the power operator ^ binds tightly to the term that precedes it; in particular, it binds more tightly than the * operator, so you don't need to write **=15000*((100%+INTEREST_RATE)^LIFE_EXPECTANCY)** explicitly.

 Copy the format from cell **B4** to cell **B5** so that it is formatted as a currency.

The value of cell **B5** should now be **£64,829.14**, as shown in Figure 4.7. Since this is less than the £66,438.85 you would have from the £1000-a-year option, this confirms the conclusion you came to by looking at the present values of the two choices.

B5 | fx =15000*(100%+INTEREST_RATE)^LIFE_EXPECTANCY

	A	B	C	D	E
1	Interest Rate	5%			
2	Life Expectancy (years)	30			
3	PV of £1000/year	-£15,372.45			
4	FV of £1000/year after 30 years	£66,438.85			
5	FV of £15000 after 30 years	£64,829.14			
6					

Figure 4.7: Calculating the future value of the £15,000 lump sum

Suppose that, instead of a £15,000 lump sum, you were offered £15,372.45. Remember that this is the present value calculated from the £1000-a-year option. Can you guess what £15,372.45 will be worth after 30 years?

 Give cell **B5** the name **FV_OF_LUMP_SUM**.

 In cell **A6**, type the label **="FV of £15,372.45 after "&LIFE_EXPECTANCY&" years"**.

 In cell **B6**, type the formula **=15372.45*(100%+INTEREST_RATE)^LIFE_EXPECTANCY**.

 Copy the format from cell **B5** to cell **B6**.

You end up with a value of £66,438.84. This means that you end up with exactly the same final sum regardless of whether you invest £1000 a year or an initial amount of £15,372.45 (ignoring the penny difference, which is due to the fact that the calculated PV of the £1000-a-year option is rounded to the nearest penny). If this is what you predicted, and you understand why, then give yourself a pat on the back!

Payments: PMT()

Suppose you want to accumulate only £50,000 at the end of the 30 years; how much of your £1000 a year can you spend if you invest the remainder in a savings account with a 5% interest rate? We can use the **PMT** function to find out what your annual savings must be in order to end up with £50,000.

> **PMT(rate, nper, pv, [fv], [type])**
>
> **rate** is the interest **rate** per period.
>
> **nper** is the **n**umber of payment **per**iods.
>
> **pv** is the **p**resent **v**alue of the loan or investment.
>
> **fv** is the **f**uture **v**alue; the value after all of the payments have been made. The default value of **fv** is **0**.
>
> **type** specifies when the payments are made: **0** (default) for the end of the period, or **1** for the beginning of the period.

 In cell **A7**, enter the label **Annual payment for £50,000**.

 In cell **B7**, type the formula **=PMT(INTEREST_RATE, LIFE_EXPECTANCY, 0, 50000)**.

This gives a value of **-£752.57**, as shown in Figure 4.8; in other words, a payment of £752.57 each year for 30 years, given an interest rate of 5%, will give a total of £50,000. This means you could spend (£1000 - £752.57 =) £247.43 of your annual winnings and still amass a £50,000 lump sum.

B7 fx =PMT(INTEREST_RATE,LIFE_EXPECTANCY,0,50000)

	A	B	C	D	E
1	Interest Rate	5%			
2	Life Expectancy (years)	30			
3	PV of £1000/year	-£15,372.45			
4	FV of £1000/year after 30 years	£66,438.85			
5	FV of £15000 after 30 years	£64,829.14			
6	FV of £15372.45 after 30 years	£66,438.84			
7	Annual payment for £50000	-£752.57			
8					

Figure 4.8: Calculating the annual payment that would be required to limit the total after 30 years to £50,000

This scenario assumes that you make one annual payment into your savings account and that your interest is also paid annually. If you were making monthly savings, and being paid interest monthly, then you would use the formula **=PMT(INTEREST_RATE/12, LIFE_EXPECTANCY*12, 0, 50000)** instead to work out what your monthly payment should be. (This assumes that **INTEREST_RATE** is given uncompounded. Otherwise, you would need to replace **INTEREST_RATE/12** with the more complicated **POWER(1+INTEREST_RATE, 1/12) - 1**, which rolls back the effect of the compound interest). You won't be asked to do this in the exam, but it's useful to know.

Right-click the **Sheet3** tab at the bottom of the window, and select **Rename** from the menu that appears.

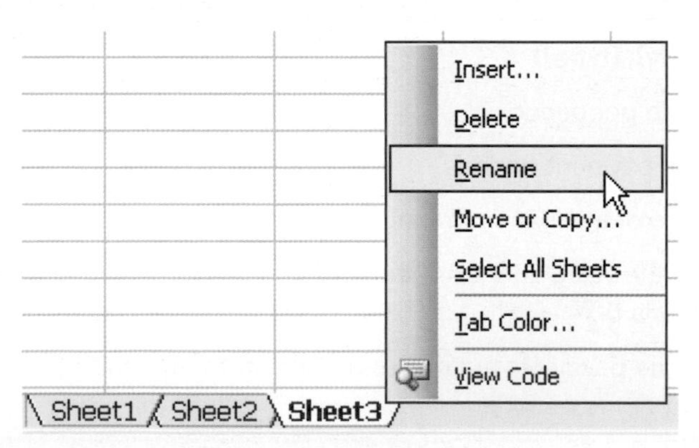

Figure 4.9: Renaming a worksheet

Type the new name **Cornflake Competition**, then press **Enter**.

Rename **Sheet1** and **Sheet2** as **Sofa Deals** and **Sofa Discount** respectively.

Save your worksheet as **Financial Functions.xls**.

Test yourself

These questions are quite challenging. You can download the answers from www.payne-gallway.co.uk/ecdl but I encourage you to try them for yourself first.

1. Suppose you already have savings of £2,500 and want to invest another £175 at the end of each month over five years in a bank or building society. Use the **RATE** function to calculate the minimum monthly rate of interest (to two decimal places) you need in order to achieve a lump sum of £15,000 after 5 years.
   [Hint: you can do the whole calculation in a single cell.]

Suppose you get a mortgage to buy a house. The house costs £150,000, and the annual interest rate is 5% (non-compounded). You have savings of £22,500 to use as a deposit. The mortgage term is 25 years and you pay at the start of each month.

2. Use the **PMT** function to calculate what your monthly mortgage payment will be (assuming the interest rate remains the same).

3. How much will you pay in total over the 25-year term? [Hint: this is a simple multiplication.] Change the interest rate down to **0%** and check that the total amount repaid exactly matches the amount borrowed (£150,000 – £22,500 = **£127,500**).

Imagine you found a magic lamp, and the genie offered to make you rich. Suppose he offered you a choice. The first option would be £1,000,000 straight away. For the second option, the genie would make a pile of coins, starting with one penny on the first day, replacing it with double the amount (2p) on the second day, again replacing it with double the amount (4p) on the third day and so on. After 27 days he would give you the money in the pile.

4. Use the **FV** function with a **rate** of **100%** to decide between the two options.

5. What if the rate of inflation suddenly shot up to 1.25% **per day**! Every day you had to wait for the genie's money, it would be worth 1.25% less. Use the **NPV** function to decide which option you should take now. [Hint: you get nothing for 26 days, then you get the lump sum.]

6. Suppose the genie made a further offer. This time, he agreed to pay £1,200,000 in equal daily instalments for 30 days. If the daily inflation rate was still 1.25%, is this a better or worse deal than taking £1,000,000 immediately? Use the **PV** function to find out.

5 Scenarios & Data Tables

Introduction

This chapter introduces a couple of techniques – **scenarios** and **data tables** – that are commonly used in financial worksheets.

A **scenario** is a set of stored values that you can recall later. Typically, you might choose to define three scenarios for the best-case, expected and worst-case sales figures. This would allow you to create a model for your cash flow and to switch quickly between the three different trading outlooks.

Data tables let you explore how a computed value changes in response to changes in the values on which it is based. These are often used to show how the monthly repayment of a loan is affected by the interest rate.

In this chapter you will

create three **scenarios** to help you decide which prize you should accept (an annual payment or a lump sum) based on interest rates and your life expectancy

generate a **scenario summary** showing how much prize money you would receive for each of the scenarios you have created

learn how **data tables** can be used to display the result of a calculation applied across a range of input values.

Scenarios

 Open the worksheet **Financial Functions.xls**, which you created in the previous chapter.

All of the calculations you've used so far to decide which prize you would accept have been based on a fixed interest rate of 5% and a fixed life expectancy of 30 years. However, you can't be sure of either of these values – to make a more informed decision, it makes sense to try out various alternatives to see what happens if interest rates drop, or if you end up living to a ripe old age.

You could just type new values into cells **B1** and **B2**, but you would lose the results from your previous 'what ifs' each time.

We can use this worksheet to investigate what effect different combinations of interest rate and life expectancy will have on the equivalent annual payment given in cell **B7**. We will look at two methods to help with this **what-if analysis**.

First, we will use **scenarios**, which allow you to store the values from a set of cells so that you can reload them later. After that, we will look at **data tables**, which show the results of applying a formula to a range of values for one or two input variables.

We will create three scenarios – best case, worst case and expected – using different values of interest rate and life expectancy for each. We'll save the current values (5% and 30 years) as the expected scenario.

Syllabus Ref: AM4.4.2.1

Create named Scenarios/Versions from defined cell ranges.

 Select cells **B1:B2** on the **Cornflake Competition** worksheet. These cells hold the values that we want to save as a scenario.

 From the menu, select **Tools**, **Scenarios**. The **Scenario Manager** dialogue appears.

 Press the **Add** button. The **Add Scenario** dialogue appears, with **Changing cells** set to **B1:B2**.

 Fill in the **Scenario name** and **Comment** as shown in Figure 5.1, then press **OK**.

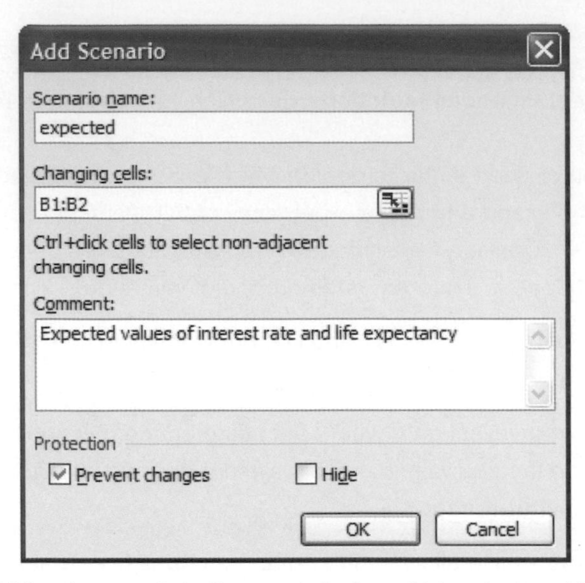

Figure 5.1: Adding the scenario for the expected values of interest rate and life expectancy

If the **Prevent changes** option is set, users won't be able to edit the scenarios if you later decide to protect the worksheet. As long as you unlock the cells that will change (see Chapter 9: Templates & Protection), users will still be able to switch between scenarios in the protected worksheet.

If the **Hide** option is set then this scenario will be hidden from users once the worksheet is protected.

The **Scenario Values** dialogue box appears, populated with the current values of the two cells as shown in Figure 5.2. These are the values we want, so just press **Add**.

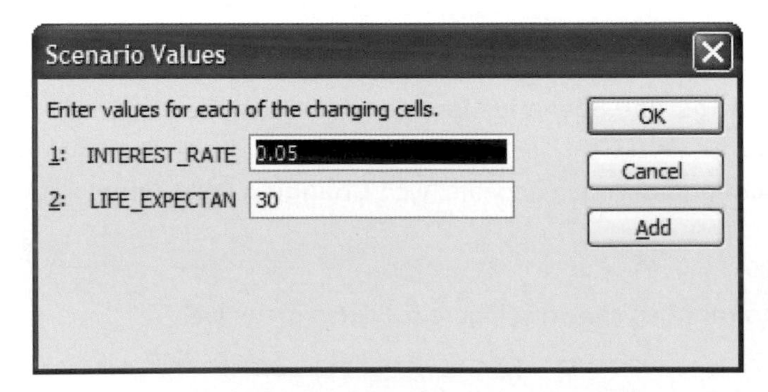

Figure 5.2: Setting values for the 'expected' scenario

Because we gave names to the two input cells, these are displayed in the **Scenario Values** dialogue box. If we hadn't done this, the cell references would be shown instead. Remember to give names to such 'driver' cells in your own worksheets, since this will make the scenarios easier to use.

Use the same technique to create another scenario. Call it **best case**, then give it an interest rate of **0.1** (equivalent to 10%) and a life expectancy of **60** years. Click **Add** in the **Scenario Values** dialogue, since there is one more scenario to add.

Create another scenario, called **worst case**, with an interest rate of **0.02** (2%) and a life expectancy of **20** years. Since this is the last scenario, click **OK** instead of **Add** in the **Scenario Values** dialogue.

The **Scenario Manager** reappears with the three scenarios listed, as shown in Figure 5.3.

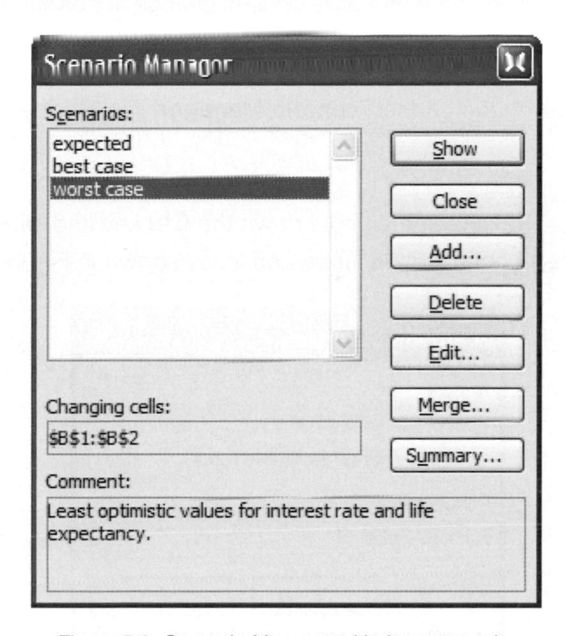

Figure 5.3: Scenario Manager with three scenarios

Select **best case** from the **Scenarios** list, then press the **Show** button. Cells **B1** and **B2** are set to **10%** and **60** respectively, and the other values are updated accordingly.

For the **best-case** scenario, the future value of £1000/year is a massive £3,034,816.40, but the future value of the £15,000 payment is even more: £4,567,224.59! Of course, this all assumes you don't spend any of the money, and the interest rate remains high, for the next 60 years.

If the three FV values in cells **B4: B6** do not fit (appear as **######**) then close the **Scenario Manager**, increase the width of column **B** and reload the **Scenario Manager** (**Tools**, **Scenarios**).

Use the **Scenario Manager** to show the **worst case** scenario.

You should get a future value of £24,297.37 for the £1000/year option and less (£22,289.21) for the lump sum. This suggests that if you are very pessimistic about both interest rates and how long you will live, you may be better off with the annual payments.

Use the **Scenario Manager** to show the **expected** scenario again.

Creating a scenario summary

Syllabus Ref: AM4.4.2.2

Create a Scenario summary/ Version report.

A **scenario summary** is a new worksheet that shows what effect the different summaries you have defined have on particular cells that you nominate as **Result cells**. We'll create a scenario summary that shows how the future values of the two prize options change according to the expected and best-case and worst-case scenarios.

Press the **Summary** button on the **Scenario Manager**. The **Scenario Summary** dialogue appears.

Click cell **B4** on the worksheet, then hold down the **Ctrl** key and click on cell **B5**. This selects the two **Result cells** we are interested in, as shown in Figure 5.4.

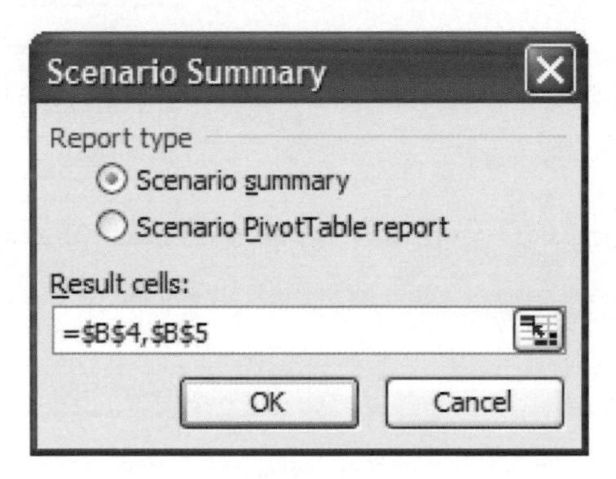

Figure 5.4: Creating a scenario summary

Press **OK**. The **Scenario Summary** dialogue disappears, and a new worksheet named **Scenario Summary** is created in your workbook, as shown in Figure 5.5.

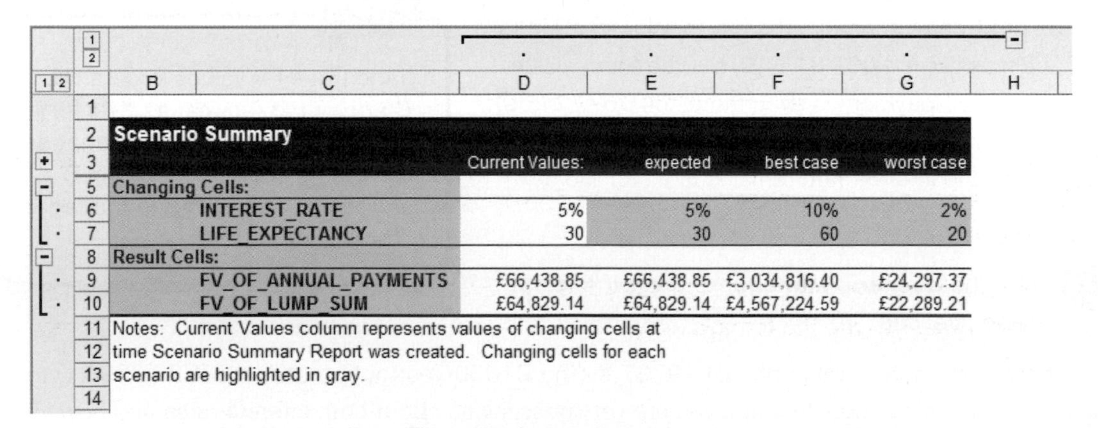

	B	C	D	E	F	G
1						
2	**Scenario Summary**					
3			Current Values:	expected	best case	worst case
5	**Changing Cells:**					
6		INTEREST_RATE	5%	5%	10%	2%
7		LIFE_EXPECTANCY	30	30	60	20
8	**Result Cells:**					
9		FV_OF_ANNUAL_PAYMENTS	£66,438.85	£66,438.85	£3,034,816.40	£24,297.37
10		FV_OF_LUMP_SUM	£64,829.14	£64,829.14	£4,567,224.59	£22,289.21
11	Notes: Current Values column represents values of changing cells at					
12	time Scenario Summary Report was created. Changing cells for each					
13	scenario are highlighted in gray.					
14						

Figure 5.5: A scenario summary

Switch back to the **Sheet3** worksheet.

Data tables

Syllabus Ref: AM4.1.2.9

Use one-input or two-input Data tables/What-if tables.

Scenarios are very useful when you need to keep track of a lot of variables. When there are only one or two, as in this case, a better approach may be to create a **data table**. Excel makes this easy to set up.

First, we need to create a list of possible life expectancies:

Enter a value of **10** into cell **D2** and a value of **15** into cell **D3**. Select cells **D2** and **D3** and use the fill handle to extend the list to cover all of the multiples of 5 years up to **60**.

For the interest rates, let's just look at the whole numbers between 3% and 8%. Of course, there would be nothing to stop you creating a much bigger table with fractional percentage values if you were doing this for real.

In cell **E1**, type the value of **3%**, and in **F1**, type **4%**. Select both cells and use the fill handle to extend the sequence up to **8%**.

Your worksheet should now look like Figure 5.6. You should be able to see the data table taking shape across cells **D1:J12**.

	A	B	C	D	E	F	G	H	I	J	K
1	Interest Rate	5%			3%	4%	5%	6%	7%	8%	
2	Life Expectancy (years)	30		10							
3	PV of £1000/year	-£15,372.45		15							
4	FV of £1000/year after 30 years	£66,438.85		20							
5	FV of £15000 after 30 years	£64,829.14		25							
6	FV of £15372.45 after 30 years	£66,430.04		30							
7	Annual payment for £50000	-£752.57		35							
8				40							
9				45							
10				50							
11				55							
12				60							
13											

Figure 5.6: Framework in place for a two-input data table

The clever bit is that, as long as we put the formula we are using in the top-left of the table, we can get Excel to automatically fill in the table's values for us. Let's fill the table with the present values for the prize of £1,000 a year.

The cell in the top-left of the data table needs to contain the formula used to generate the table's values. Type the formula **=PV(INTEREST_RATE, LIFE_EXPECTANCY, 1000)** into cell **D1**.

Select cells **D1:J12** and choose **Data**, **Table** from the menu. The **Table** dialogue appears.

Excel will use the formula in the top-left of the table (cell **D1**) to generate the table's values. Each cell in the body of the table will be generated from a pair of values: one from the top row (**3%**, **4%**, **5%**, **…**) and one from the first column (**10**, **15**, **20**, **…**). We need to tell Excel where it must temporarily copy each pair of values so that the formula in cell **D1** gives the value we want in the table. We use the **Row input cell** to specify where to copy the values from the top row, and the **Column input cell** to specify where to copy the values from the first column.

Enter **B1** as the **Row input cell** and **B2** as the **Column input cell**, as shown in Figure 5.7. Press **OK** to create the table.

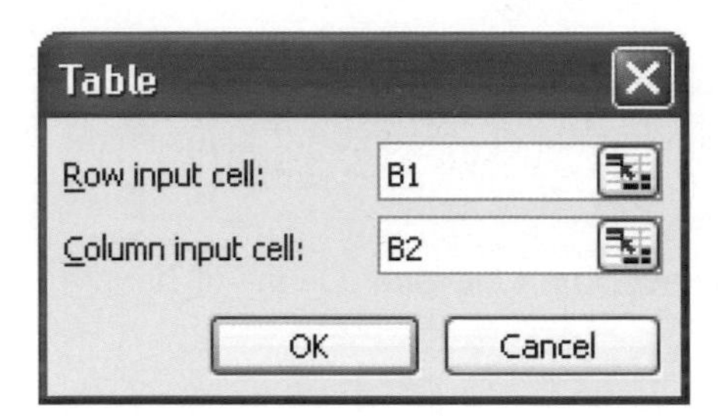

Figure 5.7: Creating a data table

We could have typed **INTEREST_RATE** and **LIFE_EXPECTANCY** instead of **B1** and **B2**. Excel does the conversion automatically, so it doesn't matter whether you use cell references or their names.

Currency

Select cells **E2:J12** and then press the **Currency** button on the **Formatting** toolbar.

	D	E	F	G	H	I	J	K
1	-£15,372.45	3%	4%	5%	6%	7%	8%	
2	10	-£ 8,530.20	-£ 8,110.90	-£ 7,721.73	-£ 7,360.09	-£ 7,023.58	-£ 6,710.08	
3	15	-£11,937.94	-£11,118.39	-£10,379.66	-£ 9,712.25	-£ 9,107.91	-£ 8,559.48	
4	20	-£14,877.47	-£13,590.33	-£12,462.21	-£11,469.92	-£10,594.01	-£ 9,818.15	
5	25	-£17,413.15	-£15,622.08	-£14,093.94	-£12,783.36	-£11,653.58	-£10,674.78	
6	30	-£19,600.44	-£17,292.03	-£15,372.45	-£13,764.83	-£12,409.04	-£11,257.78	
7	35	-£21,487.22	-£18,664.61	-£16,374.19	-£14,498.25	-£12,947.67	-£11,654.57	
8	40	-£23,114.77	-£19,792.77	-£17,159.09	-£15,046.30	-£13,331.71	-£11,924.61	
9	45	-£24,518.71	-£20,720.04	-£17,774.07	-£15,455.83	-£13,605.52	-£12,108.40	
10	50	-£25,729.76	-£21,482.18	-£18,255.93	-£15,761.86	-£13,800.75	-£12,233.48	
11	55	-£26,774.43	-£22,108.61	-£18,633.47	-£15,990.54	-£13,939.94	-£12,318.61	
12	60	-£27,675.56	-£22,623.49	-£18,929.29	-£16,161.43	-£14,039.18	-£12,376.55	
13								

Figure 5.8: A two-input data table showing how the present value of a £1,000-a-year prize varies with life expectancy and savings rate

You create a one-input data table in the same way as a two-input data table, but you fill in only one of the fields in the **Table** dialogue; the data values can be laid out in either a row or a column, and you can supply multiple formulas for the values to be substituted into.

So, what is this table telling us?

Going down each column, you can see that the magnitude of the PV increases as the life expectancy increases – this makes sense, since you would expect the £1,000-a-year option to be worth more in total if you are going to live a long time.

Slightly less intuitive is the fact that the PV decreases from left to right; that is, the value of the deal is less the higher the interest rate. This is because a high interest rate means you need less of a lump sum to generate the income that you're missing out on by not having the annual payments.

Remember that this is the present value, not the final value. The final value of the deal will increase with both life expectancy (since you receive more payments) and with interest rate (since you are getting more interest).

If you change the values for the table's headings, the table's data will be updated to match.

Save your worksheet.

Test yourself

1. Use a one-input data table to create an exchange rate 'ready reckoner' like the one shown in Figure 5.9. [Hint: cells **B3** and **C3** should have the formulas **=1.87*A2** and **=1.43*A2** respectively. You can update these values with the current exchange rates from the newspaper if you prefer. You will need to select cells **A3:C12** and use cell **A2** as the **Column input cell**.]

	A	B	C
1	**Exchange Ready Reckoner**		
2	£ 1.00	**US$**	**Euros**
3		$1.87	€ 1.43
4	**£ 50.00**	$93.50	€ 71.50
5	**£ 75.00**	$140.25	€ 107.25
6	**£ 100.00**	$187.00	€ 143.00
7	**£ 150.00**	$280.50	€ 214.50
8	**£ 200.00**	$374.00	€ 286.00
9	**£ 250.00**	$467.50	€ 357.50
10	**£ 300.00**	$561.00	€ 429.00
11	**£ 400.00**	$748.00	€ 572.00
12	**£ 500.00**	$935.00	€ 715.00

Figure 5.9: One-input data table used to create an exchange rate 'ready reckoner'

2. Use **conditional formatting** to highlight in green those values in the Cornflake Competition data table that represent a better deal than the £15,000 lump sum.

3. Suppose you inherited £1,000,000. Create a new workbook and use it to model some different ways you might spend the money. For example, you might spend half of it and invest the other half, or you might spend it all. Make sure you have a cell that contains the interest rate, and another cell that calculates the annual income you can expect from the amount you saved (you can use the **FV** function for this and assume that the interest is paid monthly). Your worksheet might look something like Figure 5.10.

	A	B
1	Interest Rate	5%
2	Amount Saved	£250,000
3	Amount Spent	£750,000
4	Annual Income From Savings	£12,790.47

Figure 5.10: One possible scenario for the £1,000,000 inheritance

4. In the worksheet you used for Question 3, create **scenarios** for different interest rates and amounts saved. Create a **scenario report** to summarise how these values affect the annual income you can expect. It should look something like Figure 5.11.

Scenario Summary	Current Values:	Thrifty with high rates	Expected	Shopaholic with low rates
Changing Cells:				
INTEREST_RATE	5%	7%	5%	2%
AMOUNT_SAVED	£250,000	£900,000	£250,000	£50,000
Result Cells:				
ANNUAL_INCOME	£12,790.47	£65,061.07	£12,790.47	£1,009.22

Notes: Current Values column represents values of changing cells at time Scenario Summary Report was created. Changing cells for each scenario are highlighted in gray.

Figure 5.11: A scenario summary showing three possible combinations of interest rate and amount saved, and the annual income that results from each

6 Lookup Functions

Introduction

This chapter demonstrates how to use the functions **VLOOKUP** and **HLOOKUP** to look up values in a table. We start with two simple examples: looking up stock and customer details in the video shop worksheet, and finding matches in a range for student exam results.

After this, we will create a time sheet that the employees of **Green Thumbs Garden Centre** can use to record their working hours. Lots of people will be using it each week, so we'll use some of Excel's functions to make filling in the time sheet as painless as possible.

In this chapter you will

- use **VLOOKUP** to find customer and stock information
- use **HLOOKUP** to find out students' grades based on their marks
- design the layout of the time sheet (this will involve adding labels, merging cells and using borders)
- use the **VLOOKUP** function to keep a task code cell in sync with a drop-down list containing the task's description.

Simple lookup

 Open **videoshop.xls**.

 Switch to the **Rentals** worksheet.

The **Rentals** worksheet (Figure 6.1) gives a simple list of all of the items that were out of the shop (that is, had been rented) after the shop shut on 9th June 2005.

The **Transaction** number increases by one every time someone rents one or more items.

The **Date out** is the date when the customer rented the item, and the **Date due back** is the date by which the rented items must be returned to the shop. Notice that the first three entries represent items that are late, so the customers will be fined when they return the items.

The **Member** number matches the **Member** number given in the membership list on the **Members** worksheet. Similarly, the **Item** number matches the **Code** number given in the **Stock** worksheet.

Syllabus Ref: AM4.3.1.6

Use lookup and reference functions: HLOOKUP; VLOOKUP.

We can use the **VLOOKUP** function to 'pull in' any information we need from the **Member** or **Stock** worksheets, based on these matching numbers.

VLOOKUP(lookup_value, table_array, col_index_num, [range_lookup])

lookup_value is the value to search for.

table_array is the range of cells to search, which must be sorted by the leftmost column.

col_index_num specifies which column to look in for the result when a matching **lookup_value** is found in the first column.

range_lookup is a flag which, if set to **TRUE** (the default) finds the closest match, and if set to **FALSE** requires an exact match.

The **V** in **VLOOKUP** means **V**ertical, since this function expects the table array to be arranged with the keys (the values which are looked up) arranged vertically in a column. There is an equivalent function, called **HLOOKUP**, which works with data arranged horizontally in rows, with the keys listed in the first row. The parameters for **HLOOKUP** are exactly the same, except that **col_index_num** is replaced by **row_index_num**.

Items Rented Out At The End Of 09/06/2005				
Transaction	Date out	Date due back	Member	Item
49005	01/06/2005	04/06/2005	2	55
49982	06/06/2005	09/06/2005	34	80
49982	06/06/2005	09/06/2005	34	51
51320	07/06/2005	10/06/2005	22	32
51321	07/06/2005	10/06/2005	99	33
51322	07/06/2005	10/06/2005	1	97
51323	07/06/2005	14/06/2005	46	41
51324	07/06/2005	10/06/2005	53	57
51324	07/06/2005	10/06/2005	53	97
51325	07/06/2005	10/06/2005	64	17
51326	07/06/2005	10/06/2005	37	65
51327	07/06/2005	10/06/2005	62	44
51328	08/06/2005	11/06/2005	86	64
51328	08/06/2005	11/06/2005	86	89
51329	08/06/2005	11/06/2005	18	89
51330	08/06/2005	11/06/2005	87	75
51331	08/06/2005	11/06/2005	45	53
51332	08/06/2005	11/06/2005	79	56
51333	08/06/2005	11/06/2005	90	90
51334	08/06/2005	11/06/2005	97	4
51335	08/06/2005	15/06/2005	38	68
51335	08/06/2005	15/06/2005	38	66
51336	08/06/2005	10/06/2005	8	99
51337	08/06/2005	10/06/2005	12	34
51338	08/06/2005	15/06/2005	40	87
51339	08/06/2005	11/06/2005	59	42
51340	08/06/2005	11/06/2005	17	80
51340	08/06/2005	10/06/2005	17	22
51341	09/06/2005	12/06/2005	54	57
51341	09/06/2005	12/06/2005	54	80
51342	09/06/2005	16/06/2005	6	83
51343	09/06/2005	12/06/2005	63	44
51343	09/06/2005	11/06/2005	63	15
51344	09/06/2005	11/06/2005	93	74
51345	09/06/2005	12/06/2005	47	90
51345	09/06/2005	11/06/2005	47	31
51346	09/06/2005	11/06/2005	72	78
51347	09/06/2005	12/06/2005	69	52
51348	09/06/2005	12/06/2005	15	96
51349	09/06/2005	11/06/2005	5	54
51350	09/06/2005	11/06/2005	76	31
51351	09/06/2005	16/06/2005	3	47
51352	09/06/2005	16/06/2005	55	77
51353	09/06/2005	12/06/2005	66	32
51354	09/06/2005	12/06/2005	33	7
51355	09/06/2005	16/06/2005	30	11
51356	09/06/2005	12/06/2005	41	16

Figure 6.1: The list of all items that are out of the shop after closing on 9th June 2005

Suppose we want to check how much money we took for rentals on 9th June 2005.

The workbook already has the name **STOCK_LIST** assigned to **A2:F100** in the **Stock** worksheet. (You can use **Insert**, **Name**, **Define** to check this.) Therefore, we can refer to this name in our lookup formula.

	A	B	C	D	E	F	G
1	Code	Type	Title	Category	Certificate	Rental price	Copies
2	1	DVD	Bourne Identity, The	Action	12	£4.00	10
3	2	DVD	Village, The	Horror	12	£4.00	18
4	3	DVD	Chitty Chitty Bang Bang	Family	PG	£3.00	8
5	4	DVD	Blade Runner	Science Fiction	15	£3.00	4
6	5	Video	Withnail And I	Comedy	15	£2.00	7
7	6	Game	Tony Hawk's Underground 2	Sport	15	£5.00	3

Figure 6.2: Top of the Stock worksheet

Look at the **Stock** worksheet. We want to find the **Rental price** based on the **Code**. The **Rental price** is in the **sixth** column, so our **col_index_num** parameter will be **6**.

In the **Rentals** worksheet, type the heading **Price** in cell **F3**.

In cell **F4**, type the formula **=VLOOKUP(E4, STOCK_LIST, 6)**.

This should result in the value **3**. Let's trace this through. We're telling Excel to look up the code from cell **E4** (**55**) in the **Stock** worksheet and return the corresponding value from column **6**.

Switch to the **Stock** worksheet and look at the row for which the **Code** is **55**. It is the *Close Encounters of the Third Kind* DVD, and its rental price is £3. This is the information we wanted.

This is a form of linking between worksheets. This subject is covered in more detail in Chapter 15.

Back in the **Rentals** worksheet, use the **fill handle** to copy the formula from cell **F4** down through cells **F5:F50**.

Select cells **F32:F50**, which are the prices for the rentals that have a **Date out** of **09/06/2005**. Look at the status bar. It should say **Sum=69** – in other words, the total value of rentals made on 9th June 2005 was £69. This is what we were trying to find out.

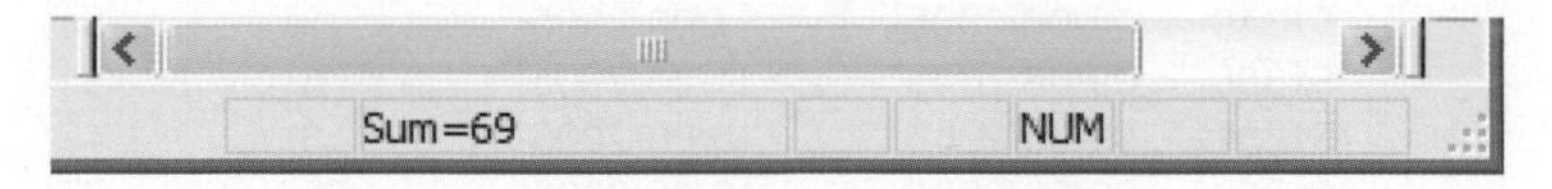

Figure 6.3: Doing a quick sum of the values in the selected cells

Let's add another column after the membership number to show the member's last name (the fourth column in the **Members** worksheet).

Right-click the column heading for column **E** and select **Insert** from the menu that appears. A new blank column is inserted between the **Member** and **Item** columns.

In cell **E3**, type the heading **Name**.

This time, we'll specify the range of cells by dragging over them instead of using a named range.

In cell **E4**, type the formula **=VLOOKUP(** then click in cell **D4** and type a comma (,). Now click on the **Members** tab and click and drag the mouse pointer over cells **A2:N100**. Then type **, 4)** and press **Enter**.

The formula in cell **E4** should now read **=VLOOKUP(D4, Members!A2:N100, 4)** and should have a value of **Thompson**.

Use the fill handle to copy the formula from cell **E4** to cells **E5:E50**.

Oops! Some of the cells are showing **#N/A**. The problem is that we did not specify a fixed reference in the formula. By the time we get to row **50**, the lookup is being made against **Members!A48:N146** instead of **Members!A2:N100**. Instead, we want all of the lookups to be made against **Members!A2:N100**.

Change the formula in cell **E4** to use a fixed reference for the lookup table: **=VLOOKUP(D4, Members!$A$2:$N$100, 4)**.

Copy the formula to the rest of the column, as before. This time all of the lookups should succeed, so there should be no **#N/A** results.

The **Rentals** worksheet should now look like Figure 6.4.

	A	B	C	D	E	F	G
1	**Items Rented Out At The End Of 09/06/2005**						
2							
3	**Transaction**	**Date out**	**Date due back**	**Member**	**Name**	**Item**	**Price**
4	49005	01/06/2005	04/06/2005	2	Thompson	55	3
5	49982	06/06/2005	09/06/2005	34	Reed	80	3
6	49982	06/06/2005	09/06/2005	34	Reed	51	3
7	51320	07/06/2005	10/06/2005	22	Mitchell	32	2
8	51321	07/06/2005	10/06/2005	99	Walker	33	3
9	51322	07/06/2005	10/06/2005	1	Henderson	97	2
10	51323	07/06/2005	14/06/2005	46	Thompson	41	5
11	51324	07/06/2005	10/06/2005	53	Clark	57	3
12	51324	07/06/2005	10/06/2005	53	Clark	97	2
13	51325	07/06/2005	10/06/2005	64	Brown	17	3
14	51326	07/06/2005	10/06/2005	37	Smith	65	2
15	51327	07/06/2005	10/06/2005	62	Bailey	44	2
16	51328	08/06/2005	11/06/2005	86	Anderson	64	3

Figure 6.4: Top of the Rentals worksheet, showing the new Name column

Save and close **videoshop.xls**.

Range lookup

You are not limited to looking up exact matches; you can look up a value that falls within a specified range. We'll see how this works by putting together a simple workbook of student grades. One worksheet will hold the actual marks that the students got, and these marks will be converted into grades by looking up the values in a table on the second worksheet.

Open a new workbook.

By default, when you create a new blank workbook, you get three worksheets (called **Sheet1**, **Sheet2** and **Sheet3**). Right-click the tab for **Sheet1** and select **Rename** from the menu that appears. Type the new name **Results**, and then press **Enter**. Double-click **Sheet2** and rename it **Grades**. Right-click **Sheet3** and select **Delete** from the menu.

Students need 76% or more for an A grade or 60% or more for a B grade. The thresholds for the grades C, D, E and F are 50%, 40%, 30% and 20% respectively. Any mark below 20% is **Ungraded**, except for 0%, which is recorded as **Zero**.

We can record this information as shown in Figure 6.5. Notice that this is a horizontal arrangement (the values that we will be looking up run across the page, instead of down) so we will need to use **HLOOKUP** instead of **VLOOKUP**.

Notice also that the values we will be looking up are in the first row; **HLOOKUP** requires that the key values are in the first row (just as **VLOOKUP** requires that the key values are in the first column). This makes sense, since we can't use any of the parameters for these lookup functions to specify the index of the information we are searching, only the index of the information we want to have returned from the search.

Type in the information shown in Figure 6.5 into the **Grades** worksheet.

	A	B	C	D	E	F	G	H	I
1	**Percent**	0%	1%	20%	30%	40%	50%	60%	76%
2	**Grade**	Zero	Ungraded	F	E	D	C	B	A

Figure 6.5: Categories of grades

Select cells **B1:I2** and give them the name **GRADES**. We can use this name in our **HLOOKUP** formula later.

In the **Results** worksheet, type in the values shown in Figure 6.6(a).

In cell **C2**, type the formula **=HLOOKUP(B2, GRADES, 2, TRUE)**. The result should be **E** since **30%** is the minimum value needed to get an **E** grade.

This tells Excel to look up the mark held in cell **B2** in the **GRADES** list. It returns the value from row **2** (**Grade**). The **TRUE** tells **HLOOKUP** to do a range search instead of an exact match: it will return the match for the largest result found that is smaller than the value being searched for. For example, a search for **45%** will return the value for **40%** (**D**).

Copy the formula for the other students. The final worksheet should look like Figure 6.6(b).

	A	B	C
1	**Student**	**Mark**	**Grade**
2	Tom	30%	
3	Sarah	48%	
4	John	71%	
5	Ranj	50%	
6	Lesley	91%	
7	Peter	59%	
8	Penny	60%	
9	Bart	5%	
10	Nasim	85%	
11	Mark	66%	
12	Sue	60%	
13	Terry	54%	

	A	B	C
1	**Student**	**Mark**	**Grade**
2	Tom	30%	E
3	Sarah	48%	D
4	John	71%	B
5	Ranj	50%	C
6	Lesley	91%	A
7	Peter	59%	C
8	Penny	60%	B
9	Bart	5%	Ungraded
10	Nasim	85%	A
11	Mark	66%	B
12	Sue	60%	B
13	Terry	54%	C

Figure 6.6: Student marks (a) before and (b) after looking up the grades

Save the workbook as **grades.xls** and close it.

Preparing the time sheet

We will now move on to a more substantial example. You are going to develop an Excel-based time sheet for Green Thumbs Garden Centre over the next several chapters. This will give another example of how to use lookup functions, as well as giving us the opportunity to look at some of the other functions that Excel has to offer.

First, let's map out what goes where on the time sheet. The main body of the time sheet will comprise a row for each task done that week, which will be broken down into a description and finance code for the task, daily totals for the hours worked on that task and a final total.

Open a new blank workbook.

Since we'll be adding a heading at the top, we'll begin the body of the time sheet on row **7**.

In cell **A7**, type the label **Description**; in cell **B7**, type **Code**; in cell **C7**, type **Hours Worked**.

We need a column for each day of the week. In cell **C8**, type **Mon**.

Rather than type in the other days of the week, we can get Excel to do it for us. You can use the **fill handle** to extend any lists that Excel knows about; if you look at **Tools**, **Options**, **Custom Lists** you will see that the sequence **Mon**, **Tue**, **...**, **Sun** is one such list.

With cell **C8** selected, drag its **fill handle** across to cell **I8** (the tooltip will show the sequence as you go, ending with **Sun** on cell **I8**, as shown in Figure 6.7).

	A	B	C	D	E	F	G	H	I	J
1										
2										
3										
4										
5										
6										
7	Descriptior	Code	Hours Worked							
8			Mon							
9										
10								Sun		

Figure 6.7: Extending a series (days of the week) using the fill handle

We need one more column: type **Total** in cell **J8**.

The rows beneath these headings will be blank until an employee fills them in; we'll use grid lines to show the extent of the time sheet. The garden centre's manager has told you that eight tasks will be sufficient – nobody should be doing more different things than that.

Select cells **A7:J16**, then use the **Borders** button on the **Formatting** toolbar to add grid lines around each of the cells in the selection, as shown in Figure 6.8.

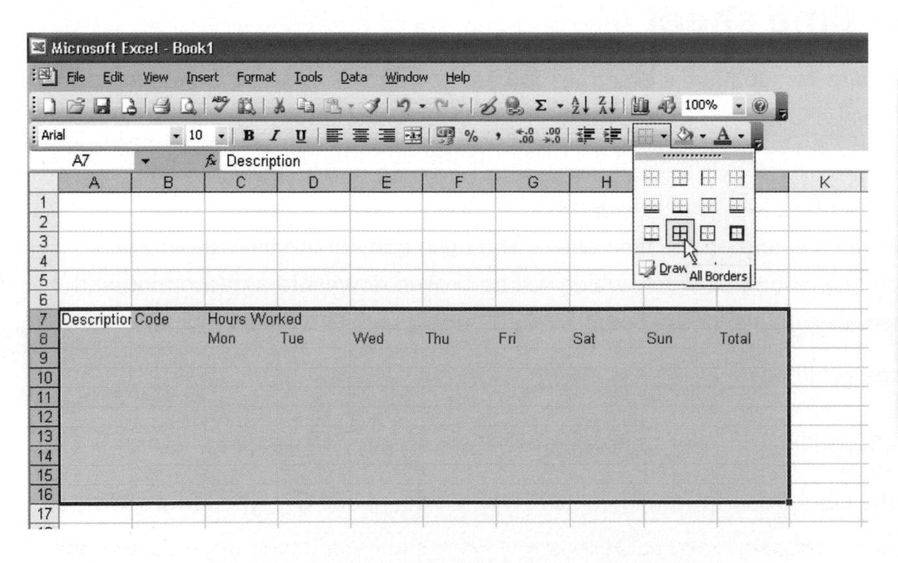

Figure 6.8: Adding border lines around selected cells

TIP

The **Borders** button changes to show the border type that it was last used for, so it may look slightly different in your Excel. Click the arrow to the right of the button to display the menu shown in Figure 6.8.

We will also want a total for the number of hours worked each day (**C17:J17**), so we'll add a grid around these cells too.

Select cells **C17:J17** and then press the **Borders** button (not the arrow next to it). The **Borders** button remembers the last type of border that you used, and reapplies those settings to the currently selected cells.

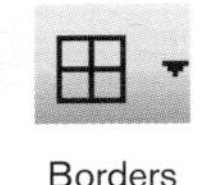

Borders

In cell **A2**, type the heading **Time Sheet**. We'll make this bigger later.

In cells **D2** and **D3**, type the headings **Name** and **Manager** respectively.

Your time sheet should now look like Figure 6.9. Now we're ready to tidy it up a bit.

	A	B	C	D	E	F	G	H	I	J
1										
2	Time Sheet			Name						
3				Manager						
4										
5										
6										
7	Descriptio	Code	Hours Worked							
8			Mon	Tue	Wed	Thu	Fri	Sat	Sun	Total
9										
10										
11										
12										
13										
14										
15										
16										
17										
18										

Figure 6.9: Framework for a time sheet for the garden centre

All of the heading cells, including where the employee types in their name and manager, can be bold. Select rows **1** to **8** by clicking and dragging down the row headings on the left, and then press **Ctrl+B** to make their contents bold.

Select cells **C7:J7**, then press the **Merge and Center** button on the **Formatting** toolbar. This makes the heading **Hours Worked** stretch across the days of the week and the **Total** columns.

Merge and Centre

The descriptions are going to be quite long, so increase the width of column **A** to about three times its default.

Because the **Hours Worked** headings take up two lines, it will look neater if we merge each of the two labels **Description** and **Code** with the blank cell beneath it.

Select cells **A7:A8**. Right-click and select **Format Cells** from the menu. The **Format Cells** dialogue appears.

Make sure the **Alignment** tab is selected. Tick the **Merge cells** checkbox and set the **Vertical text alignment** to **Top**, as shown in Figure 6.10. Press **OK**.

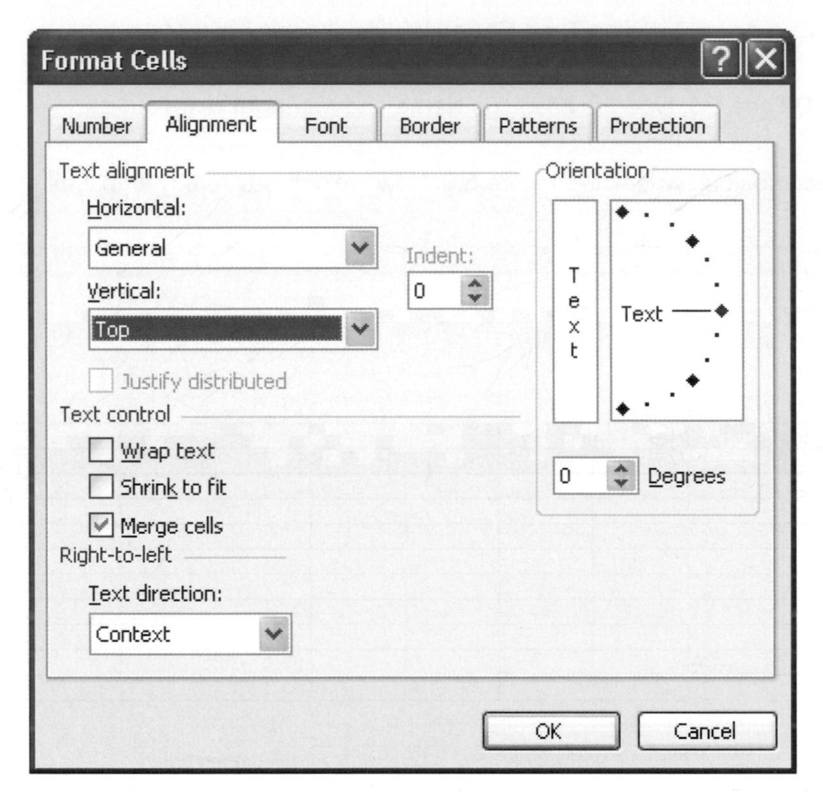

Figure 6.10: Merging cells, and making text align to the top instead of the bottom

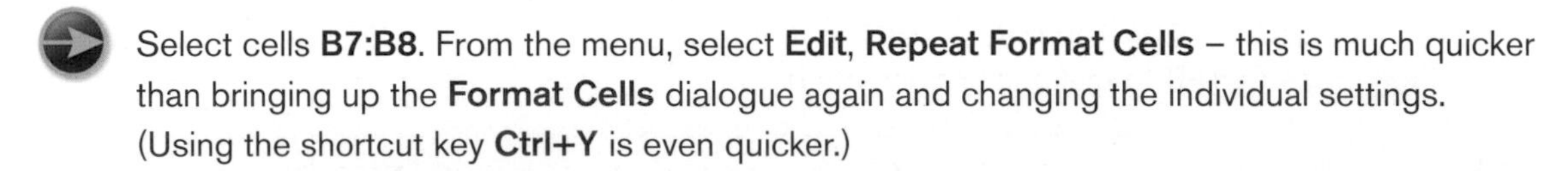
Select cells **B7:B8**. From the menu, select **Edit**, **Repeat Format Cells** – this is much quicker than bringing up the **Format Cells** dialogue again and changing the individual settings. (Using the shortcut key **Ctrl+Y** is even quicker.)

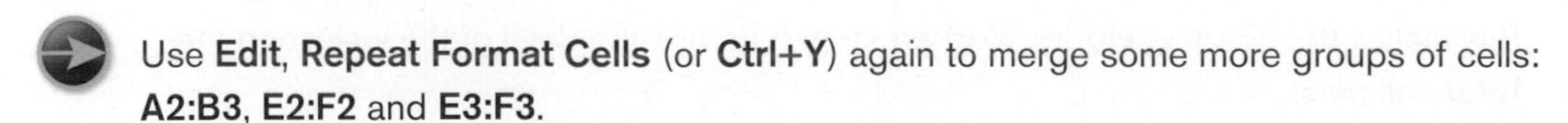
Use **Edit**, **Repeat Format Cells** (or **Ctrl+Y**) again to merge some more groups of cells: **A2:B3**, **E2:F2** and **E3:F3**.

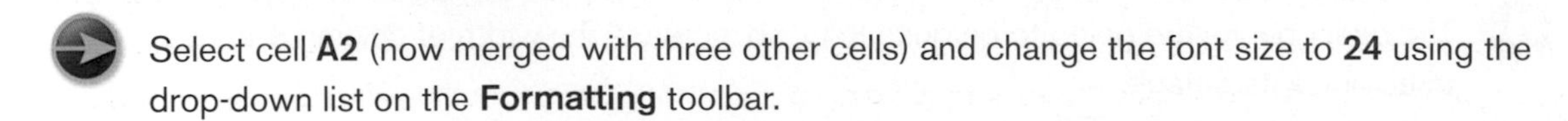
Select cell **A2** (now merged with three other cells) and change the font size to **24** using the drop-down list on the **Formatting** toolbar.

The time sheet should now look like Figure 6.11.

	A	B	C	D	E	F	G	H	I	J	K
1											
2	**Time Sheet**			**Name**							
3				**Manager**							
4											
5											
6											
7	**Description**	**Code**	**Hours Worked**								
8			**Mon**	**Tue**	**Wed**	**Thu**	**Fri**	**Sat**	**Sun**	**Total**	
9											
10											
11											
12											
13											
14											
15											
16											
17											
18											

Figure 6.11: Time sheet after initial tidying

Let's put some example entries into the time sheet to see what they look like.

Suppose an employee at the garden centre has worked on the checkouts for seven hours each weekday, and has also driven the fork lift for one hour on Tuesday and Thursday, and for five hours on Saturday. Fill in the time sheet to reflect this, as shown in Figure 6.12.

	A	B	C	D	E	F	G	H	I	J
1										
2	**Time Sheet**			**Name**						
3				**Manager**						
4										
5										
6										
7	**Description**	**Code**	**Hours Worked**							
8			**Mon**	**Tue**	**Wed**	**Thu**	**Fri**	**Sat**	**Sun**	**Total**
9	Checkouts	SALE	7	7	7	7	7			
10	Fork lift driving	FORK		1		1		5		
11										
12										
13										
14										
15										
16										
17										

Figure 6.12: Filling in an example time sheet

The store manager has provided you with a short list of the possible tasks performed by employees at the garden centre. Instead of people typing these in each time, it would be better if they could use a drop-down list to select the task they want to book hours to. This will reduce the likelihood of errors and prevent people from making up tasks as they see fit.

The first thing to do is to create a list of task descriptions and their codes. We'll do this on a separate worksheet.

 Rename **Sheet1** as **Time Sheet**, rename **Sheet2** as **Tasks** and delete **Sheet3**.

The worksheet tabs at the bottom of the window should now look like Figure 6.13.

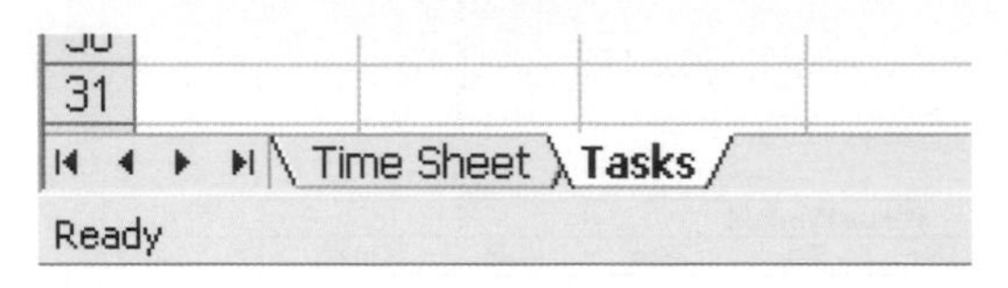

Figure 6.13: Renaming the worksheets in a workbook

 With the **Tasks** worksheet selected, type in the list of task descriptions and their codes, as shown in Figure 6.14. Make cells **A1:B1** bold so that the headings stand out.

	A	B
1	**Task Description**	**Code**
2	Checkouts	SALE
3	Customer service	CUST
4	Deliveries	DELV
5	Fork lift driving	FORK
6	Management	MNGT
7	Plant/fish care	CARE
8	Restocking	STOK
9	Training, Giving	TRNG
10	Training, Receiving	TRN2
11		

Figure 6.14: Task descriptions and codes

 Select cells **A2:A10** and give the range the name **TASK_NAMES** using the **Name Box**. Remember to press **Enter** to apply the new name.

 Switch back to the **Time Sheet** worksheet and select cell **A9**. We're going to change this to a drop-down list that contains the values in **TASK_NAMES**.

 From the menu, select **Data, Validation**. The **Data Validation** dialogue appears. Change the **Allow** value to **List**. In the **Source** box type **=TASK_NAMES** (the equals sign is important: if you don't include it, you will end up with a drop-down list that contains the string '**TASK_NAMES**'). The dialogue should look like Figure 6.15. Press **OK** to create the list.

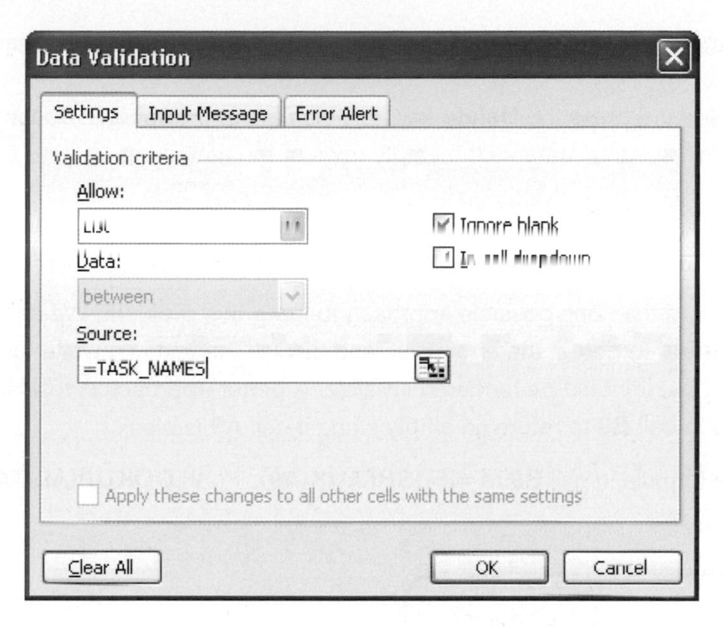

Figure 6.15: Adding a drop-down list to a cell

Cell **A9** now contains a drop-down list, as shown in Figure 6.16. Try it out.

A9 | Checkouts

	A	B	C	D	E	F	G	H	I	J	K
1											
2	Time Sheet			Name				Week Ending		03/02/2006	
3				Manager							
4											
5			Enter best estimate; corrections can be made later.								
6											
7	Description	Code	Hours Worked								
8			Mon	Tue	Wed	Thu	Fri	Sat	Sun	Total	
9	Checkouts	LE	7	7	7	7	7			35	
10	Checkouts	RK		1		1		5		7	
11	Customer service Deliveries										
12	Fork lift driving										
13	Management										
14	Plant/fish care										
15	Restocking Training, Giving										
16											
17			7	8	7	8	7	5		42	
18											

Figure 6.16: Using the drop-down list

It would be useful if the task code updated automatically whenever a different task was selected from the drop-down list. We can use the function **VLOOKUP** to achieve this.

Switch to the **Tasks** worksheet and select the cells **A1:B10**. Give this range the name **TASK_TABLE**. We can then pass this name to the **VLOOKUP** function as the **table_array** parameter.

Change back to the **Time Sheet** worksheet. Select cell **B9**. Type the formula **=VLOOKUP(A9, TASK_TABLE, 2, 0)**. This tells Excel to find an exact match for the value of cell **A9** in the first column of the **TASK_TABLE**, and to return the value from the corresponding second column.

 Try changing the value of cell **A9**. The code in cell **B9** should change to match.

 Select cell **A9** and press the **Delete** key; this blanks out the value (it doesn't delete the list), resetting it to the same state as the empty rows of the timesheet.

Notice how the value of cell **B9** has changed to **#N/A**, which means 'not available'. This is because there is no code in the **TASK_TABLE** that corresponds to a blank value in the left-hand column.

As usual, there is more than one possible approach to fixing this problem. We could use **conditional formatting** to detect the error value and display the text in a white font – the **#N/A** would still be there, but it would be rendered invisible. A better approach is to wrap an **IF** command around the formula in cell **B9** to return an empty string if cell **A9** is blank.

 Change the formula in cell **B9** to **=IF(ISBLANK(A9), " ", VLOOKUP(A9, TASK_TABLE, 2, 0))**

> The **IF** function is covered in Chapter 8.

 Cell **B9** should now be blank. Try setting different values for cell **A9** to check that cell **B9** still updates as expected.

 Select cells **A9:B9** and drag the **fill handle** down to copy the contents into cells **A10:B16**. Check that each of the description rows now has a drop-down list, and that whenever you select a new description, its code updates to match.

Adding new bookable tasks

It's worth considering what needs to happen if new tasks are to be added to the list. Let's add tasks for holiday and sickness bookings to show the process.

 Switch to the **Tasks** worksheet.

In the two rows beneath the existing table, add two more entries: **Holiday**, with a code of **HOLS**, and **Sickness**, with a code of **SICK**, as shown in Figure 6.17(a).

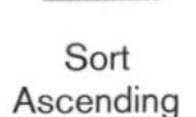
Sort Ascending

Remember that the left-hand column needs to be in alphabetical order for the **VLOOKUP** function to work. Select cells **A2:B12** and then press the **Sort Ascending** button on the **Standard** toolbar. The list should now be in the order given in Figure 6.17(b).

> We'll look in more detail at sorting in Chapter 11.

	A	B
1	**Task Description**	**Code**
2	Checkouts	SALE
3	Customer service	CUST
4	Deliveries	DELV
5	Fork lift driving	FORK
6	Management	MNGT
7	Plant/fish care	CARE
8	Restocking	STOK
9	Training, Giving	TRNG
10	Training, Receiving	TRN2
11	Holiday	HOLS
12	Sickness	SICK
13		

	A	B
1	**Task Description**	**Code**
2	Checkouts	SALE
3	Customer service	CUST
4	Deliveries	DELV
5	Fork lift driving	FORK
6	Holiday	HOLS
7	Management	MNGT
8	Plant/fish care	CARE
9	Restocking	STOK
10	Sickness	SICK
11	Training, Giving	TRNG
12	Training, Receiving	TRN2
13		

Figure 6.17: Extended list of tasks (a) before and (b) after sorting

We also need to redefine the range **TASK_TABLE** so that it covers the two new rows.

- From the menu select **Insert**, **Name**, **Define**. The **Define Name** dialogue appears.
- Click on the name **TASK_TABLE** in the list. Notice that the **Refers to** value is still **=Tasks!$A$1:$B$10**.
- Click on the **Minimize Dialog** button to the right of the **Refers to** area.

Minimize Dialog

- A dashed area appears, showing the current area to which the name refers. Click and drag the mouse pointer over the new area it should use (cells **A1:B12**).

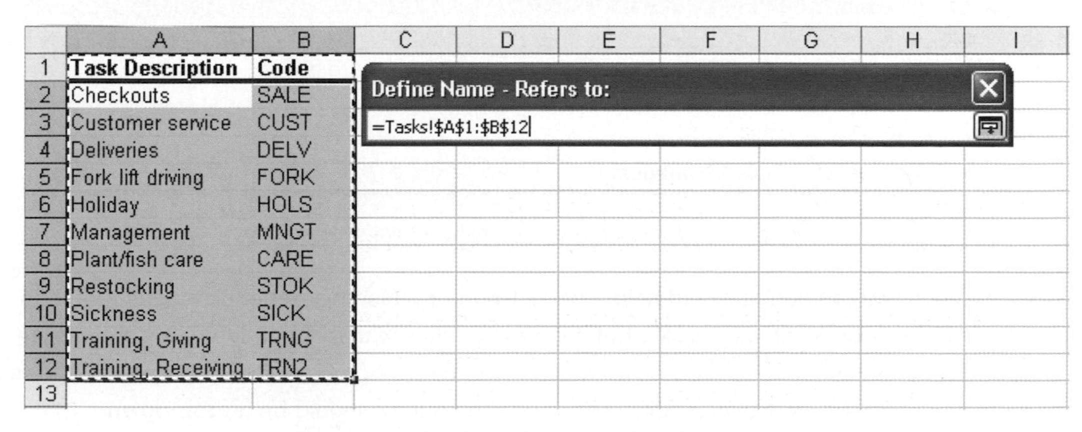

	A	B
1	**Task Description**	**Code**
2	Checkouts	SALE
3	Customer service	CUST
4	Deliveries	DELV
5	Fork lift driving	FORK
6	Holiday	HOLS
7	Management	MNGT
8	Plant/fish care	CARE
9	Restocking	STOK
10	Sickness	SICK
11	Training, Giving	TRNG
12	Training, Receiving	TRN2
13		

Figure 6.18: Redefining the range referred to by a name

Restore Dialog

Press the **Restore Dialog** button, then press **OK** to confirm the change.

Back in the **Time Sheet** worksheet, confirm that the two new tasks (**Holiday** and **Sickness**) appear in all of the drop-down menus, and that the correct codes are filled in for them.

If you insert a row or column in the middle of a named range, the name is automatically expanded to cover the new cells. Therefore, in this case, we could have added two new blank rows in appropriate places in the task list and then filled in the values, so that we did not need to perform the steps for sorting or for expanding **TASK_LIST**. However, it was worth covering these techniques because you will find that they come in handy.

Save the workbook as **timesheet.xls**.

Test yourself

1. Add a new worksheet, called **Managers**, to the workbook. (To insert a worksheet, right-click the worksheet tabs and choose **Insert** from the menu that appears. Select **Worksheet** and press **OK**.) Fill it out to look like Figure 6.19 (obviously, a real garden centre would have more employees, but this number will suffice for this exercise). Notice how this list is arranged in rows. Use the **HLOOKUP** function to automatically fill in the manager's name in the **Time Sheet** cell when the employees type theirs. Excel uses the value **#N/A** in the **Manager** cell whenever the lookup fails – this is OK.

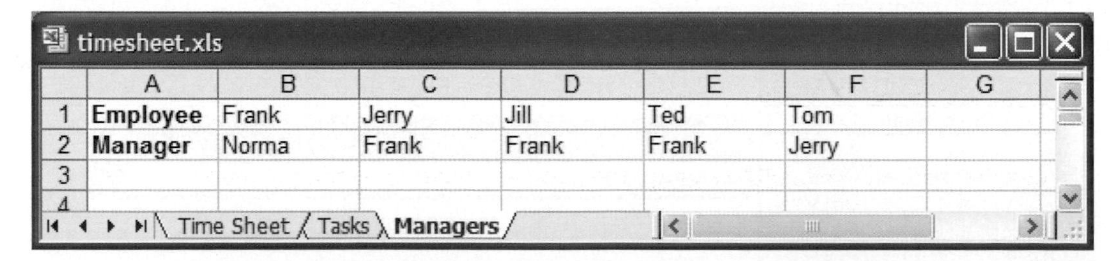

timesheet.xls

	A	B	C	D	E	F	G
1	**Employee**	Frank	Jerry	Jill	Ted	Tom	
2	**Manager**	Norma	Frank	Frank	Frank	Jerry	
3							
4							

Time Sheet / Tasks / **Managers**

Figure 6.19: A list, arranged in rows, of employees and their managers

2. Create a new workbook that would help a collector to organise his or her collection. You can choose whatever collectibles you like, but it is best to stick with just one type. The main page should list the collection. Use drop-down menus where appropriate; for example, if you choose to create a workbook for a stamp collection, then the country should be a drop-down.

7 Database & Mathematical Functions

Introduction

In this chapter, we will use database functions to look up information about the video shop. We will also use the mathematical functions **SUMIF** and **ROUND**.

In this chapter you will

- use the **DCOUNT** function to count the number of rows that match certain criteria
- use the **DSUM** function to add together values from a specified column of all the rows that match certain criteria
- use the **DMIN** and **DMAX** functions to find minimum and maximum values from a specified column of all the rows that match certain criteria
- learn how to specify criteria to search more than one column at once (an **AND search**)
- learn how to specify multiple sets of criteria so that a match is found whenever a row matches any of the sets of criteria (an **OR search**)
- use the **SUMIF** function to add together values without having to set aside an area of your worksheet for search criteria
- use the **ROUND** function to change the accuracy used for storing numbers.

Database functions

 Open the file **videoshop.xls**.

Database functions let you look up specific values from your set of structured data. We will create a new worksheet in the video shop workbook and use it to find out information about the shop's stock and customers.

Syllabus Ref: AM4.3.1.8
Use available database functions: DSUM; DMIN; DMAX and DCOUNT.

Setting up the Queries worksheet

 Right-click any of the worksheet tabs at the bottom of the Excel window and select **Insert**. The **Insert** dialogue appears, as shown in Figure 7.1.

 Select **Worksheet** on the **General** tab and then press **OK**.

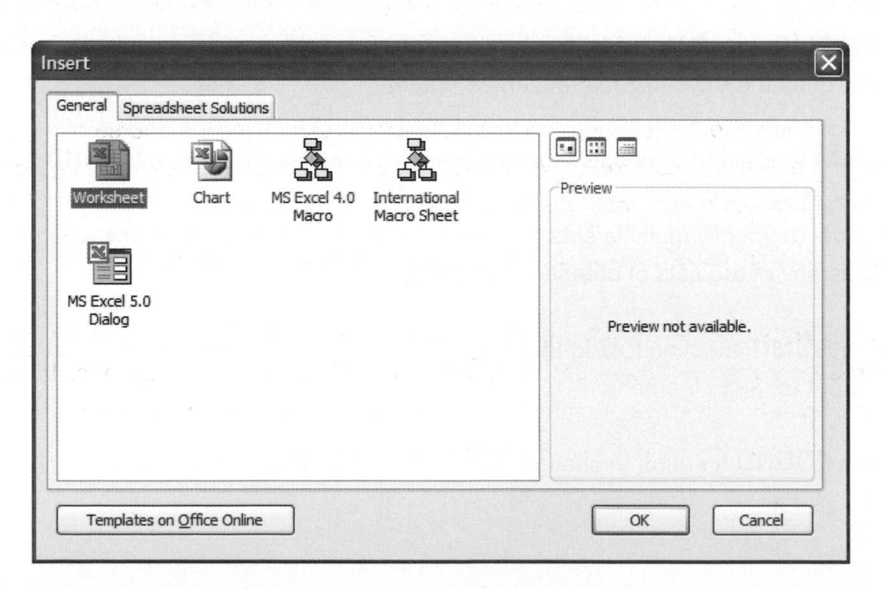

Figure 7.1: Inserting a new worksheet

 Double-click in the tab for the new worksheet, type **Queries** as its new name and press **Enter**.

 Click and drag the **Queries** tab so that it moves to the right of the other tabs.

 In cell **A1**, type **Queries**. Make it **bold** and size **16**.

Counting rows with DCOUNT

The video shop stocks DVDs, videos and games. Videos are slowly being phased out and replaced by DVDs. It would be useful to be able to see a summary of the number of different titles stocked in each category. We can use Excel's database functions to find out.

The four database lookup functions are **DSUM**, **DMIN**, **DMAX** and **DCOUNT**. Each of these takes three parameters: a **database**, the name of the **field** to return and the **criteria**.

DMIN (and **DMAX**) return the minimum (or maximum) field value from the subset of records that match the criteria. **DSUM** adds together the fields from records that match the criteria. **DCOUNT** returns the number of matching records.

In cell **B2**, type the heading **Unique Titles**. In cells **A3**, **A4** and **A5**, type the category names **Videos**, **DVDs**, and **Games**. Make these four cells bold.

The **criteria** parameter for the database functions must be a reference to a range of cells. The first row in the range contains heading names matching those in the database. The second and subsequent rows contain the values or ranges to look up – a record matches if any of these rows match.

Don't worry too much about this for now; it should become clear over the course of the exercise. For now, you just need to be aware that we must set aside a portion of the worksheet to contain our criteria for filtering the different types of stock items.

In cell **B7**, enter the value **Type**. In cell **B8**, type the value that we want to find: **Video**.

Let's just try to get the number of video titles for now. We will use **DCOUNT** to find the number of matching records. The **field** parameter is optional: if it is included then only records that have numbers in the specified field are counted; if it is omitted then all matching records are counted. We can omit it because there are no empty cells in the database.

In cell **B3**, enter the formula **=DCOUNT(STOCK_DB, , B7:B8)**.

The cell range **A1:G100** on the **Stock** worksheet has been assigned the name **STOCK_DB**, so we can use this to query it.

Your worksheet should now look like Figure 7.2.

B3 | =DCOUNT(STOCK_DB, , B7:B8)

	A	B	C	D	E	F
1	**Queries**					
2		**Unique Titles**				
3	**Videos**	20				
4	**DVDs**					
5	**Games**					
6						
7		Type				
8		Video				
9						

Figure 7.2: Using DCOUNT to count the number of videos

We need two more criteria, one each for DVDs and games.

 Enter **Type** in cell **C7** and **DVD** in cell **C8**.

 Enter **Type** in cell **D7** and **Game** in cell **D8**.

 Use these new criteria to add appropriate **DCOUNT** functions to cells **B4** and **B5**.

Your worksheet should now look like Figure 7.3.

	A	B	C	D
1	**Queries**			
2		**Unique Titles**		
3	**Videos**	20		
4	**DVDs**	54		
5	**Games**	25		
6				
7		Type	Type	Type
8		Video	DVD	Game

Figure 7.3: Three DCOUNT queries

Summing matching values with DSUM

This is useful information. We can see that there are 20 different videos, 54 different DVDs and 25 different games. However, for each of these unique titles we have a different number of boxes actually on the shelf. This information is held in the **Copies** column in the **Stock** worksheet. We can use the **DSUM** function to add together all of the matching copies for each type.

 Type the heading **Total Stock** in cell **C2** and make it bold.

In cell **C3**, enter the formula **=DSUM(STOCK_DB, "Copies", B7:B8)**.

This formula tells Excel to look in the **STOCK_DB** database, summing all of the values in the **Copies** column whenever the criteria in cells **B7:B8** (**Type** = **Video**) are met.

The result in cell **C3** is **189**. Now we know that there are 189 video cassettes distributed over the 20 titles.

Create similar formulas in cells **C4** and **C5**. The results should come out as **570** and **197**.

Remember that the **Field** parameter was optional for **DCOUNT**. It is mandatory for **DSUM**, though, since we must always specify something to be added up.

Finding minimum and maximum values with DMIN and DMAX

We now know how many videos, DVDs and games there are. It would also be useful to know the minimum and maximum number of copies held for each different category. For example, are there any DVD titles for which there is only one copy? If so, you might want to buy some more stock.

We can set up a table below the criteria we set up before and reuse them.

In cell **A9**, type the label **Minimum Copies**. In cell **A10**, type the label **Maximum Copies**.

Make cells **A9**, **A10**, **B8**, **C8** and **D8** bold. Increase the column width so that the labels fit.

We're 'borrowing' the headings in row 8 as table headings. We can hide row 7 when we've finished with it.

In cell **B9**, enter the formula **=DMIN(STOCK_DB, "Copies", B7:B8)**.

The result is **2**, which means that at least one video title has only two copies.

In cell **B10**, enter the equivalent **DMAX** formula: **=DMAX(STOCK_DB, "Copies", B7:B8)**.

Complete the **DMIN** and **DMAX** formulas for DVDs and games.

Because the criteria are above the formulas in each case, and the criteria references are relative (no **$**s), you can simply copy the formulas or use the fill handle.

 Hide row **7**.

Your worksheet should now look like Figure 7.4.

	A	B	C	D	E
1	**Queries**				
2		**Unique Titles**	**Total Stock**		
3	**Videos**	20	189		
4	**DVDs**	54	570		
5	**Games**	25	197		
6					
8		**Video**	**DVD**	**Game**	
9	**Minimum Copies**	2	1	2	
10	**Maximum Copies**	20	22	12	
11					

Figure 7.4: DMIN and DMAX formulas in place

TIP

Notice how we have hidden the top row of the search criteria and used the criteria values as table headings. This is a useful technique when you are just breaking things up by category.

The value in cell **D10** shows that at least one game has **12** copies. Imagine that there was supposed to be a maximum of ten copies of each game. Let's use database functions to find out how many game titles have more than ten copies.

Multiple search criteria ('AND')

 In cell **A12**, type the text **How many games have more than ten copies?** Make it italic.

We need to set up criteria for the **DCOUNT** function. We only want to count those rows where **Type = Game** and **Copies >10**.

 In cell **C13**, type the text **Type**. In cell **C14**, type **Game**.

 In cell **D13**, type the text **Copies**. In cell **D14**, type **>10** (with or without a space; it doesn't matter).

 In cell **A13**, enter the formula **=DCOUNT(STOCK_DB, , C13:D14).**

The result of this formula is **1**, telling us that there is exactly one game title that has more than ten copies. (We already know that it has 12 copies.)

Since there is exactly one result, we can do another lookup to find out which one it is. This uses the **DGET** function, which isn't in the ECDL syllabus but is useful to know about nonetheless.

 In cell **A16**, type the text **Which game is it?** and make it italic.

 In cell **A17**, enter the formula **=DGET(STOCK_DB, "Title", C13:D14).**

This formula tells Excel to search the **STOCK_DB** for the **Title** of the item matching the criteria in cells **C13:D14**. Now we know that it is the game **Juiced** that has 12 copies.

Choice of search criteria ('OR')

Sometimes you want to find rows that match any one of several criteria. Suppose you are interested in the number of customers who have not spent much money (perhaps you want to send them a money-off coupon to encourage them to come into the shop).

Two categories of customer fall into this group: long-term customers who have spent less than £100 in total, and any customers who have spent less than £10 in total regardless of how long they have been customers.

 In cell **A19**, type **Number of low-spending customers**. Make it italic.

 In cell **C20**, type **Date Joined**, and in cell **D20**, type **Total Spend**.

These are the names of the two columns we need to query in the **Members** worksheet. Again, we have given the data cells a name – in this case **MEMBERS_DB**.

The first category is long-term customers (say, those who joined before 2001) who have spent less than £100.

 In cell **C21**, type **<1/1/2001**. In cell **D21**, type **<100**.

The other category is any customers who have spent less than £10. For this, we can leave the **Date Joined** cell blank (which will match all dates) and just give **<10** as the criterion for the **Total Spend**.

 In cell **D22**, type **<10**.

 In cell **A20**, enter the formula **=DCOUNT(MEMBERS_DB, , C20:D22)**.

This gives the value **21**.

	A	B	C	D
19	*Number of low-spending customers*			
20	21		Date Joined	Total Spend
21			<1/1/2001	<100
22				<10

Figure 7.5: A query using two criteria rows

Mathematical functions

An alternative to **DSUM** is **SUMIF**, which can be useful when the selection criteria are simple and won't change.

The shop's customers come from the main town of Middlington and from its surrounding villages. Let's use the **SUMIF** function to find out how much people in these different areas have spent in the shop.

Syllabus Ref: AM4.3.1.2

Use mathematical functions: SUMIF; SUMPOSITIVE; ROUND.

In cell **A24**, type **Sales by area.** Make it italic.

In cells **A25:A28**, type the area names: **Blakely**, **Pickerington**, **Hamshaw**, and **Middlington**.

SUMIF(range, criteria, [sum_range])

Finds the sum of those cells in the supplied **sum_range** (or **range** if **sum_range** is not supplied) for which the **criteria** (passed in as a string) evaluate to **true**.

For the **range**, we will supply the **Village** values from the **Members** worksheet. The values are blank for Middlington itself. The **criteria** will be the string to match – the name of the village. The **sum_range** will be the **Total Spend** column from the **Members** worksheet.

In cell **B25**, start to type a formula. Type **=SUMIF(**, then click on the **Members** worksheet tab. Click and drag the mouse pointer to select cells **H2:H100**, then type **, "Blakely",** as the second parameter. Finally, select cells **N2:N100**, type **)** and press **Enter**.

B25 | fx =SUMIF(Members!H2:H100,"Blakely",Members!N2:N100)

	A	B	C	D	E	F
24	*Sales by area*					
25	Blakely	356.57				
26	Pickerington					
27	Hamshaw					
28	Middlington					
29						

Figure 7.6: Using SUMIF to calculate the total spent by residents of Blakely

This tells us that residents of Blakely have spent £356.57 in total.

Create similar formulas for Pickerington, Hamshaw and Middlington. For Middlington you will need to use an empty string (" ") as the **criteria** parameter.

The results are shown in Figure 7.7. Check that you have used rows **2** to **100** in each case.

	A	B
24	*Sales by area*	
25	Blakely	356.57
26	Pickerington	[illegible]
27	Hamshaw	[illegible]
28	Middlington	9073.13

Figure 7.7: Completed list of sales by area

The **SUMIF** function is not restricted to exact matches; it can do simple comparisons too. We will use it to find out who has spent more: customers who joined before 2003 or those who have joined since. We'll also see how to use the **ROUND** function to change the accuracy at which these figures are stored.

In cell **A30**, type **Customers who joined before 2003 have spent**. Make it italic.

In cell **A31**, type **Customers who joined since 2003 have spent**. Make it italic.

Look at the **Members** worksheet. The date they joined is in column **M** and the total they have spent is in column **N**. We can specify these columns using the notation **M:M** and **N:N** when we type our **SUMIF** formulas, as an alternative to using the mouse.

In the **Queries** worksheet, select cell **D30**. Enter the formula **=SUMIF(Members!M:M, "<1/1/2003", Members!N:N).**

This results in 4886.21 – members who joined before 2003 have spent £4886.21 in total.

In cell **D31**, enter the formula **=SUMIF(Members!M:M, ">=1/1/2003", Members!N:N).**

We have used **>=**, which means **greater than or equal to.** Similarly, **<=** means **less than or equal to**. You can also use **<>** to specify **not equal to.**

Members who joined on or after 1st January 2003 have spent £5297.84.

The ECDL syllabus mentions the **SUMPOSITIVE** function. This does not exist in Excel, but you can get the same effect by using **SUMIF** with a criteria of **> 0.**

The ROUND function

The **ROUND** function changes the accuracy used for storing a number. This changes the value of the cell, not just how it is displayed.

> **ROUND(number, num_digits)**
>
> Rounds the supplied **number** to **num_digits** decimal places. For example, **ROUND(543.21, 1)** results in **543.2**.
>
> If **num_digits** is a negative number, then the rounding is applied to the left of the decimal point. For example, **ROUND(1234567.89, -3)** results in **1235000** (i.e. rounding to the nearest thousand).

A quick example will demonstrate how this is typically used.

From the menu, select **Tools**, **Options**. The **Options** dialogue appears.

Switch to the **Edit** tab and make sure that the **Fixed decimal** option is **not** ticked, as shown in Figure 7.8. Press **OK** to close the dialogue.

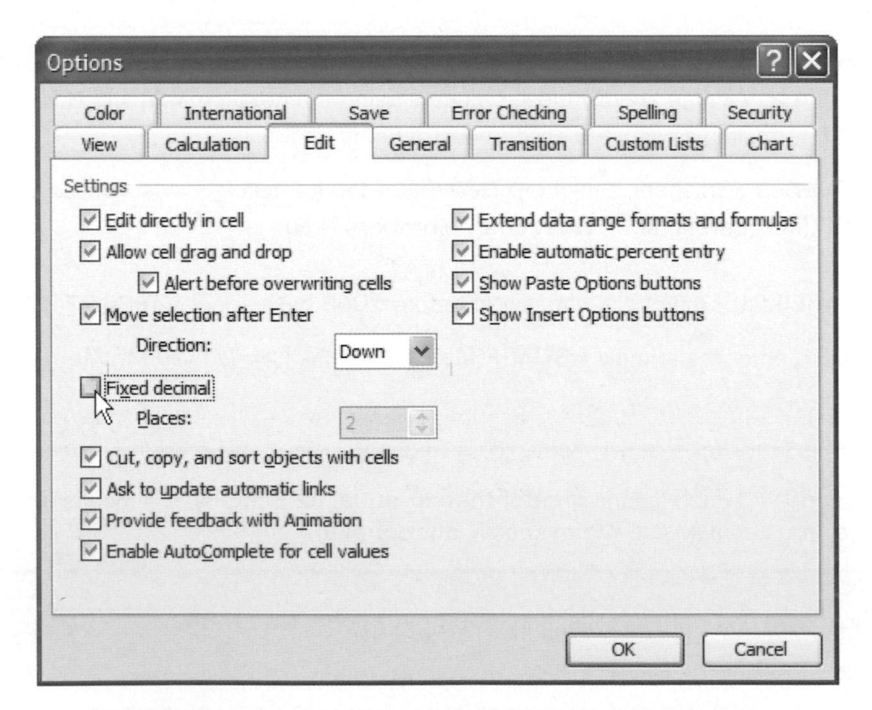

Figure 7.8: Turning off the option to display a fixed number of decimal places

Make columns **D** and **E** wide enough to show long numbers. In cell **D34**, type the formula **=D33**. In cell **E34**, enter the formula **=E33**.

We will use cells **D34** and **E34** to tell us the true values held in cells **D33** and **E33** as unformatted numbers. Both values are initially **0** because cells **D33** and **E33** are blank.

 In cell **D33**, enter the formula **=ROUND(1234.5678, 2)**.

This rounds the number **1234.5678** to **2** decimal places, resulting in **1234.57**. Cell **D34** also changes to **1234.57**.

 Give cell **E33** the value **1234.5678**. Cell **E34** also changes to **1234.5678**.

Let's set the value in cell **E33** to display to **2** decimal places.

 Select cell **E33** and, from the menu, select **Format Cells**. The **Format Cells** dialogue appears.

 Click the **Number** tab and set the **Category** to **Number**. Type **2** in the **Decimal places** box. Press **OK** to accept the change.

Cell **E33** is now displayed as **1234.57**, but cell **E34** shows that the true value of cell **E33** is still **1234.5678**.

This shows that **ROUND** changes the value, but cell formatting changes only the display.

	D	E
33	1234.57	1234.57
34	1234.57	1234.5678

Figure 7.9: Value rounding versus display rounding

 Now you've got the hang of rounding, delete the values in these four cells.

If you give **ROUND** a negative number of decimal places, it rounds to the equivalent multiple of ten. That is, **-1** rounds to the nearest ten, **-2** rounds to the nearest hundred, **-3** rounds to the nearest thousand and so on.

Let's wrap the two 2003 queries each in a **ROUND** function, rounding the amounts spent to the nearest £100.

 Edit the formula in cell **D30**, adding **ROUND(** after the = at the beginning and appending **, -2)** after the last **,**. Press **Enter**. The new value should be **4900**.

 Do the same for cell **D31**. The new value should be **5300**.

 Save your worksheet, you're done!

Test yourself

At the bottom of the **Queries** worksheet, use the database functions (**DSUM**, **DMIN**, **DMAX**, and **DCOUNT**) to answer the questions that follow.

1. How many types of stock are there with PG certificates? Use **DCOUNT** to find out.

2. How many items in total are there with PG certificates? Use **DSUM** to find out.

3. How many members joined in February 2003? You will need to use the **DCOUNT** function and two **Date Joined** parameters.

4. When did the first member from Pickerington join? Use **DMIN** to find out. You will have to format the number you get so that it is displayed as a date.

5. Which member has spent the most? Use **DMAX** and **DGET** to find out. You will need to supply criteria even though you want to search across the whole database – pairing any field name with a blank criterion cell should work.

6. From the **Rentals** worksheet, what is the total price of items due back before 12/06/2005? Use **SUMIF** to find out.

7. Given that there are 30 matching results for the previous question, calculate the average price of the items due back before 12/06/2005. Use the **ROUND** function to round the result to the nearest pound.

8 Other Functions

Introduction

In this chapter, we will add some more functionality to the time sheet for the **Green Thumbs Garden Centre**, which you created in Chapter 6. This will allow us to explore the other functions offered by Excel.

In this chapter you will

- use **AutoSum** to total up the hours worked
- learn various methods for **suppressing zero values**
- use Excel's date and time functions: **TODAY**, **DAY**, **MONTH** and **YEAR**
- use the logical functions **IF**, **AND** and **OR** to create formulas that test whether certain conditions are met
- learn how functions can be nested (that is, written one inside the other) to build up powerful formulas (formalising what you have already learnt about this)
- use **WordArt** to add an impressive title to the time sheet and use colour to simplify the task of filling it in by marking out the areas in which the users need to enter values.

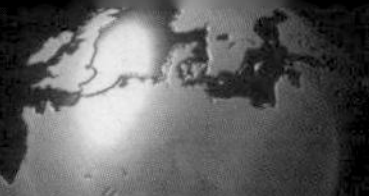

AutoSum

Open the workbook **timesheet.xls** that you created in Chapter 6.

Look at the time sheet. There are two sets of totals: the hours worked for each task (running down column **J**) and the total hours worked each day (across row **17**). We can get Excel to fill in these values automatically.

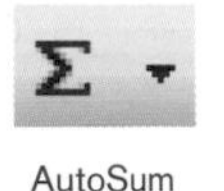
AutoSum

Select cells **J9:J16**, which will hold the total hours worked on each task. Press the **AutoSum** button – this command guesses what you are trying to sum and fills in the formula automatically.

Select cell **J9** – you will see that the **AutoSum** command has correctly worked out that this cell should contain the sum of cells **C9:I9**, as shown in Figure 8.1.

Arial 10 | J9 | =SUM(C9:I9)

	A	B	C	D	E	F	G	H	I	J
1										
2				Name						
3	Time Sheet			Manager						
4										
5										
6										
7	Description	Code	Hours Worked							
8			Mon	Tue	Wed	Thu	Fri	Sat	Sun	Total
9	Checkouts	SALE	7	7	7	7	7			35
10	Fork lift driving	FORK		1		1		5		7
11										0
12										0
13										0
14										0
15										0
16										0
17										

Figure 8.1: Result of applying the AutoSum command to the column of totals

This is quite helpful. The two totals – 35 hours spent on the checkout and 7 hours driving the fork lift – have been calculated automatically. Unfortunately, all of the blank lines give a zero total; it would look neater if the totals were displayed only if they were non-zero.

There are (at least) three ways we could keep the sums working but hide the zero values:

1. We could hide all zero values on the worksheet by selecting **Tools**, **Options**, changing to the **View** tab and unticking the option **Zero values**.

2. We could use a **custom number format** (see Chapter 3) to suppress the display of zeroes in the cells that hold the totals. The format code **#** will suffice – both positive and negative values will still be displayed, but cells with zero values will look blank.

3. We could use the logical function **IF**, which we will look at later, to work out in advance what the value of the cell will be and to change it from **0** to an empty string if necessary. This is similar to what we did for **VLOOKUP** Chapter 6 (page 80).

Given that there is no reason why there should be any zeros in the time sheet (booking zero hours to a task and leaving it blank are the same thing), we can use the simplest option: suppressing the display of any zeros in the worksheet.

From the menu, select **Tools**, **Options**. Make sure the **View** tab is selected, untick the option **Zero values**, then press **OK**.

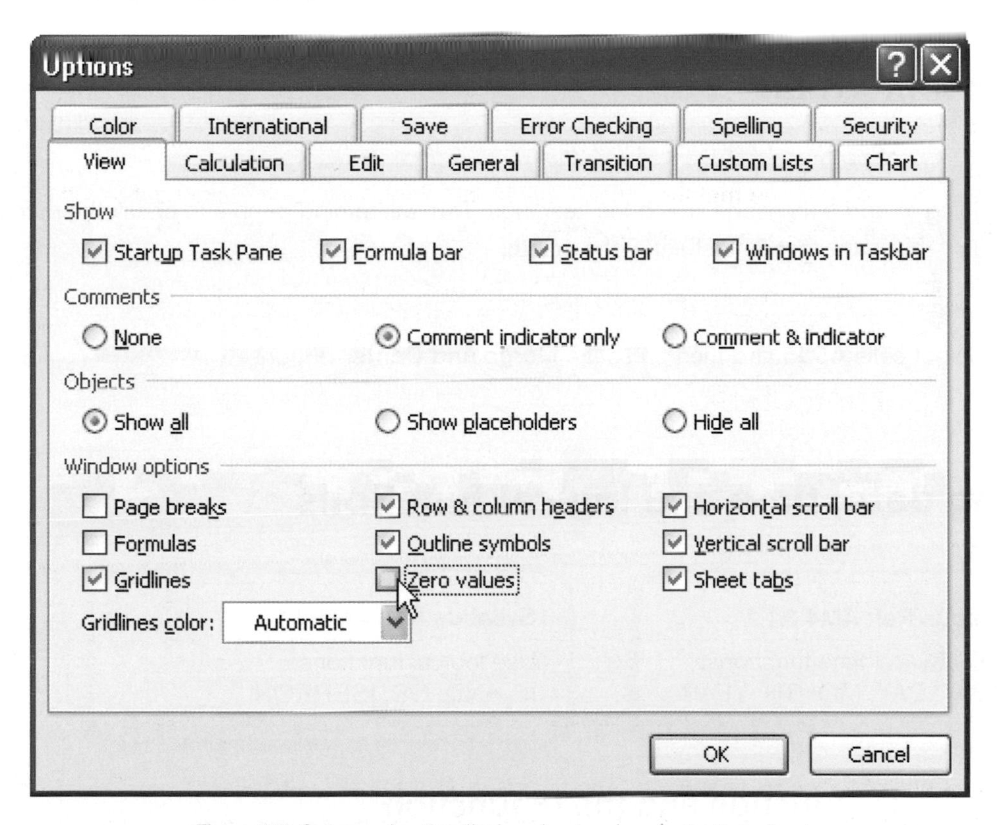

Figure 8.2: Suppressing the display of zero values in the time sheet

Select cells **C17:J17** and press the **AutoSum** button. This fills in the total hours worked for each day and, in cell **J17**, the total hours worked for the week.

All employees of the garden centre have to fill in their time sheets every Friday, print them out and get them signed. To help with filing, Friday's date must be in the top right-hand corner of the time sheets. Employees who are working at the weekend should enter their rostered hours and guess which activities they will be doing; corrections can be made in subsequent weeks if the guess turns out to be wrong, but this is much more complicated after the month's end because the figures have been entered into the accounts.

In cell **H2**, type the label **Week Ending**. In cell **J2**, enter the date **30/06/2006** (this is just a dummy value for now). Make sure your **Regional Options** are set correctly, as explained on page 14.

Since we're going to use this date for calculations, we'll give a name to the cell.

Select cell **J2**. In the **Name Box** (see Figure 8.3), type the name **END_OF_WEEK** and press **Enter**.

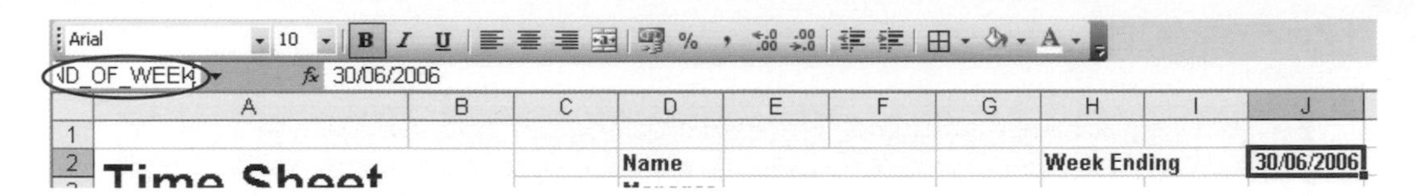

Figure 8.3: Giving the name END_OF_WEEK to cell J2

We're going to add a message line to the headings. This will remind people to check their time bookings if this is the last time sheet of the month.

Merge and Center

Select cells **A5:J5** and then press the **Merge and Center** button.

Using date, time and logical functions

Syllabus Ref: AM4.3.1.1

Use date and time functions:
TODAY; DAY; MONTH; YEAR.

Syllabus Ref: AM4.3.1.7

Use logical functions:
IF; AND; OR; ISERROR.

The MONTH function and the IF function

We want cell **A5** to display a reminder if this is the last time sheet of the month, and a general message otherwise. To do this, we can use the **MONTH** function to get the month part of the date, and the **IF** function to test which message to display.

ISERROR is a simple function that returns **TRUE** if the parameter you pass it causes an error, and **FALSE** otherwise. For example, ISERROR (1/0) returns **TRUE** because division by zero causes an error. **ISERROR** is usually used inside an **IF** function.

Don't skip the following box, even if you think you already understand the **IF** function: the default values are more complicated than you might realise.

IF(logical_test, [value_if_true], [value_if_false])

Tests whether a condition is true or false and returns different values depending on the result of this test.

logical_test is any expression that evaluates to **TRUE** or **FALSE**.

value_if_true is the value that the cell will have if the **logical_test** evaluates to **TRUE**. If **value_if_true** is left blank (that is, if there are just two commas between **logical_test** and **value_if_false**), it defaults to **0**.

value_if_false is the value that the cell will have if the **logical_test** evaluates to **FALSE**. If **value_if_false** is omitted completely (that is, if there is a closing parenthesis immediately after **value_if_true**), then the logical value **FALSE** is returned; if a blank value is used for **value_if_false** (that is, there is a comma and closing parenthesis after **value_if_true**), then the value **0** is returned.

For example:

IF(A6 > 6, 10, 20) yields **10** if cell **A6** has a value greater than **6**; otherwise, it yields **20**.

IF(C4 = "Price", "Sales") yields the string **Sales** if cell **C4** contains the string **Price**; otherwise, it yields **FALSE**. Note that this comparison is not case-sensitive: if cell **C4** has a value of **PRICE**, **price** or even **pRiCe**, the logical test will still be true.

MONTH(serial_number)

Returns the month part of a date.

serial_number is a date. Internally, Excel stores dates as numbers starting with **1** for **1st January 1900**. Since this parameter will usually be a reference to a cell containing a date, you won't need to worry about the internal representation of dates.

In cell **A5**, enter the following formula all on one line: **=IF(MONTH(END_OF_WEEK) <> MONTH(END_OF_WEEK+7), "Please ensure that any corrections have been entered.", "Enter best estimate; corrections can be made later.")**

As well as **MONTH**, you also need to know how to use the **DAY** and **YEAR** functions; these work in exactly the same way, but return different parts of the date. The **YEAR** function returns a four-digit year, even if it is passed a reference to a cell containing a date formatted with a two-digit year.

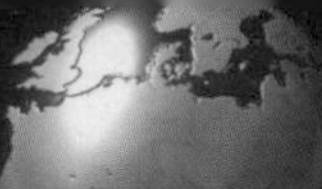

The symbol <> means **not equal** (actually **less than or greater than**, hence the < and > characters). We could instead have used = to test for equality and swapped the order of the two strings.

The formula says that if the current month is different from the month of the date in one week's time (meaning that this is the last week of the month), then display the first message; otherwise, display the second message.

Since the test date we used (**30/06/2006**) is right at the end of the month, cell **A5** displays the message **Please ensure that any corrections have been entered.**

Change the date in cell **J2** to **15/06/2006**. Since this is not in the last week of June, cell **A5** will change to **Enter best estimate; corrections can be made later.**

Nested functions

Syllabus Ref: AM4.3.1.9
Use nested functions.

Notice how the formula we entered uses the **MONTH** function inside the **IF** function – this is called **nesting** one function inside another.

It can be useful to nest IF functions if you need to choose between more than two possibilities. For example, **IF(EXAM_RESULT >= 80%, "DISTINCTION", IF(EXAM_RESULT > 60%, "PASS", "FAIL"))** will display **DISTINCTION**, **PASS** or **FAIL** depending on the value of **EXAM_RESULT**.

Because of the Christmas holidays, time sheets in December have to be finalised by the 15th instead of the last week of the month. We can use the conditional functions **AND** and **OR** to add this extra check.

AND(logical1, [logical2], ...)

Returns **TRUE** only if all of its parameters are **TRUE**.

logical*n* is any expression that can be evaluated to **TRUE** or **FALSE**.

OR(logical1, [logical2], ...)

Returns **TRUE** if one or more of its parameters is **TRUE**.

logical*n* is any expression that can be evaluated to **TRUE** or **FALSE**.

Select cell **A5** and edit its formula to add
**=IF(OR(MONTH(END_OF_WEEK) <> MONTH(END_OF_WEEK+7),
AND(MONTH(END_OF_WEEK)=12, DAY(END_OF_WEEK)>=15)),
"Please ensure that any corrections have been entered.",
"Enter best estimate; corrections can be made later.")**

The new logic is as follows: **IF** it is the last week of the month, **OR** (it is the twelfth month **AND** it is day 15 or later) then display the first message; otherwise, display the second one.

Test this logic by changing cell **J2** to **20/12/2006**. Even though it's not the last week of the month, the '**Please ensure...**' message should be displayed.

The TODAY function

At the moment, we have to manually type the date in the top-right of the time sheet. Instead, we can get Excel to fill in the current date; this will be OK as long as the employees fill in their time sheets on a Friday.

> **TODAY()**
>
> Returns the current date. Note that Excel requires brackets after a function name, even if, as in this case, the function takes no parameters.

Change the contents of cell **J2** to **=TODAY()**.

The cell should change to display today's date. Cell **A5** should show the appropriate message for the date, based on the rules we discussed earlier.

Sometimes employees will need to fill in a time sheet before Friday – for example, if they will be on holiday on the Friday. We can extend the formula in cell **J2** to take account of this, by using the **WEEKDAY** function (which you don't need to know for the exam).

> **WEEKDAY(serial_number, [return_type])**
>
> Returns a number representing the day of the week.
>
> **serial_number** is a date.
>
> **return_type** specifies which numbering scheme should be used: **1** (the default value) represents **Sunday** as day **1** through to **Saturday** as day **7**; **2** represents **Monday** as day **1** through to **Sunday** as day **7**; **3** represents **Monday** as day **0** through to **Sunday** as day **6**).

Change cell **J2** to **=TODAY()+5 - WEEKDAY(TODAY(), 2)**.

The term **WEEKDAY(TODAY(), 2)** evaluates to **1** if today is a Monday, **2** if today is a Tuesday, up to **7** if today is a Sunday. Therefore, **5 - WEEKDAY(TODAY(), 2)** represents the number of days until Friday. Therefore the formula as a whole gives the date of Friday in the current week.

Adding some colour

A few quick changes can make this time sheet look a lot more professional and visually appealing.

 From the menu, select **Insert**, **Picture**, **WordArt**. The **WordArt Gallery** appears.

 Select the arc shape (the third one on the top row – see Figure 8.4) and press **OK**.

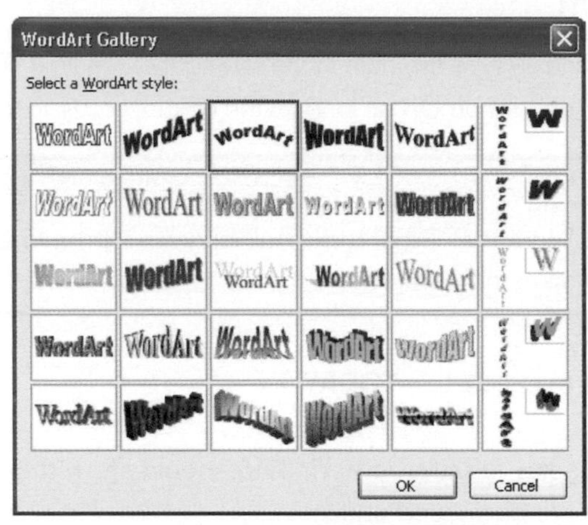

Figure 8.4: The WordArt Gallery

 The **Edit WordArt Text** dialogue appears. Set the **Size** to **32** and type the text **Green Thumbs Garden Centre**. Press **OK**.

Figure 8.5: Typing the heading text for the time sheet

The **WordArt** text **Green Thumbs Garden Centre** appears, together with the **WordArt** toolbar. Press the **Format WordArt** button (highlighted in Figure 8.6).

Figure 8.6: The WordArt toolbar, with the Format WordArt button highlighted

The **Format WordArt** dialogue appears. Make sure the **Colors and Lines** tab is selected. Change the **Fill Color** to **Green** and then press **OK**.

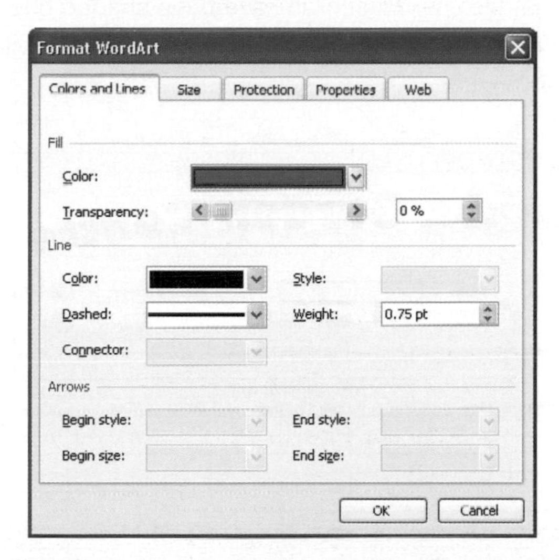

Figure 8.7: Changing the fill colour of the WordArt text

Increase the height of row **1** by clicking the border between rows **1** and **2** and dragging down, as shown in Figure 8.8.

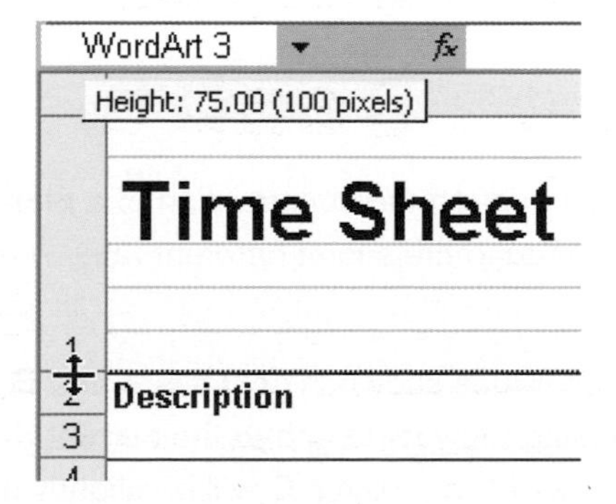

Figure 8.8: Increasing the height of a row

Click and drag the **WordArt** into place in row **1**.

 Apply thick borders around cells **E2** and **E3**, then use **Format**, **Cells**, **Patterns** to apply fill colours to the cells as shown in Figure 8.9.

You can hold down the **Ctrl** key to select several different parts of a worksheet at once. You will probably find it quicker to use this technique to select all of the cells that you want to set to a particular colour, rather than selecting them bit by bit and changing the colours each time.

Notice how all of the cells that the user must fill in have been shaded one colour, and all of the cells with calculated values have been shaded a different colour – this will help people to fill in the correct parts of the time sheet.

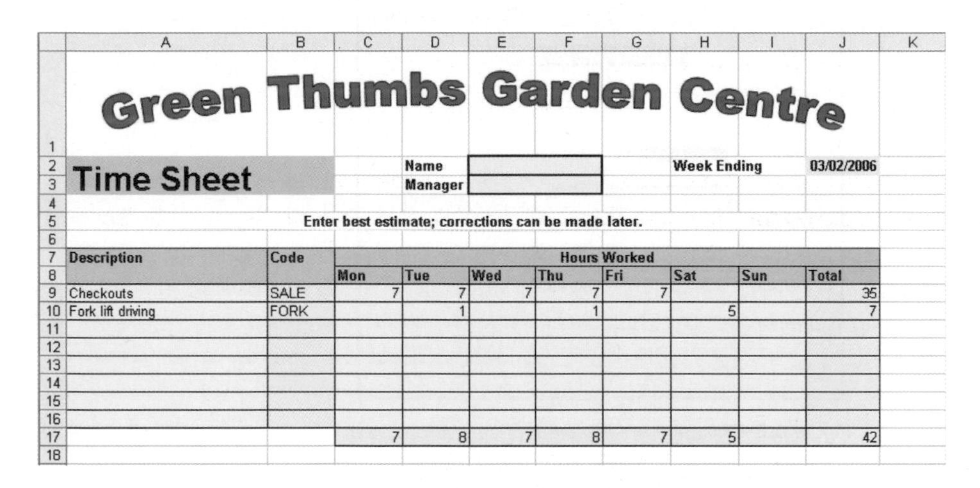

	A	B	C	D	E	F	G	H	I	J	K
1	Green Thumbs Garden Centre										
2	Time Sheet			Name				Week Ending		03/02/2006	
3				Manager							
4											
5		Enter best estimate; corrections can be made later.									
6											
7	Description	Code	Hours Worked								
8			Mon	Tue	Wed	Thu	Fri	Sat	Sun	Total	
9	Checkouts	SALE	7	7	7	7	7			35	
10	Fork lift driving	FORK		1		1		5		7	
11											
12											
13											
14											
15											
16											
17			7	8	7	8	7	5		42	
18											

Figure 8.9: Colouring the time sheet

 Save and close the time sheet.

Test yourself

The following questions guide you through the construction of a **planetary calendar**. The various planets in the solar system travel around the sun at different rates – the further they are from the sun, the longer their years are.

1. In a new workbook, fill out the values shown in columns **A** and **B** of Figure 8.10. Calculate the dates in column **C** by adding the year length to the current date found using the **TODAY** function (so, of course, your values for column **C** will be slightly different).

	A	B	C
1	**Planet**	**Year Length (Earth Days)**	**Earth Date in 1 Planet Year**
2	Mercury	87.97	07/09/2005
3	Venus	224.70	22/01/2006
4	Earth	365.26	12/06/2006
5	Mars	686.98	29/04/2007
6	Jupiter	4332.60	22/04/2017
7	Saturn	10759.30	26/11/2034
8	Uranus	30684.00	15/06/2089
9	Neptune	60188.30	27/03/2170
10	Pluto	90777.30	26/12/2253

Figure 8.10: Framework for the planetary calendar

These dates show when each of these planets will next be in its current position, having travelled once round the sun. As you can see, Neptune and Pluto will take quite some time!

To the right of each of these dates, we want to display the date in words. For example, **07/09/2005** should be shown as **7th September 2005**. We'll tackle this bit by bit.

2. Extracting the day and year numbers is straightforward: we can use the **DAY** and **YEAR** functions. Do this, putting the days in column **E** and the years in column **H**.

3. The months are a bit trickier, since we need to replace the numbers with the month names. We need to create a lookup table. In cell **A13**, type **1** and in cell **B13**, type **January**. Select these two cells and use the fill handle to copy the values down, as shown in Figure 8.11. Use the **MONTH** function nested within a **VLOOKUP** function to generate the month names in column **G**. The result should look something like Figure 8.12.

	A	B
13	1	January
14	2	February
15	3	March
16	4	April
17	5	May
18	6	June
19	7	July
20	8	August
21	9	September
22	10	October
23	11	November
24	12	December
25		

Figure 8.11: A lookup table for month names

	A	B	C	D	E	F	G	H
1	**Planet**	**Year Length (Earth Days)**	**Earth Date in 1 Planet Year**					
2	Mercury	87.97	07/09/2005		7		September	2005
3	Venus	224.70	22/01/2006		22		January	2006
4	Earth	365.26	12/06/2006		12		June	2006
5	Mars	686.98	29/04/2007		29		April	2007
6	Jupiter	4332.60	22/04/2017		22		April	2017
7	Saturn	10759.30	26/11/2034		26		November	2034
8	Uranus	30684.00	15/06/2089		15		June	2089
9	Neptune	60188.30	27/03/2170		27		March	2170
10	Pluto	90777.30	26/12/2253		26		December	2253

Figure 8.12: Months shown as words in column G

4. The final task is to get column **F** to show **st**, **nd**, **rd** or **th**, depending on the values in column **E**. Get the formula working in cell **F2** and then copy it to the others later. You will need to use lots of tested **IF** and **OR** functions, but you can build the formula up one step at a time. Use **=IF(OR(E2=1, E2=21, E2=31), "st", "th")** as a starting point. When you have finished, your calendar should look something like Figure 8.13.

	A	B	C	D	E	F	G	H
1	**Planet**	**Year Length (Earth Days)**	**Earth Date in 1 Planet Year**					
2	Mercury	87.97	07/09/2005		7	th	September	2005
3	Venus	224.70	22/01/2006		22	nd	January	2006
4	Earth	365.26	12/06/2006		12	th	June	2006
5	Mars	686.98	29/04/2007		29	th	April	2007
6	Jupiter	4332.60	22/04/2017		22	nd	April	2017
7	Saturn	10759.30	26/11/2034		26	th	November	2034
8	Uranus	30684.00	15/06/2089		15	th	June	2089
9	Neptune	60188.30	27/03/2170		27	th	March	2170
10	Pluto	90777.30	26/12/2253		26	th	December	2253

Figure 8.13: The completed planetary calendar

Revision from previous chapters

5. Apply **conditional formatting** to the time sheet's cell **A5** so that it gets a red background if the warning message is displayed. [Tip: you can use the formula **=LEFT(A5, 13)="Please ensure"**, as shown in Figure 8.14(a), to achieve this]. Don't forget to test that it works by changing the formula in cell **J2** so that you can see the effect come and go.

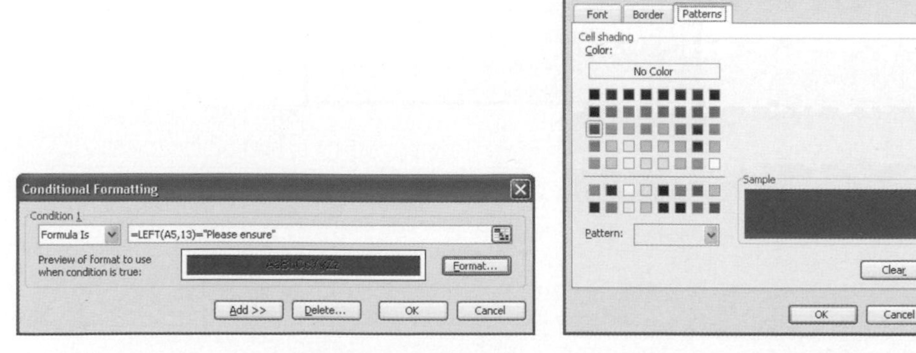

Figure 8.14: Applying conditional formatting to the message cell – (a) the formula and (b) setting a red background

9 Templates & Protection

Introduction

In this chapter, we will save the time sheet as a template, which garden centre employees could use as the basis for their time sheets each week. Then we will look at how cells, worksheets and workbooks can be protected against change.

In this chapter you will

- save the time sheet as a **template** so that creating new weekly time sheets is easy
- learn how to **use and edit templates**
- learn how to use **protection** to prevent unauthorized changes to complete worksheets or to specific cells on those worksheets
- add **password protection** to an entire workbook.

The instructions in this chapter assume that you do not have the **Hide extension for known file types** option set in Windows. If you do, you won't see the **xlt** file extensions for Excel templates. This isn't a problem. You can still distinquish between **xls** workbooks and **xlt** templates because the icons for the latter have yellow bars across the top.

Templates

A template is a saved workbook that you can use as a basis for new workbooks that you create. Excel comes with some templates, and you can get more from **Office Online** if you are connected to the Internet.

You can also create your own templates. We'll save a blank time sheet as a template, so that it's easy to create new time sheets every week.

Open the workbook **timesheet.xls**.

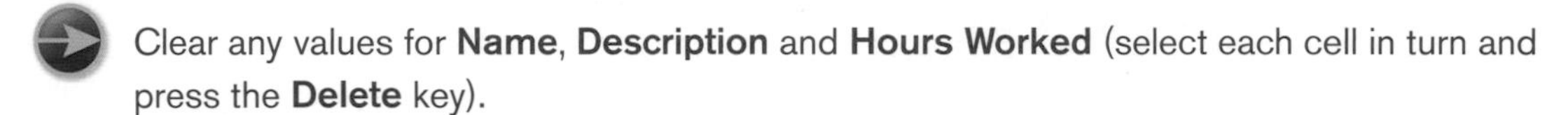

Clear any values for **Name**, **Description** and **Hours Worked** (select each cell in turn and press the **Delete** key).

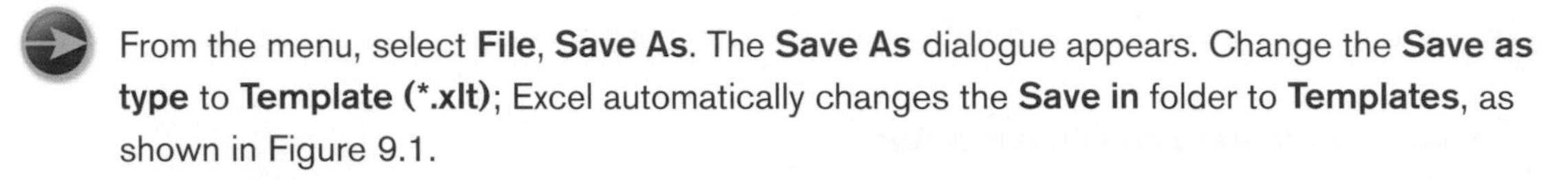

From the menu, select **File**, **Save As**. The **Save As** dialogue appears. Change the **Save as type** to **Template (*.xlt)**; Excel automatically changes the **Save in** folder to **Templates**, as shown in Figure 9.1.

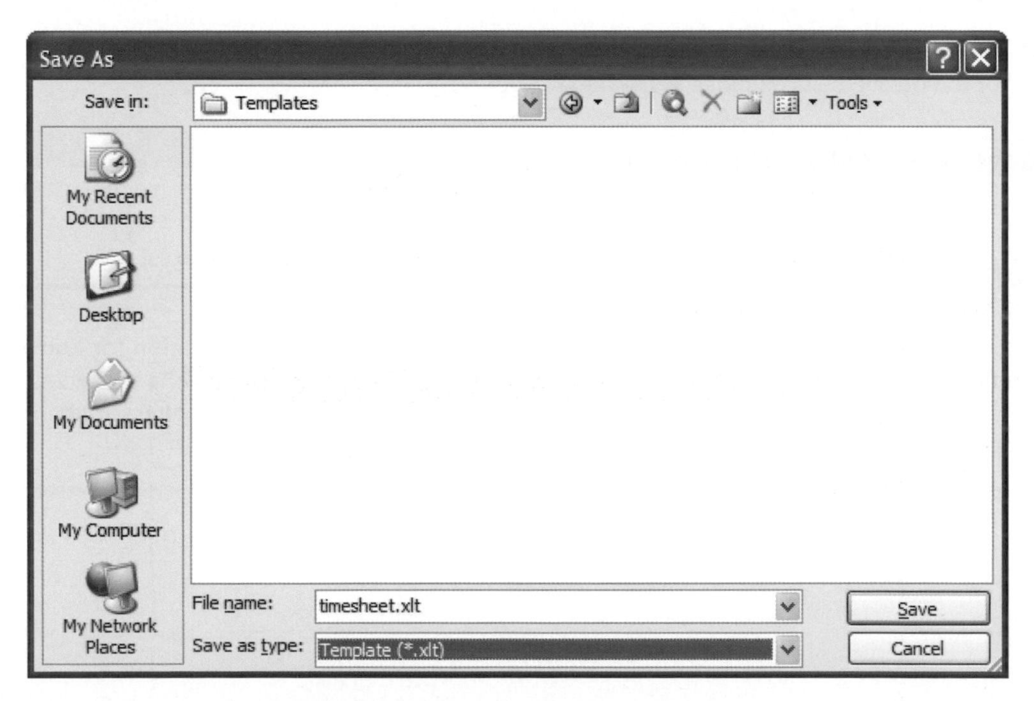

Figure 9.1: Saving a document as a template

Press the **Save** button to accept the default name of **timesheet.xlt**.

From the menu, select **File**, **Close** to close the template.

Syllabus Ref: AM4.2.4.1
Use a template.

Now, let's go through the process that a garden centre employee would use to create a new time sheet for the week.

From the menu, select **File**, **New**. The **New Workbook** task pane appears. Click the option **On my computer**, as shown in Figure 9.2

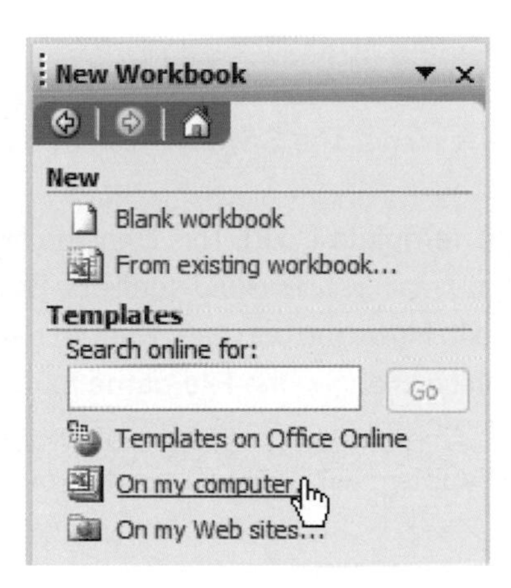

Figure 9.2: Choosing to create a new workbook from a local template

The **Templates** dialogue appears, with **timesheet.xlt** as one of the available templates.

Select **timesheet.xlt** and press **OK**.

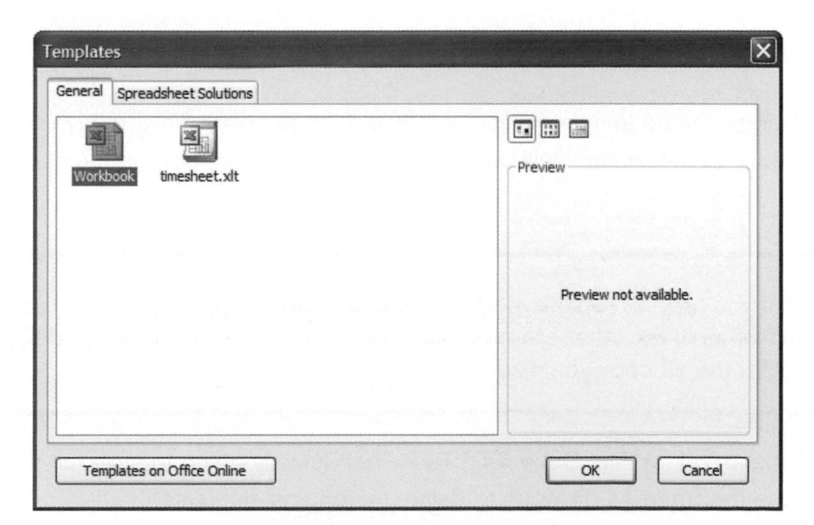

Figure 9.3: List of available templates

A new blank time sheet appears. The employee would now proceed to fill it in, print it, save it and so on.

Syllabus Ref: AM4.2.4.2
Edit a template.

There is no difference between a spreadsheet and a template apart from the file extension that is used (**xls** for spreadsheet and **xlt** for templates). Because of this, if you need to modify a template you can either open the **xlt** file directly (via **File**, **Open**) or you can create a new spreadsheet from the template (via **File**, **New**) and then save it over the top. We'll use the second approach, creating a time sheet template specifically for employee Jerry.

 Type **Jerry** in the name area. Frank is automatically filled in as Jerry's manager.

 Select **File**, **Save As** from the menu. The **Save As** dialogue appears, as before.

 Change the **Save as type** to **Template (*.xlt)**. This time, the file we created before – **timesheet.xlt** – appears in the main list. To avoid conflicts, Excel gives the file we are saving a different name: **timesheet1.xlt**. However, we really want to save it over the top of the original, so click on **timesheet.xlt** (which changes the **File name** to match) and then press **Save**.

 A warning dialogue box will appear, asking if you want to overwrite the file. Press **Yes** to confirm that you do.

 Close the template file.

 Create a new workbook based on **timesheet.xlt**; that is, select **File**, **New**, click on **My Computer** and double-click your new template. Confirm that **Jerry** and **Frank** are filled in.

Tidying up

Now you know how to create templates, you can delete the template file you have saved. This is particularly important if other people will be running through this exercise on the same PC later.

Remember that you have already saved the time sheet as an **xls** worksheet in the same folder you have used for all of the other exercises in this book. You are just going to delete from the **Templates** folder the **xlt** copy you made.

 From the menu, select **File**, **Save As**. We are not actually going to save the file; we are just going to use the **Save As** dialogue to delete the original template.

 Change the **Save as type** to **Template (*.xlt)**. Highlight the **timesheet.xlt** file by clicking on it once, and then press the **Delete** button, as shown in Figure 9.4.

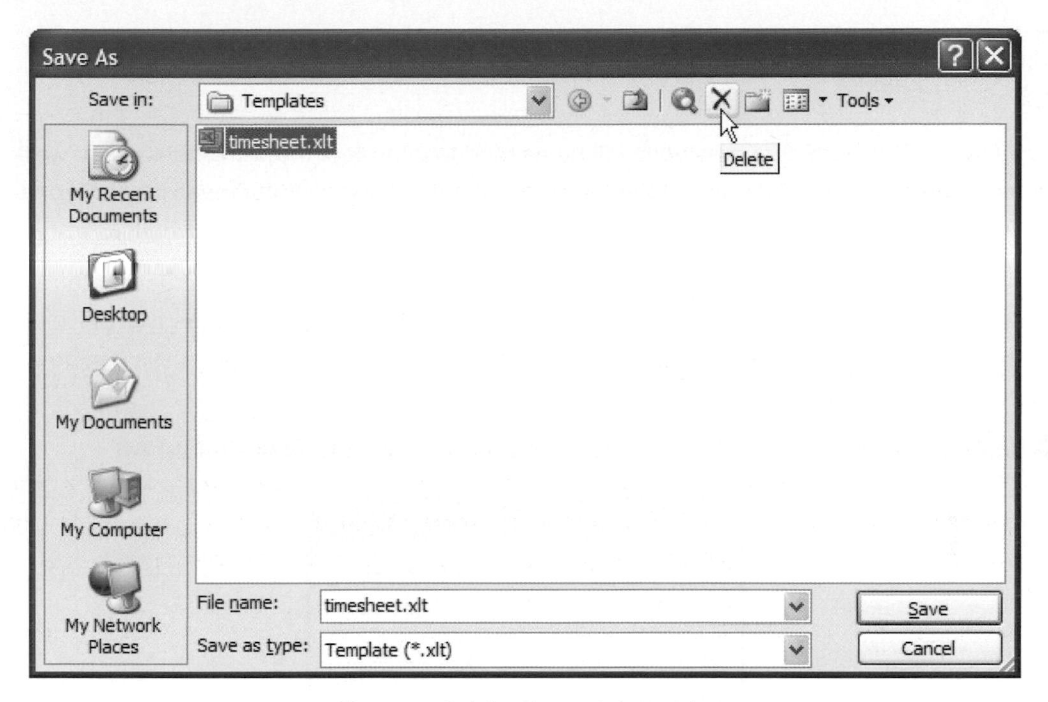

Figure 9.4: Deleting the example template

A dialogue box appears, asking if you want to move **timesheet.xlt** to the **Recycle Bin**. Press **Yes** to confirm that you do.

Press **Cancel**. Remember that we never intended to save the file.

Close the time sheet file. For the exercises that follow, you can reopen the **timesheet.xls** file you saved earlier.

Protection

Syllabus Ref: AM4.1.3.1

Protect/unprotect a worksheet with a password.

Protecting worksheets

In Excel, you can password-protect worksheets or individual cells, preventing people from making changes. We will use this facility to restrict users of the time sheet so that they can only change the cells we have shaded light yellow.

First, we'll lock the whole of the **Tasks** worksheet, since employees shouldn't be allowed to create or change task definitions.

Select the **Tasks** worksheet.

From the menu, select **Tools**, **Protection**, **Protect Sheet**. The **Protect Sheet** dialogue appears.

If you supply a password, that password will be needed to unprotect the worksheet again; we'll leave the password blank – this still prevents changes to the worksheet but means that anyone could easily turn that protection off if they wanted to.

The checkboxes on the **Protect Sheet** dialogue allow you to control exactly what users are permitted to do on a protected worksheet (see Figure 9.5). In most situations, the two default options – **Select locked cells** and **Select unlocked cells** – are what you want: cells can be selected, but their contents cannot be changed.

Just press **OK** to select the default settings and to protect the **Tasks** worksheet.

Figure 9.5: Protecting a worksheet

Now try to change the contents of one of the cells in the **Tasks** worksheet. You should get the warning dialogue shown in Figure 9.6, telling you that you can't make the change. Press **OK** to dismiss the dialogue.

Figure 9.6: An error message appears if you try to change a protected worksheet

Syllabus Ref: AM4.1.3.2
Protect/unprotect designated cells in a worksheet with a password.

We also want to protect the **Time Sheet** worksheet, but this is more complicated because we want to allow our users to make changes to some specific cells. We do this by unlocking those cells before protecting the worksheet.

Click and drag the mouse pointer over cells **F2:F3** on the **Time Sheet** worksheet. Hold down the **Ctrl** key and click and drag the mouse pointer over the two other ranges that we want people to be able to edit: **A9:A16** and **C9:I16**. All three areas should be selected at once.

From the menu, select **Format**, **Cells**. The **Format Cells** dialogue appears. Change to the **Protection** tab and untick the **Locked** checkbox, as shown in Figure 9.7. Press **OK**.

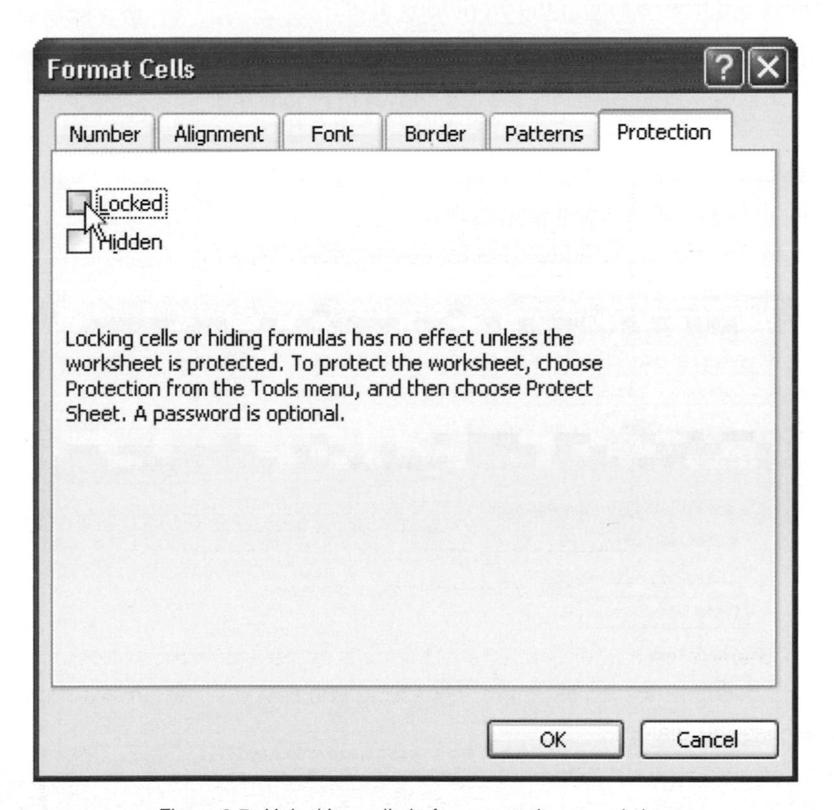

Figure 9.7: Unlocking cells before protecting a worksheet

Now we can lock the worksheet. From the menu, select **Tools**, **Protection**, **Protect Sheet** to display the **Protect Sheet** dialogue. Press **OK** to accept the default settings.

Confirm that you can edit the values held in the light-yellow cells, but that you get the error dialogue if you try to change any of the other cells.

You can use the **Tab** key to move between the unlocked cells in a protected worksheet – it automatically skips over the cells that you are not allowed to modify.

To remove protection from a worksheet you would select **Tools**, **Protection**, **Unprotect Sheet**. If a password was entered when the worksheet was protected, you will be asked to type it in before you are allowed to unprotect the worksheet.

Save the workbook as **timesheet.xls**.

Protecting workbooks

Syllabus Ref: AM4.1.4.1
Add password protection to a spreadsheet.

You can go one stage further and prevent users who do not know the password from opening the workbook at all.

From the menu, select **Tools**, **Options**. The **Options** dialogue appears. Change to the **Security** tab, as shown in Figure 9.8.

For **Password to open**, type **password** and press **OK**. Obviously, you'd use something a bit more difficult to guess in a real workbook!

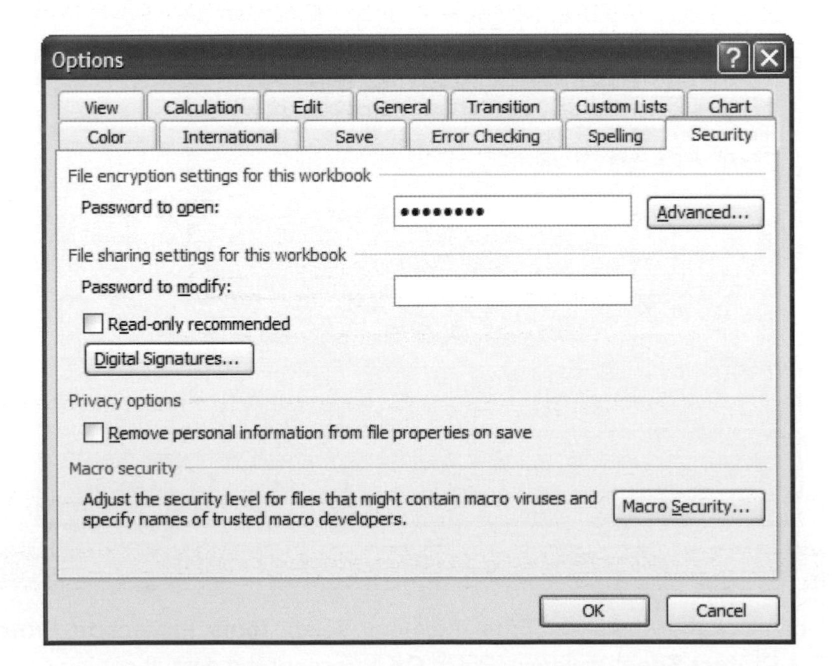

Figure 9.8: Protecting a workbook with a password – step 1 of 2

 The confirmation dialogue shown in Figure 9.9 appears. Type **password** again and press **OK**.

Figure 9.9: Protecting a workbook with a password – step 2 of 2

 Save and close your workbook.

 Open your workbook again. The easiest way to do this is to open the **File** menu and choose the option at the top of the list of recently used files, which appears at the bottom of the menu.

Now, instead of opening the file straight away, Excel pops up the dialogue box shown in Figure 9.10.

Figure 9.10: Opening a password-protected worksheet

 Deliberately type an incorrect password, such as **letmein**, to check that the worksheet doesn't load.

 You should get the error message shown in Figure 9.11. Press **OK** to dismiss it.

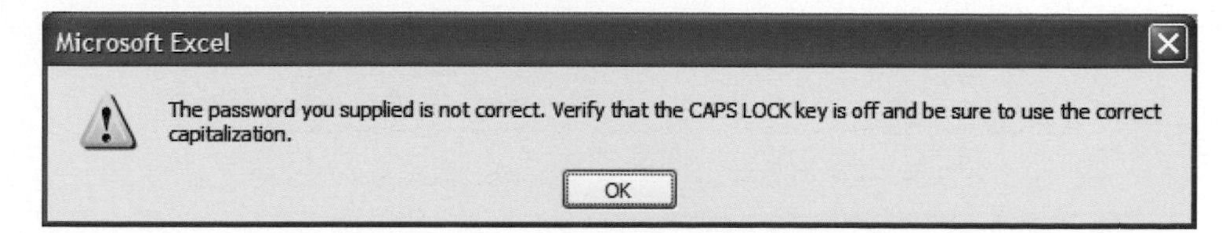

Figure 9.11: Error message – the password was incorrect

 Reopen the worksheet and, this time, supply the correct password: **password**.

This time, the worksheet opens. Let's remove the password protection.

Syllabus Ref: AM4.1.4.2

Remove password protection from a spreadsheet.

 From the menu, select **Tools**, **Options**. The **Options** dialogue will open, and the **Security** tab will still be on display (unless you changed to a different tab after setting the password).

 Delete everything in the **Password to open** field and press **OK**.

 Save and close the workbook.

 Open the workbook again and check that you are not asked for a password.

Test yourself

1. Cell **E3** in the **Time Sheet** worksheet is calculated automatically from the value in cell **E2**. Lock cell **E3** using **Format**, **Cells** as before. Change the colour of cell **E3** to match the other cells that contain calculated values. Protect all of the worksheets.

2. Practise unprotecting the worksheets and protecting them again. Notice how the cells that were unlocked keep their settings, so that they are still editable when you reprotect the **Time Sheet** worksheet.

3. Experiment with creating workbooks based on the templates that come with Excel, or those available on **Office Online**. Are they easy to fill in, and if so, why? Could you make any improvements? You might like to save your altered versions as new templates, but take care not to overwrite the originals.

10 Subtotals

Introduction

This chapter is all about generating subtotals. Excel has some very powerful options for generating different types of subtotals for ordered sets of information. We will use the stock information from the video shop and see how we can extract useful information from the raw data using subtotals.

In this chapter you will

- create typical subtotals using the **SUM** function
- learn about the different **options** available when creating subtotals
- learn how to **replace or remove subtotals**
- learn about the **other functions** that can be applied instead of **SUM**
- **add new subtotals** without losing the existing ones
- learn how to use the **grouping area** to summarise results.

Subtotals

Subtotals are used to extract information from lists. The easiest way to understand exactly what they are and how they work is to plunge straight into an exercise. Let's use subtotals to count the number of DVDs, videos and games in the shop.

 Open **videoshop.xls** and switch to the **Stock** worksheet.

The records are currently sorted in **Code** order. In order to use subtotals we need to group together everything we want to subtotal – that is, all the videos together, all the DVDs together and all the games together. We can do this by sorting on the **Type** column. However, later on we may want to dig deeper by generating subtotals for the categories within each type (for example, comparing action DVDs with horror videos). Because of this, we'll sort by **Category** first.

Sort Ascending

 Sort the rows by **Category**.

 Sort the rows by **Type**.

Excel preserves the order of records for any equal values it finds when sorting. This means that, within each type (**DVD**, **Video**, **and so on**), the records are still sorted by category (**Action**, **Children's**, **and so on**). This is a useful technique – you can quickly sort by any number of columns by doing a simple sort in reverse order (that is, to sort in the order **A**, **B**, sort first on **B** and then on **A**).

The top of your worksheet should now be sorted by type, and by category within type, as shown in Figure 10.1. We'll cover sorting in more depth in the next chapter; for now, we just need the rows in this order so that we can create subtotals.

	A	B	C	D	E	F	G
1	Code	Type	Title	Category	Certificate	Rental price	Copies
2	1	DVD	Bourne Identity, The	Action	12	4	10
3	15	DVD	Collateral	Action	15	4	5
4	22	DVD	King Arthur	Action	15	4	14
5	37	DVD	Lord Of The Rings, The - The Two Towers	Action	12	3	11
6	39	DVD	Die Hard	Action	18	3	13
7	46	DVD	Spider-Man 2	Action	PG	4	1
8	51	DVD	Charlie's Angels: Full Throttle	Action	12	3	18
9	78	DVD	Kill Bill - Vol. 2	Action	18	4	10
10	80	DVD	Starsky And Hutch	Action	15	3	22
11	84	DVD	Troy	Action	15	4	10
12	90	DVD	Pirates Of The Caribbean - The Curse Of The Black Pearl	Action	12	3	14
13	95	DVD	Lord Of The Rings, The - The Return Of The King	Action	12	4	10
14	9	DVD	Fantasia	Childrens	U	3	5
15	13	DVD	Everybody Loves Mickey	Childrens	U	3	5
16	16	DVD	Box Of Delights, The	Childrens	U	3	9
17	17	DVD	Toy Story	Childrens	U	3	1
18	45	DVD	101 Dalmatians	Childrens	U	3	9
19	53	DVD	Grinch, The	Childrens	PG	3	8
20	57	DVD	Shrek	Childrens	U	3	16
21	67	DVD	Harry Potter and the Prisoner of Azkaban	Childrens	PG	4	4
22	70	DVD	Fireman Sam - To The Rescue!	Childrens	U	3	10
23	73	DVD	Goodnight Mister Tom	Childrens	PG	3	14
24	74	DVD	Shrek 2	Childrens	U	4	11
25	86	DVD	Lady And The Tramp	Childrens	U	3	6

Figure 10.1: Stock sorted by Type and Category

Suppose we just want to find out how many copies there are for each of the three different stock types (how many video cassettes exist, and so on).

Select any of the cells with information in. Excel is clever enough to work out the extent of the data given a starting point.

Syllabus Ref: AM4.1.2.8
Use subtotalling features.

From the menu, select **Data**, **Subtotals**. The **Subtotal** dialogue appears.

Every time the **Type** changes (for example, from **DVD** to **Game**), we want to know the total number of **Copies**.

Set **At each change in** to **Type**. Set **Use function** to **Sum**. Make sure that only **Copies** is ticked in **Add subtotal to**. Since there aren't any subtotals yet, it doesn't matter whether **Replace current subtotals** is ticked. Make sure **Page break between groups** is not ticked, but that **Summary below data** is. All of this is shown in Figure 10.2. Press **OK**.

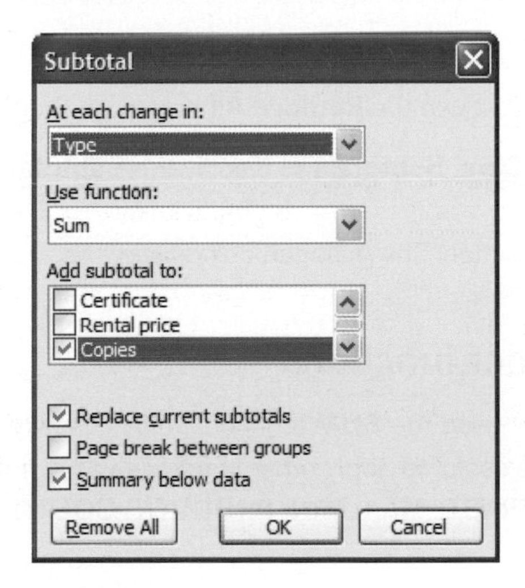

Figure 10.2: Creating Copies subtotals for each change in Type

The three tick boxes at the bottom of the **Subtotal** dialogue allow you to further customise the way the subtotalling works.

You can add more than one set of subtotals; we will do this later. The **Replace current subtotals** option allows you to choose between making changes to the existing subtotals or adding a new set.

The **Page break between groups** option works as you might expect, and it can be useful for splitting up very large sets of data.

The subtotals can be added either above or below each group of rows; if **Summary below data** is ticked then the subtotals appear at the bottoms of the groups; otherwise they appear at the tops.

You should notice a couple of changes in your worksheet. First, on the left is a **grouping area** containing vertical lines and dots – we'll look at this later in this chapter. Second, if you scroll down to row **56**, you'll see the first subtotal we have created: **DVD Total 570**.

This tells us that the sum of all the **Copies** where the **Type** is **DVD** comes to **570**. There are similar rows for **Game** (**197**) and **Video** (**189**). At the very bottom is a **Grand Total** of **956**.

This is the information we wanted to find out. As long as we clear the **Replace current subtotals** checkbox, we can add a second level of subtotals. Let's add in subtotals by **Category**.

From the menu, select **Data**, **Subtotals**. This time, set **At each change in** to **Category**, untick **Replace current subtotals**, then press **OK**.

New rows have appeared showing **Action Total**, **Children's Total**, and so on. The original subtotals (such as **DVD total**) are still there too: if we had ticked the **Replace current subtotals** box then these would have been removed.

Removing subtotals

It's easy to remove subtotals. Just use the **Remove All** button on the **Subtotal** dialogue box.

From the menu, select **Data**, **Subtotals** to display the **Subtotal** dialogue box.

Press the **Remove All** button. The dialogue box closes and the subtotals disappear.

Subtotalling with other functions

So far, all of the subtotals have used the **SUM** function. This is usually what you need to do. However, sometimes it can be useful to apply other functions to the subtotalled groups; Excel supports **SUM**, **COUNT**, **AVERAGE**, **MAX**, **MIN**, **PRODUCT**, **COUNT NUMS**, **STDDEV**, **STDDEVP**, **VAR** and **VARP**.

SUM adds the group's values together. This is the default function for subtotalling, and by far the most common function to use.

COUNT counts the number of values in the group.

AVERAGE returns the mean of the values in the group.

MAX returns the maximum value in the group.

MIN returns the minimum value in the group.

PRODUCT multiplies the group's values together.

COUNT NUMS returns the count of the group's values that contain numeric data.

The last four functions below are used for statistical analysis. Don't worry if you don't understand the descriptions; you won't need to understand these for the exam.

STDDEV estimates the standard deviation of the values in the group, where those values represent only a sample of the total population.

STDDEVP calculates the standard deviation of the values in the group, assuming that the values represent the whole population.

VAR estimates the variation of the values in the group, where those values represent only a sample of the total population.

VARP calculates the variation of the values in the group, assuming that the values represent the whole population.

Let's use the **COUNT** function to count the number of different titles for each different type of stock. In other words, how many DVD titles are there? How many video titles are there? How many game titles are there?

From the menu, select **Data**, **Subtotals**. Select **Type** and **Count** in the first two drop-down lists. Make sure that **Copies** is ticked in the **Add subtotal to** list. (For the **COUNT** function, this just controls the column that will display the subtotals, since the values themselves aren't used.) Press **OK**.

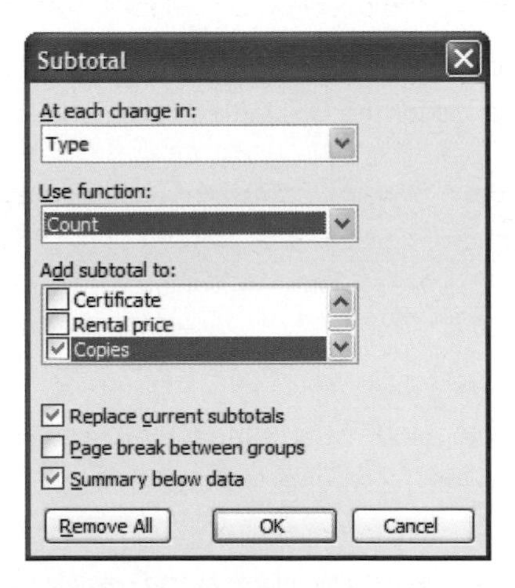

Figure 10.3: Creating subtotals by counting the number of records for each change in Type

Four subtotals are generated, telling us that there are 54 DVDs, 25 games and 20 videos, making 99 in total.

We can add a second subtotal applying a different function to a different column. Let's display subtotals for the average rental price of each category.

Display the **Subtotal** dialogue again. This time, choose **Category** and **Average** in the top two drop-down lists. In the **Add subtotal to** list, tick **Rental price** and untick **Copies**. Untick **Replace current subtotals** and press **OK**.

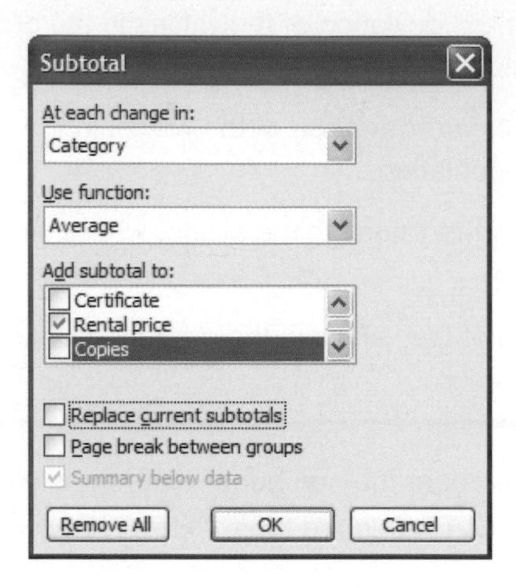

Figure 10.4: Finding the average rental price for each category

Select column **F** and change the cell format to **Currency** with **2** decimal places. If you get some currency other than pounds sterling (£), check the regional settings in your PC's **Control Panel**.

The top of your worksheet should now look like Figure 10.5. Notice the **Action Average** on row **14**, showing that the average rental price for the DVD titles of action films is **£3.58**.

	A	B	C	D	E	F	G
1	Code	Type	Title	Category	Certificate	Rental price	Copies
2	1	DVD	Bourne Identity, The	Action	12	£4.00	10
3	15	DVD	Collateral	Action	15	£4.00	5
4	22	DVD	King Arthur	Action	15	£4.00	14
5	37	DVD	Lord Of The Rings, The - The Two Towers	Action	12	£3.00	11
6	39	DVD	Die Hard	Action	18	£3.00	13
7	46	DVD	Spider-Man 2	Action	PG	£4.00	1
8	51	DVD	Charlie's Angels: Full Throttle	Action	12	£3.00	18
9	78	DVD	Kill Bill - Vol. 2	Action	18	£4.00	10
10	80	DVD	Starsky And Hutch	Action	15	£3.00	22
11	84	DVD	Troy	Action	15	£4.00	10
12	90	DVD	Pirates Of The Caribbean - The Curse Of The Black Pearl	Action	12	£3.00	14
13	95	DVD	Lord Of The Rings, The - The Return Of The King	Action	12	£4.00	10
14				**Action Average**		£3.58	

Figure 10.5: Worksheet after adding average rental price subtotals

Notice the **grouping area** on the left of the worksheet. There are three vertical lines (called **row level bars**). The leftmost bar spans all of the rows apart from the headings at the top and the two grand totals at the bottom. In the middle of the grouping area are three more **row level bars** one on top of the other, so that each bar spans a different value in the **Type** column. To the right of this come the **row level bars** for each of the **Category** types.

Click the boxed minus sign in the grouping area for row **14**. This collapses all of the **Action** DVDs.

The minus sign has changed into a plus sign. Click this to display the detail again.

Experiment with collapsing and expanding other branches.

Expanding and collapsing individual 'branches' can be useful, but often you want to display or hide all of the information at a particular level at once. The boxed numbers (**row level symbols**) at the top of the grouping area make this easy.

Click the boxed **1**. This hides everything apart from the titles and grand totals. You can see at a glance that the average rental price is **£3.48** and there are **99** distinct items in stock.

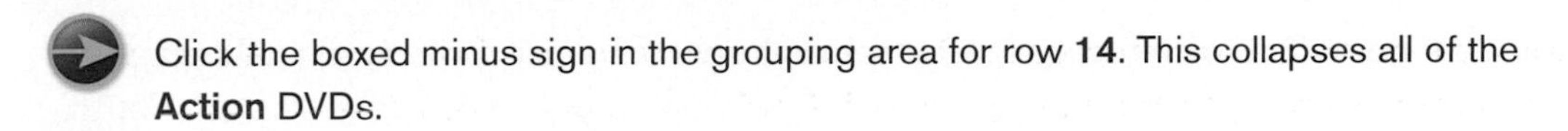
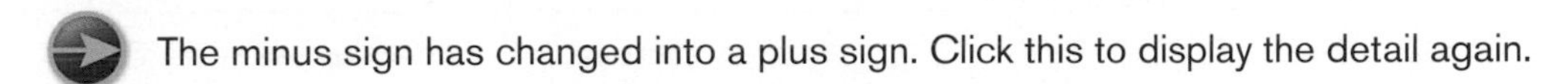

	A	B	C	D	E	F	G
1	Code	Type	Title	Category	Certificate	Rental price	Copies
130				Grand Average		£3.48	
131		Grand Count					99

Figure 10.6: Displaying level 1 subtotals

Now click the boxed **2**. This displays the next level of detail. Now you can see the subtotals for the **Type** counts.

	A	B	C	D	E	F	G
1	Code	Type	Title	Category	Certificate	Rental price	Copies
68		DVD Count					54
100		Game Count					25
129		Video Count					20
130				Grand Average		£3.48	
131		Grand Count					99

Figure 10.7: Displaying level 2 subtotals

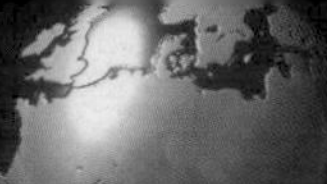

Click the boxed **3**. Now you get all of the subtotals, but the detail rows remain hidden.

	A	B	C	D	E	F	G
1	Code	Type	Title	Category	Certificate	Rental price	Copies
14				Action Average		£3.58	
27				Childrens Average		£3.17	
35				Comedy Average		£3.43	
37				Documentary Average		£3.00	
41				Drama Average		£3.00	
44				Family Average		£3.50	
48				Horror Average		£3.67	
52				Romantic Drama Average		£3.00	
56				Science Fiction Average		£3.33	
60				Thriller Average		£3.33	
63				War Average		£3.00	
67				Western Average		£3.00	
68		DVD Count					54
77				Adventure Average		£5.00	
80				Beat 'Em Up Average		£5.00	
86				First Person Shooter Average		£5.00	
90				Racing Average		£5.00	
96				Sport Average		£5.00	
99				Strategy Average		£5.00	
100		Game Count					25
102				Action Average		£2.00	
111				Childrens Average		£2.00	
116				Comedy Average		£2.25	
118				Family Average		£2.00	
120				Romantic Drama Average		£2.00	
122				Science Fiction Average		£2.00	
124				War Average		£2.00	
128				Western Average		£2.00	
129		Video Count					20
130				Grand Average		£3.48	
131		Grand Count					99

Figure 10.8: Displaying level 3 subtotals

Finally, click the boxed **4**. This causes everything to be displayed.

Tidying up

To return the worksheet to its original state, we must remove the subtotals and sort the stock items by their codes.

Remove the subtotalling, as before.

Sort the rows by the **Code** column.

Test yourself

Shops that have lots of branches often employ **mystery shoppers**. Their job is to visit one of the shops pretending to be a real customer, and to make a record of how good the staff and facilities are. Head Office can then see where improvement is needed and where praise is due.

For these questions, we'll set up a Mystery Shopper Report that will list the findings of 100 of those visits done in January 2005. Don't worry, there won't be too much typing – we'll cheat by getting Excel to generate random results for us.

First, type in the headings shown in Figure 10.9.

	A	B	C	D	E	F	G	H	I	J	K
1	**Mystery Shopper Report**										
2											
3					**STAFF**				**FACILITIES**		
4											
5	**Shop**	**Date of visit**	**Politeness**	**Appearance**	**Efficiency**	**Helpfulness**	**Product knowledge**	**Cleanliness**	**Layout**	**Stock levels**	**Parking**

Figure 10.9: Headings for the Mystery Shopper Report

Notice that we have left row **4** blank. Both sorting and subtotals work much more smoothly with only a single row of heading information above the data.

Suppose there are ten shops in the chain. Use the formula **=INT(RAND()*10)+1** in cell **A6** to generate a random number between 1 and 10. We can use the same formula to generate results for the inspection: copy the formula to cells **C6:K6**. For the date, use the formula **=DATE(2005, 1, 1)+RAND()*31** in cell **B6**. If Excel doesn't automatically reformat this cell to be a date then do so manually (select **Format**, **Cells** and choose **Date** on the **Number** tab). Don't worry if you don't understand these formulas; you won't need to do anything like this for the exam.

Select cells **A6:K6** and use the fill handle to copy the formulas down to row **105**. This gives us the results of 100 mystery shopper visits.

To fix the values, select cells **A6:K105** and copy them. Then use **Edit**, **Paste Special** to replace the formulas with their **Values**, as shown in Figure 10.10. Now the numbers are fixed, so they won't keep changing as you edit the worksheet.

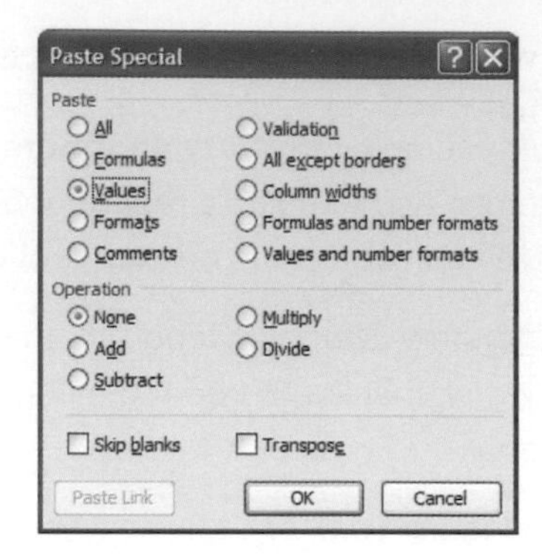

Figure 10.10: Replacing volatile data with snapshot values

Sort the rows so that they are sorted in shop-number order and in date order for each shop. The top of your worksheet should look something like Figure 10.11.

	A	B	C	D	E	F	G	H	I	J	K
3					STAFF				FACILITIES		
4											
5	Shop	Date of visit	Politeness	Appearance	Efficiency	Helpfulness	Product knowledge	Cleanliness	Layout	Stock levels	Parking
6	1	05/01/2005	1	8	1	9	7	9	8	1	7
7	1	10/01/2005	9	6	1	6	3	10	8	4	5
8	1	10/01/2005	9	1	4	1	8	1	2	4	9
9	1	10/01/2005	2	8	5	10	3	7	4	7	5
10	1	12/01/2005	2	7	8	6	4	6	1	9	5
11	1	18/01/2005	7	1	3	7	6	3	10	5	8
12	1	20/01/2005	6	2	6	4	3	1	7	1	5
13	1	21/01/2005	3	6	2	5	5	5	10	2	9
14	1	26/01/2005	7	8	8	4	2	7	6	8	6
15	1	30/01/2005	9	9	3	5	3	3	6	7	1
16	2	01/01/2005	9	10	3	4	4	10	7	10	2
17	2	02/01/2005	4	1	10	2	1	2	4	5	6
18	2	02/01/2005	6	1	9	10	4	5	8	1	4
19	2	03/01/2005	10	8	5	1	5	8	4	7	8
20	2	11/01/2005	8	8	4	8	2	4	8	6	1
21	2	14/01/2005	9	4	1	10	1	6	5	8	4
22	2	21/01/2005	1	4	3	5	7	6	3	2	6
23	2	25/01/2005	4	7	2	4	9	3	2	4	7
24	2	26/01/2005	3	8	5	10	2	3	3	6	9
25	2	29/01/2005	1	8	10	9	8	2	1	2	5
26	3	03/01/2005	8	9	10	6	7	8	2	1	9

Figure 10.11: Data generated for the Mystery Shopper Report

1. Use subtotals to show the **COUNT** of the number of visits to each shop, shown in the **Shop** column. Change the **row level** to show just the totals. It should look something like Figure 10.12.

	A	B	C	D	E	F	G	H	I	J	K	L
1		Mystery Shopper Report										
2												
3						STAFF				FACILITIES		
4												
5		Shop	Date of visit	Politeness	Appearance	Efficiency	Helpfulness	Product knowledge	Cleanliness	Layout	Stock levels	Parking
16	1 Count	10										
27	2 Count	10										
37	3 Count	9										
49	4 Count	11										
58	5 Count	8										
70	6 Count	11										
81	7 Count	10										
91	8 Count	9										
100	9 Count	8										
115	10 Count	14										
116	Grand Count	100										

Figure 10.12: Using subtotals to show the number of visits to each shop

2. Replace the current subtotals with subtotals showing the average scores across **all** of the categories for each shop, as shown in Figure 10.13.

	A	B	C	D	E	F	G	H	I	J	K
1	**Mystery Shopper Report**										
2											
3					**STAFF**				**FACILITIES**		
4											
5	Shop	Date of visit	Politeness	Appearance	Efficiency	Helpfulness	Product knowledge	Cleanliness	Layout	Stock levels	Parking
6	1	05/01/2005	1	8	1	9	7	9	8	1	7
7	1	10/01/2005	9	6	1	6	[illegible]	10	[illegible]	1	[illegible]
8	1	[illegible]	9	1	4	1	8	1	2	4	9
9	1	10/01/2005	2	8	5	10	3	7	4	7	5
10	1	12/01/2005	2	7	8	6	4	6	1	9	5
11	1	18/01/2005	7	1	3	7	6	3	10	5	8
12	1	20/01/2005	6	2	6	4	3	1	7	1	5
13	1	21/01/2005	3	6	2	5	5	5	10	2	9
14	1	26/01/2005	7	8	8	4	2	7	6	8	6
15	1	30/01/2005	9	9	3	5	3	3	6	7	1
16	**1 Average**		5.5	5.6	4.1	5.7	4.4	5.2	6.2	4.8	6
17	2	01/01/2005	9	10	3	4	4	10	7	10	2
18	2	02/01/2005	4	1	10	2	1	2	4	5	6
19	2	02/01/2005	6	1	9	10	4	5	8	1	4
20	2	03/01/2005	10	8	5	1	6	8	4	7	8
21	2	11/01/2005	8	8	4	8	2	4	8	6	1
22	2	14/01/2005	9	4	1	10	1	6	5	8	4
23	2	21/01/2005	1	4	3	5	7	6	3	2	6
24	2	25/01/2005	4	7	2	4	9	3	2	4	7
25	2	26/01/2005	3	8	5	10	2	3	3	6	9
26	2	29/01/2005	1	8	10	9	8	2	1	2	5
27	**2 Average**		5.5	5.9	5.2	6.3	4.3	4.9	4.5	5.1	5.2

Figure 10.13: Average scores recorded for each shop

3. Add subtotals showing the minimum scores recorded each day in each shop, without removing the average subtotals, as shown in Figure 10.14.

	A	B	C	D	E	F	G	H	I	J	K
1	**Mystery Shopper Report**										
2											
3					**STAFF**				**FACILITIES**		
4											
5	Shop	Date of visit	Politeness	Appearance	Efficiency	Helpfulness	Product knowledge	Cleanliness	Layout	Stock levels	Parking
7		**05/01/2005 Min**	1	8	1	9	7	9	8	1	7
11		**10/01/2005 Min**	2	1	1	1	3	1	2	4	5
13		**12/01/2005 Min**	2	7	8	6	4	6	1	9	5
15		**18/01/2005 Min**	7	1	3	7	6	3	10	5	8
17		**20/01/2005 Min**	6	2	6	4	3	1	7	1	5
19		**21/01/2005 Min**	3	6	2	5	5	5	10	2	9
21		**26/01/2005 Min**	7	8	8	4	2	7	6	8	6
23		**30/01/2005 Min**	9	9	3	5	3	3	6	7	1
24	**1 Average**		5.5	5.6	4.1	5.7	4.4	5.2	6.2	4.8	6
26		**01/01/2005 Min**	9	10	3	4	4	10	7	10	2
29		**02/01/2005 Min**	4	1	9	2	1	2	4	1	4
31		**03/01/2005 Min**	10	8	5	1	5	8	4	7	8
33		**11/01/2005 Min**	8	8	4	8	2	4	8	6	1
35		**14/01/2005 Min**	9	4	1	10	1	6	5	8	4
37		**21/01/2005 Min**	1	4	3	5	7	6	3	2	6
39		**25/01/2005 Min**	4	7	2	4	9	3	2	4	7
41		**26/01/2005 Min**	3	8	5	10	2	3	3	6	9
43		**29/01/2005 Min**	1	8	10	9	8	2	1	2	5
44	**2 Average**		5.5	5.9	5.2	6.3	4.3	4.9	4.5	5.1	5.2

Figure 10.14: Minimum scores recorded each day for each shop

Bonus question

4. How does the day of the week affect the scores across the shops as a whole? Perhaps staff are always grumpy on a Monday, so are less polite. Perhaps stock levels are at their highest on Thursdays because this is when new deliveries come in. Look up the **WEEKDAY** function in the help, and use it with subtotals to investigate this relationship. If you get the time, try drawing a graph of the results.

11 Filtering & Sorting

Introduction

This chapter covers two important techniques for handling long lists of information: filtering and sorting. **Filtering** is the process of hiding certain unwanted information so that you can concentrate on what is important, or to allow you to answer particular questions about the information you are working with. **Sorting** is self-explanatory; here, we look at some more advanced sorting topics, such as using **custom sort orders**.

In this chapter you will

- filter the video shop's membership data using **AutoFilter**
- create a **custom AutoFilter**
- build an **advanced filter** with multiple criteria
- learn how to use **formulas in advanced filters** to build more complex queries
- **sort** the video shop's stock by **multiple columns**
- create and use a **custom sort order** for situations in which you need something other than alphabetical order.

Filtering

A **filter** is a means of hiding those rows in a worksheet that do not meet some specified criteria. The act of compressing a group, which you saw with subtotals in the previous chapter, can be thought of as a type of filter.

There are two ways of applying filters to a table of data: **AutoFilter**, which uses drop-down lists to set the criteria, and **Advanced Filter**, for which the criteria are typed into cells in the worksheet. We'll look at these two filter types in turn.

AutoFilter

> **Syllabus Ref: AM4.2.2.1**
> Create a single or multiple criteria query using available options.

 Open **videoshop.xls** and display the **Members** worksheet.

 Select any of the cells in the body of the table (for example, **D14**). From the menu, select **Data**, **Filter**, **AutoFilter**.

You will notice that the cells in the top row have changed into drop-down lists. Let's have a look at the contents of the **Village** list, as shown in Figure 11.1.

G	H	I
Address2	Village	Town/Ci
Mill Road		Middlington
		Middlington
Hampton Str		Middlington
		Middlington
		Middlington
		Middlington
Mill Road		Middlington
		Middlington
		Middlington

Sort Ascending
Sort Descending
(All)
(Top 10...)
(Custom...)
Blakely
Hamshaw
Pickerington
(Blanks)
(NonBlanks)

Figure 11.1: Options for an AutoFiltered column of villages

The first two options are **Sort Ascending** and **Sort Descending**. These won't work in our table, unless we first remove the automatic subtotals, but they are often useful for sets of data with many rows.

The **(All)** option, which is selected by default, does not filter the column at all. You can choose this setting to remove a filter.

(Top 10...) displays a dialogue upon selection (Figure 11.2) that lets you choose only the highest or lowest values from a numerical list.

As you might expect, **(Custom...)** provides the most powerful filtering options. We'll see shortly how to use this.

The list then contains an entry for each of the unique values in that column. For example, to display only those rows that correspond to the village of Blakely, you would select **Blakely**.

The final two options – **(Blanks)** and **(Nonblanks)** – let you find or hide blank cells.

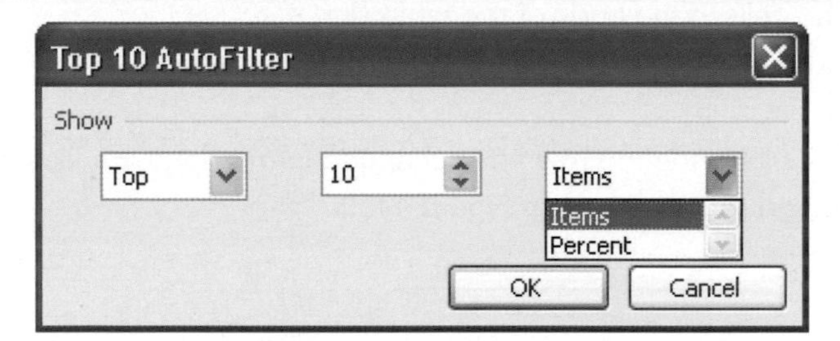

Figure 11.2: Filtering to display only the top ten items in a list

From the **Village** list, select **Pickerington**.

The filter is applied, and only the seven customers who live in Pickerington are displayed, as shown in Figure 11.3.

	A	B	C	D	E	F	G	H	I
1	Memb	Tit	Initi	Surnam	Date of bir	Address1	Address2	Village	Town/Ci
15	14	Ms	T	Stewart	05/01/1987	6 Little Row		Pickerington	Middlington
24	23	Ms	W	Miller	17/07/1969	1 London Road		Pickerington	Middlington
58	57	Mr	J	Baker	27/10/1970	3 Little Row		Pickerington	Middlington
74	73	Mrs	E	Chang	01/10/1976	14 London Road		Pickerington	Middlington
83	82	Ms	S	Jones	22/11/1980	17 Little Row		Pickerington	Middlington
92	91	Ms	N	Harris	14/02/1984	23 Regent Street		Pickerington	Middlington
97	96	Mrs	J	Clark	30/11/1971	22 London Road		Pickerington	Middlington
101									

Figure 11.3: Filtering the customer list to show only customers from Pickerington

Notice that the arrow for the **Village** drop-down list is now blue, whereas the others remain black. This shows you which column has the filter applied.

Suppose an existing customer (whose name you don't remember) came into the shop asking about a particular DVD, but you didn't have it in stock. He was a bit annoyed, since he had driven in from Pickerington specially. After he had gone, you found a cuff link on the floor and guessed it belonged to the man from Pickerington.

Let's apply a second filter to the list so you can find out who he was and give him a call.

 From the **Title** drop-down list, select **Mr**. This second filter is applied in addition to the existing one (notice that the arrows for both **Title** and **Village** are now blue).

Applying these two filters has identified the mystery man. It was Mr J Baker, and you now have his contact details. Hopefully, finding out that his lost cuff link has been found will make him forget his disappointment about the DVD being out of stock!

 Set both of the filters back to **(All)**. The two arrows become black again, and all of the rows are displayed.

Custom AutoFilter

Suppose we want to see a list of all customers who have spent over £200. We can use a custom AutoFilter to do this.

 From the **Total Spend** list, select **Custom**. The **Custom AutoFilter** dialogue appears.

 Change the first drop-down list to **is greater than** and set a value of **200**, as shown in Figure 11.4. Press **OK**.

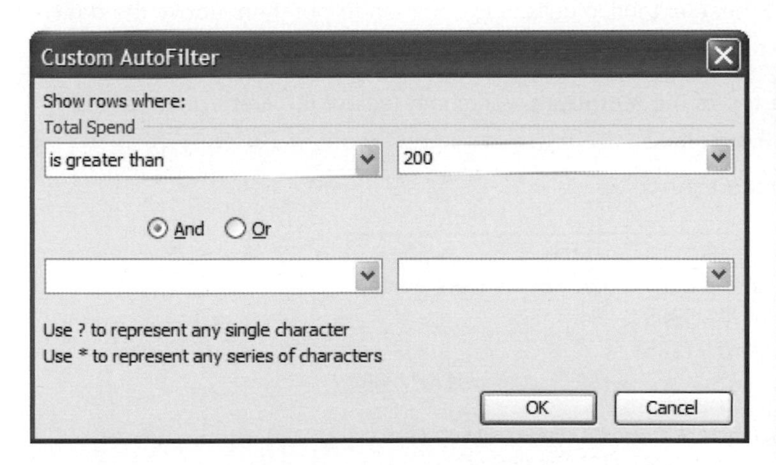

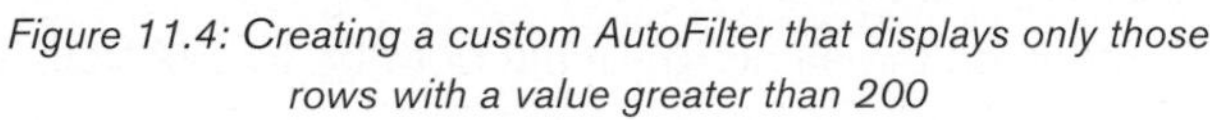
Figure 11.4: Creating a custom AutoFilter that displays only those rows with a value greater than 200

This filter has reduced the list down to just those 14 customers who have spent over £200.

Remove the **AutoFilter** by selecting from the menu **Data**, **Filter**, **AutoFilter** (which should be ticked). All of the rows are displayed again.

Syllabus Ref: AM4.2.2.2

Use advanced query/filter options.

Advanced filters

More complicated queries can be constructed by using an **advanced filter**. Instead of being selected from drop-down lists, the criteria for an advanced filter are written as text into cells in a worksheet, just as for the database functions we used in Chapter 7. Remember that the first row identifies the columns that are being used, and each row below this lists the criteria that must evaluate to **TRUE** if a record is to be displayed.

If a criteria row has more than one test then all of the tests (columns) must pass; if multiple criteria rows are used then any of the rows may pass. This allows us to build arbitrarily complex filters as long as they fit the general pattern:

IF(criterion_1.1 **AND** criterion_1.2 **AND** …) **OR** (criterion_2.1 **AND** criterion_2.2 **AND** …) **OR** …

Don't worry if this seems complicated: it really isn't, as the following example will show.

The average age of customers in the video shop is around 30. In order to attract more of the older and younger customers, you want to send out a flyer offering people a free rental for each friend they introduce. You want to pick certain customers to send this offer to: those born before 1965, those born since 1985 and also your highest-spending customers (those who have joined since 2004 and already spent at least £150).

Remember that we will have to put these criteria in cells. It is common to put them above the data to which they refer, so let's make some room.

Insert five blank rows at the top of the **Members** worksheet (select the first five rows and choose **Insert**, **Rows** from the menu).

Enter the criteria shown in Figure 11.5.

	A	B	C
1	Date of birth	Total Spend	Date Joined
2	<01/01/1965		
3	>01/01/1985		
4		>150	>01/01/2004

Figure 11.5: Criteria for the advanced filter

If you work through this, remembering that criteria on the same row must both be true (**AND**), and only one row needs to pass (**OR**), then you can read this as follows:

(Date of birth before 1965) OR (Date of birth after 1985) OR
(Total spend over £150 AND Date joined after 2004).

 Click in any of the cells containing information (for example, cell **A7**).

 From the menu, select **Data**, **Filter**, **Advanced Filter**. The **Advanced Filter** dialogue appears.

 Make sure that the **Action** is set to **Filter the list, in-place**. The **List range** of **$A$6:$N$105** should be detected automatically. Set the **Criteria range** to **$A$1:$C$4** (the cells you have just typed values for). All of our member records are unique, so it doesn't matter whether **Unique records only** is ticked. Press **OK**.

Figure 11.6: Setting the criteria range for an advanced filter

The member data is filtered down to the 23 records that match one or more of the search criteria. Notice that there are no down arrows as there were for **AutoFilter**.

 Change the value in cell **B4** to **>200**.

Nothing happens! You might have expected the filtered data to be automatically updated. Instead, you have to reapply the filter whenever you change the criteria.

 From the menu, select **Data**, **Filter**, **Advanced Filter**. The **Advanced Filter** dialogue appears, and remembers the information you entered last time. Press **OK** to apply the change.

This time, there are only 20 matching records.

You can remove any filter you apply, by selecting **Data**, **Filter**, **Show All** from the menu. However, if you are simply replacing one filter with another then you don't need to do this step in the middle – the new filter always completely replaces any existing filter; they are not cumulative.

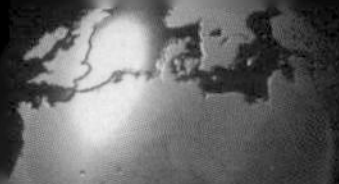

Filtering with formulas

Some companies send their customers birthday cards. You think this might be a good marketing idea, so you want a list of all of your customers whose birthdays fall in May.

You can use an advanced filter together with a formula to generate the list.

From the menu, select **Data**, **Filter**, **Show All**. This removes the filter and displays all of the rows.

In cell **E1**, type the text **BornInMay**.

It doesn't matter what text you type in this cell, as long as it does **not** match any of the headings. This tells Excel that you are using a formula.

In cell **E2**, type the formula = **MONTH(E7) = 5**.

The date of birth in cell **E7** is **21/04/1976**. Therefore **MONTH(E7)** has the value **4** (April). As a result, the whole comparison = **MONTH(E7) = 5** evaluates to **FALSE**.

The clever bit is that when you use a formula in the criteria for an advanced filter, Excel automatically evaluates it for each row in turn using relative references. Therefore, the test will be = **MONTH(E8) = 5** for row **8**, and so on. This is rather like the way **data tables** work (see Chapter 5).

From the menu, select **Data**, **Filter**, **Advanced Filter**. Change the **Criteria range** to **E1:E2** (leave the **List range** as it is) and press **OK**.

Your worksheet should now look like Figure 11.7.

	A	B	C	D	E	F
1	Date of birth	Total Spend	Date Joined		BornInMay	
2	<01/01/1965				FALSE	
3	>01/01/1985					
4		>200	>01/01/2004			
5						
6	**Member**	**Title**	**Initial**	**Surname**	**Date of birth**	**Address1**
17	11	Mrs	S	Honeywell	15/05/1971	211 St. John's Road
22	16	Ms	K	Bennett	29/05/1973	13 Broad Street
31	25	Mr	T	Russell	27/05/1970	The Old Rectory
32	26	Ms	V	Wilson	17/05/1968	2 Bridge Row
33	27	Mr	L	Clark	23/05/1986	51 St. John's Road
48	42	Ms	K	Garcia	05/05/1986	2 Elmer St
53	47	Mr	S	Cook	01/05/1957	1 Compton Drive
71	65	Ms	L	Rodriguez	28/05/1969	2 Shepherd's Pass
74	68	Ms	C	Turner	21/05/1983	1 Pellow Place
99	93	Mrs	S	Bagnal	08/05/1980	Treetops
105	99	Mr	S	Walker	01/05/1978	6 Milber Rise
106						

Figure 11.7: Filtered list of members with birthdays in May

Tidy up by removing the filter and deleting rows **1** to **5**.

Sorting

You already know how to sort a table of data by a single column using the **Sort Ascending** and **Sort Descending** buttons on the **Standard** toolbar. You have also seen (page 118) that, because Excel's sort preserves the relative order of matching values, you can sort by several columns by doing simple sorts in reverse order.

Sort Ascending

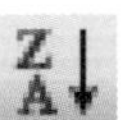

Sort Descending

Sorting by multiple columns

Excel also has a **Sort** dialogue box, which lets you sort by several columns at once. Let's try sorting the **Stock** worksheet's data by **Type** and **Title**.

Syllabus Ref: AM4.2.1.1

Sort data by multiple columns.

 Change to the **Stock** worksheet and select any of the cells in the **Stock** table.

 From the menu, select **Data**, **Sort**. The **Sort** dialogue appears.

 Change the top drop-down list to **Type** and make sure its sort order is **Ascending** (that is, A to Z). Set the second drop-down list to **Title** (**Ascending**). The **Sort** dialogue should look like Figure 11.8. Notice how Excel has guessed that our table has a **Header row** – this is correct, since we don't want row **1** to be sorted. Press **OK**.

Figure 11.8: Sorting by two fields – first by Type and then by Title within each Type

The sort order should now be as shown in Figure 11.9. The DVDs come first, with their titles sorted alphabetically.

	A	B	C
1	Code	Type	Title
2	45	DVD	101 Dalmatians
3	99	DVD	24 Hour Party People
4	64	DVD	Blade
5	4	DVD	Blade Runner
6	1	DVD	Bourne Identity, The
7	60	DVD	Bowling For Columbine
8	16	DVD	Box Of Delights, The
9	88	DVD	Bridge On The River Kwai, The
10	93	DVD	Butch Cassidy And The Sundance Kid
11	54	DVD	Butterfly Effect, The
12	25	DVD	Cannonball Run, The

Figure 11.9: Result of sorting on two columns

Custom sorts

Sometimes you need a sort order that is not alphabetical. The following step shows such a situation.

Do a standard ascending single-column sort on the **Certificate** column.

Notice how the sort order is numbers first (**12**, **15** and **18**) followed by letters (**PG** and **U**). A more natural sort order would be from most to least accessible: **U**, **PG**, **12**, **15**, **18**.

U stands for **Universal** and is used for entertainment that is suitable for all.

PG stands for **Parental Guidance.** Such entertainment is suitable for general viewing, but parents are advised to consider how young or sensitive children might react.

12, **15** and **18** indicate entertainment that is not suitable for anyone younger than 12, 15 or 18 respectively.

If you are a parent, don't fall for your child's ruse that 'PG' stands for 'Pretty Good' and the numbers are scores out of 20!

Syllabus Ref: AM4.2.1.2

Perform custom sorts.

We can use a custom sort to sort the stock items into this more natural order. The first step is to create a **custom list**.

From the menu, select **Tools, Options**. The **Options** dialogue appears.

Switch to the **Custom Lists** tab. With **NEW LIST** selected in the left-hand list, type **U**, **PG**, **12**, **15** and **18** (pressing **Enter** after all but the last one) into the **List entries** box, as shown in Figure 11.10(a). Press the **Add** button, which creates the new list, as shown in Figure 11.10(b). Press **OK** to dismiss the **Options** dialogue and save the new custom list.

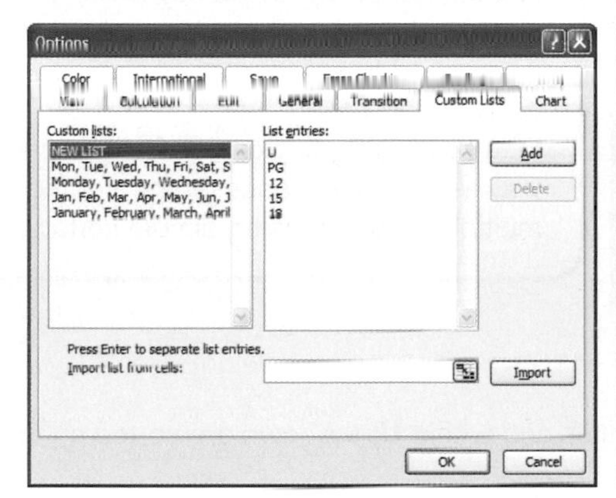

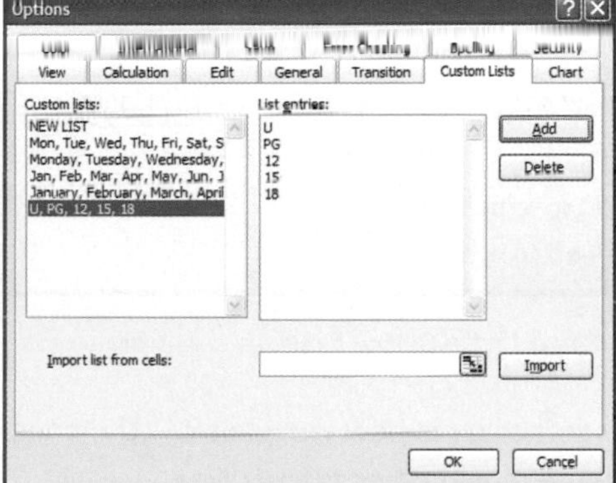

Figure 11.10: Adding a custom list – (a) typing it in and (b) after pressing Add

From the menu, select **Data**, **Sort**. The **Sort** dialogue appears.

Change **Sort by** to **Certificate** and **Then by** to **Copies**. Make the **Copies** sort **Descending**, as shown in Figure 11.11. Press the **Options** button.

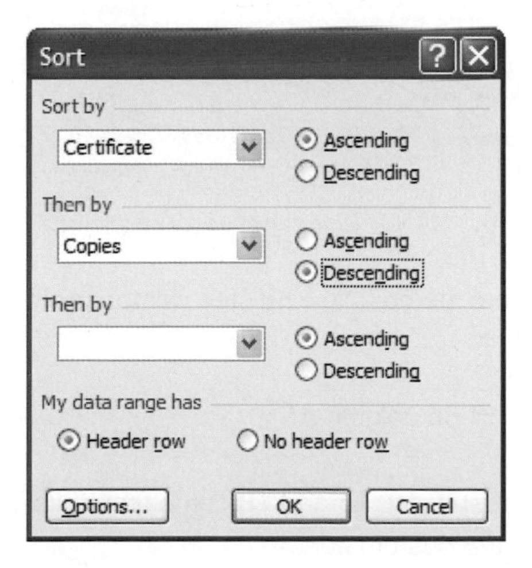

Figure 11.11: Sorting by Certificate (U to 18 custom order) and then Copies (descending order)

 The **Sort Options** dialogue appears. As the **First key sort order**, select your newly defined list: **U**, **PG**, **12**, **15**, **18**, and press **OK**. Press **OK** on the **Sort** dialogue.

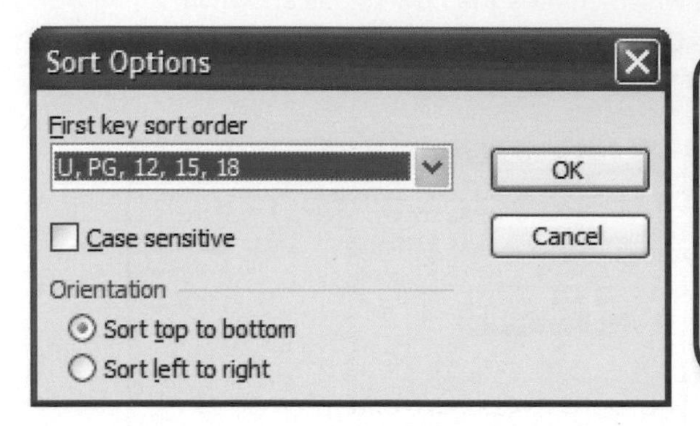

Figure 11.12: Setting a custom sort order

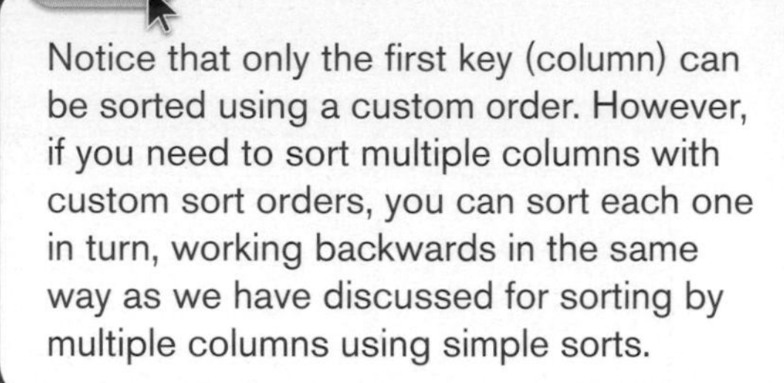

Notice that only the first key (column) can be sorted using a custom order. However, if you need to sort multiple columns with custom sort orders, you can sort each one in turn, working backwards in the same way as we have discussed for sorting by multiple columns using simple sorts.

The new sort order is how we want it – **U** comes first, and within **U**, the rows are sorted so that the item with the most copies comes first.

	A	B	C	D	E	F	G
1	Code	Type	Title	Category	Certificate	Rental price	Copies
2	50	Video	Toy Story	Childrens	U	£2.00	20
3	57	DVD	Shrek	Childrens	U	£3.00	16
4	74	DVD	Shrek 2	Childrens	U	£4.00	11
5	35	Video	Shrek	Childrens	U	£2.00	11
6	26	Video	Teletubbies - Teletubbies Go!	Childrens	U	£2.00	11
7	70	DVD	Fireman Sam - To The Rescue!	Childrens	U	£3.00	10
8	45	DVD	101 Dalmatians	Childrens	U	£3.00	9
9	16	DVD	Box Of Delights, The	Childrens	U	£3.00	9
10	86	DVD	Lady And The Tramp	Childrens	U	£3.00	6
11	13	DVD	Everybody Loves Mickey	Childrens	U	£3.00	5
12	9	DVD	Fantasia	Childrens	U	£3.00	5
13	65	Video	101 Dalmatians	Childrens	U	£2.00	3
14	30	Video	Fantasia	Childrens	U	£2.00	3
15	79	Video	Lady And The Tramp	Childrens	U	£2.00	3
16	62	Video	The Complete Ivor The Engine	Childrens	U	£2.00	2
17	17	DVD	Toy Story	Childrens	U	£3.00	1
18	89	Video	Chitty Chitty Bang Bang	Family	PG	£2.00	20

Figure 11.13: Table sorted with a custom order

However, there is a slight problem as the following step demonstrates.

Sort Ascending

Do a simple ascending sort on column **A**.

This gives a rather unexpected result: **12**, **15** and **18** come first, followed by the other numbers in order. Excel is still trying to use the custom sort.

This isn't normally a problem, since most custom sorts are done just on words. However, it is important to remember that simple sorts will continue to use your custom sort order until you turn it off. Let's do that now.

 From the menu, select **Data**, **Sort**. The **Sort** dialogue appears. Press the **Options** button and change the **First key sort order** to **Normal**, as shown in Figure 11.14. Press **OK**.

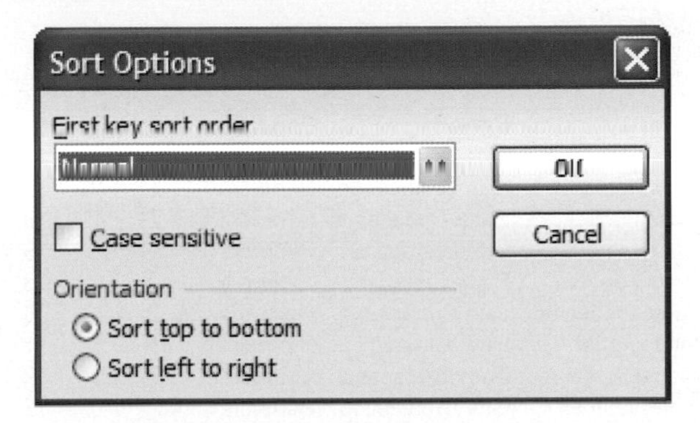

Figure 11.14: Turning off the custom sort order

 Back in the **Sort** dialogue, sort by the single field **Code** in **Ascending** order.

The expected sort order (**1**, **2**, **3**, …) is returned.

Test yourself

First, type the following information about dinosaurs into a new workbook (or you can download it from www.payne-gallway.co.uk/ecdl).

	A	B	C	D	E	F	G	H
1	Order	Name	Period	Food	Legs	Height (ft)	Length (ft)	Weight (lbs)
2	Ornithischian	Corythosaurus	Late Cretaceous	Herbivore	2	16	30	8860
3	Ornithischian	Hadrosaurus	Late Cretaceous	Herbivore	2	15	30	6000
4	Ornithischian	Iguanodon	Early Cretaceous	Herbivore	2	18	30	10000
5	Ornithischian	Lambeosaurus	Late Cretaceous	Herbivore	2	18	30	14000
6	Ornithischian	Ouranosaurus	Early Cretaceous	Herbivore	2	10	23	8000
7	Ornithischian	Shantungosaurus	Late Cretaceous	Herbivore	2	25	51	14000
8	Ornithischian	Stegosaurus	Late Jurassic	Herbivore	4	11	30	6000
9	Saurischian	Acrocanthosaurus	Early Cretaceous	Carnivore	2	19	40	6000
10	Saurischian	Albertosaurus	Late Cretaceous	Carnivore	2	15	30	6000
11	Saurischian	Allosaurus	Late Jurassic	Carnivore	2	17	40	4000
12	Saurischian	Apatosaurus	Late Jurassic	Herbivore	4	15	75	66000
13	Saurischian	Argentinosaurus	Late Cretaceous	Herbivore	4	70	120	220000
14	Saurischian	Brachiosaurus	Late Jurassic	Herbivore	4	50	100	100000
15	Saurischian	Diplodocus	Late Jurassic	Herbivore	4	24	89	50000
16	Saurischian	Mamenchisaurus	Late Jurassic	Herbivore	4	35	69	60000
17	Saurischian	Megalosaurus	Middle Jurassic	Carnivore	2	12	26	2000
18	Saurischian	Seismosaurus	Late Jurassic	Herbivore	4	84	150	200000
19	Saurischian	Supersaurus	Late Jurassic	Herbivore	4	66	100	120000
20	Saurischian	Tyrannosaurus	Late Cretaceous	Carnivore	2	23	50	14000
21	Saurischian	Ultrasaurus	Late Jurassic	Herbivore	4	53	100	140000

Figure 11.15: Dinosaur statistics

1. Define a custom list of historical periods in chronological order: **Early Jurassic**, **Middle Jurassic**, **Late Jurassic**, **Early Cretaceous**, **Middle Cretaceous** and **Late Cretaceous**. Sort the table using two keys: **Period** (using the custom sort order you have just defined) and **Name**. Delete the custom list to tidy up, since you won't need it again.

The dinosaurs should now be sorted with **Megalosaurus** (the oldest) at the top and **Tyrannosaurus** at the bottom.

Suppose you want to concentrate on those dinosaurs likely to have the thickest bones. You decide that two-legged dinosaurs over 16 ft tall, or four-legged dinosaurs at least 50 ft tall, are likely to have thick bones. The same is true for any dinosaur at least 100 ft long. Finally, you also want to include any dinosaur that has to carry 15,000 lbs or more on each leg.

2. Create a **custom filter** that will reduce the list down to just those dinosaurs (13 out of 20) that fall into one or more of the above groups.

3. Add **average subtotals** for the **Height**, **Length** and **Weight** values, grouped by **Period**. Set all of these to display whole numbers only.

12 Macros

Introduction

In this chapter, we will record some macros (sets of commands that can be played back later). We will run these macros and assign them to a custom toolbar. We will use two scenarios: changing the page setup and cracking codes.

In this chapter you will

- **record a macro** to turn on gridlines in the page setup, and another to turn them back off
- **run the macros** to test them
- **create two more macros** for revealing and hiding a secret message using a mask (blacking out some of the cells)
- create a **new toolbar** and assign these macros to **custom buttons** on it
- learn about **macro security**.

Scenario 1: page setup changes

Syllabus Ref: AM4.5.1.1

Record a simple macro (e.g. page setup changes).

Recording a macro

A macro is a sequence of commands, which you can apply in one go. Since the syllabus suggests recording a macro to do page setup changes, this seems like a good place to start. We will also use macros to do something a little more fun – decoding secret messages!

Sometimes it's useful to turn on gridlines (borders around each cell) when printing a worksheet, particularly if there are a lot of blank cells. It's a pain having to go in and manually change the page setup, so let's create a couple of macros to turn this setting on and off.

Open a new blank workbook.

From the menu, select **Tools**, **Macro**, **Record New Macro**. The **Record Macro** dialogue appears. Fill in the **Macro name** and **Description** as shown in Figure 12.1.

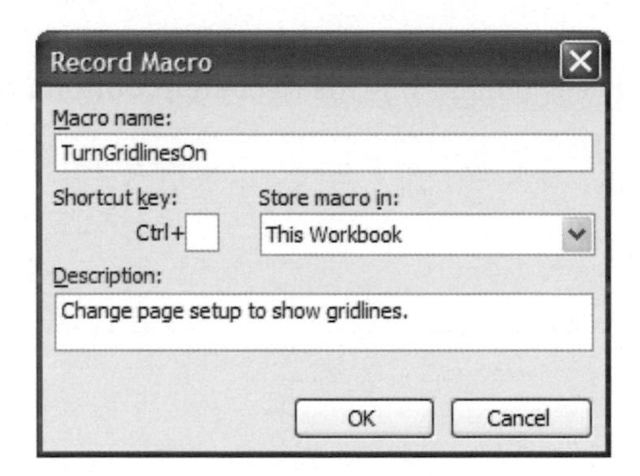

Figure 12.1: Starting to record a macro

Make sure that **Store macro in** is set to **This Workbook**, then press **OK**.

The **Stop Recording** toolbar appears. It only has two buttons (**Stop Recording** and **Relative Reference**), as shown in Figure 12.2.

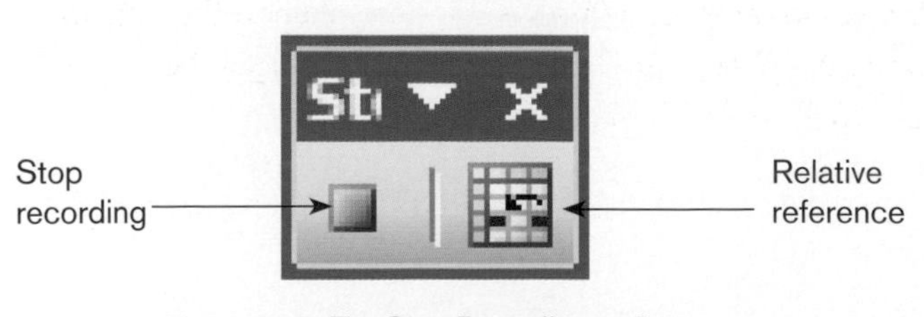

Figure 12.2: The Stop Recording toolbar

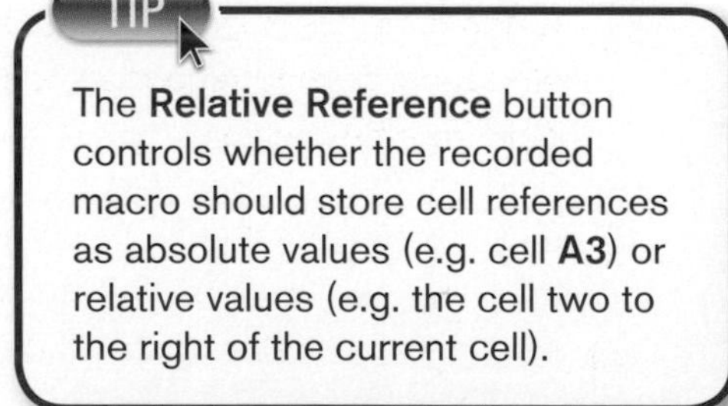

The **Relative Reference** button controls whether the recorded macro should store cell references as absolute values (e.g. cell **A3**) or relative values (e.g. the cell two to the right of the current cell).

From the menu, select **File**, **Page Setup**. The **Page Setup** dialogue appears.

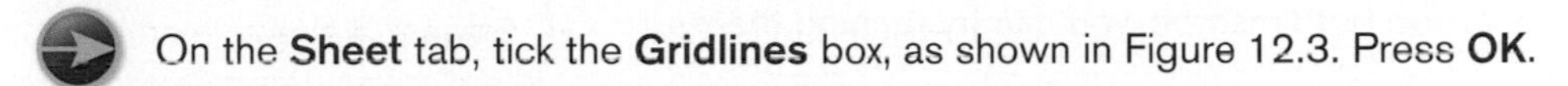
On the **Sheet** tab, tick the **Gridlines** box, as shown in Figure 12.3. Press **OK**.

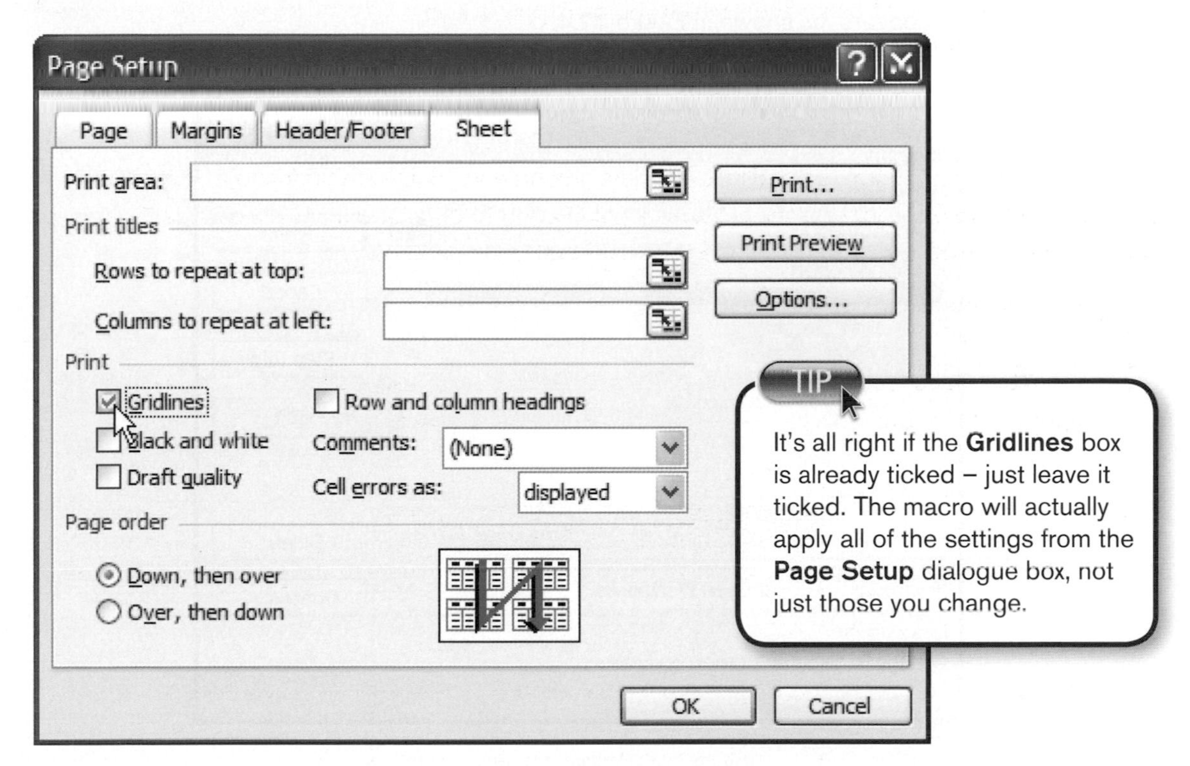

Figure 12.3: Turning on gridlines

- Select **Tools**, **Macro**, **Stop Recording**. (An equivalent alternative would have been to press the **Stop Recording** button on the **Stop Recording** toolbar.)

- Do a **Print Preview** (you will need to type something into one or more of the cells first, since you cannot preview an empty worksheet). You should be able to see gridlines around the cells.

- Close the **Print Preview**, then use the same technique (start recording, change the setting, stop recording) to record a second macro, called **TurnGridlinesOff**, that unticks the **Gridlines** box again.

Running a macro

Syllabus Ref: AM4.5.1.2

Run a macro.

Now you have recorded both macros, you can try running them.

 From the menu, select **Tools**, **Macro**, **Macros**. The **Macro** dialogue box appears, as shown in Figure 12.4.

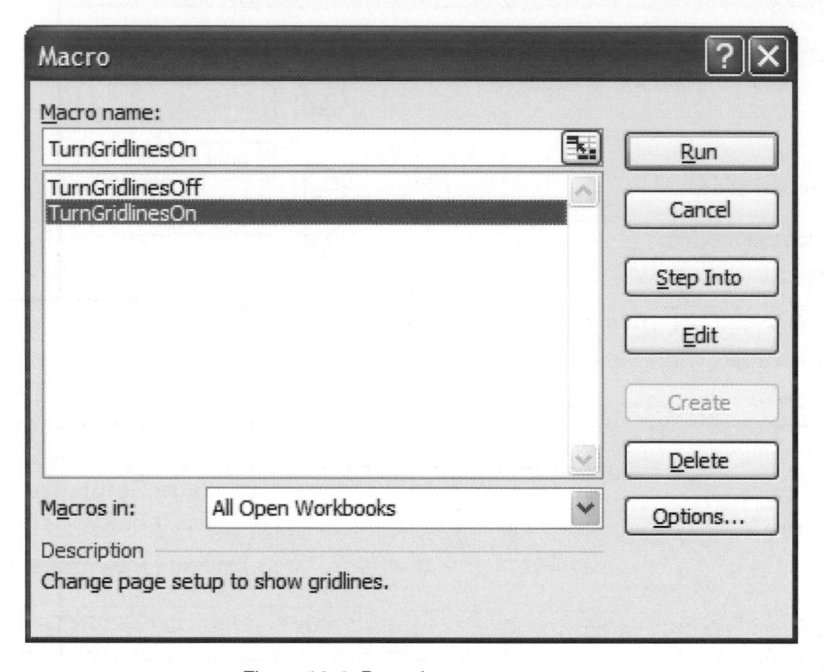

Figure 12.4: Preparing to run a macro

 Select **TurnGridlinesOn** and press the **Run** button. You may see the screen flicker a bit.

 Do a **Print Preview**. The gridlines should be on, as shown in Figure 12.5.

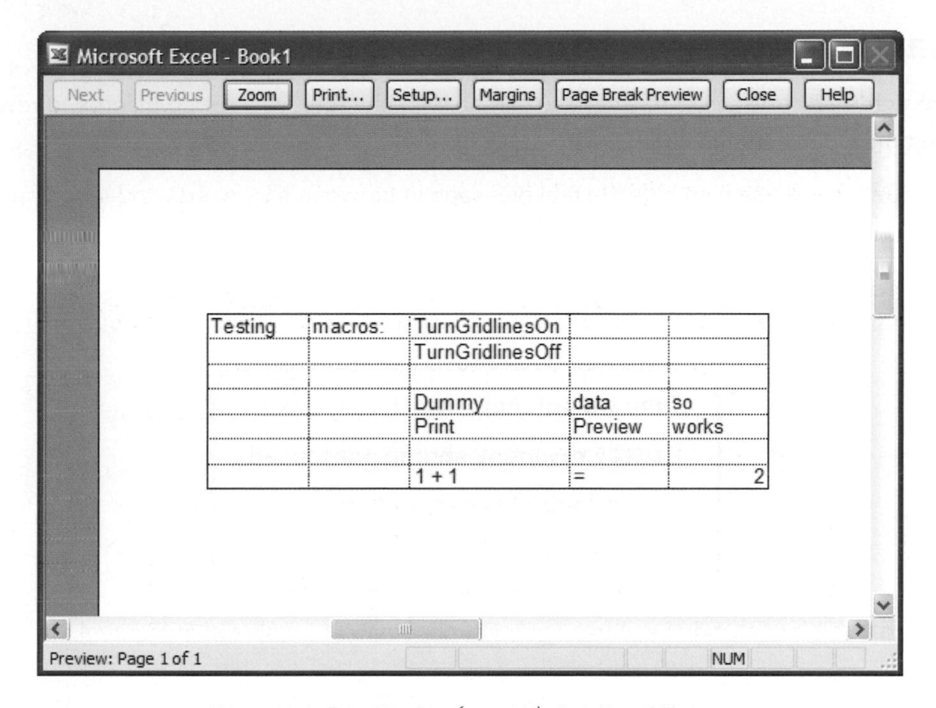

Figure 12.5: Print Preview (zoomed) showing gridlines on

Close the **Print Preview**, then use the same method to run thc **TurnGridlinesOff** macro. Now the **Print Preview** should show that gridlines are off, as in Figure 12.6.

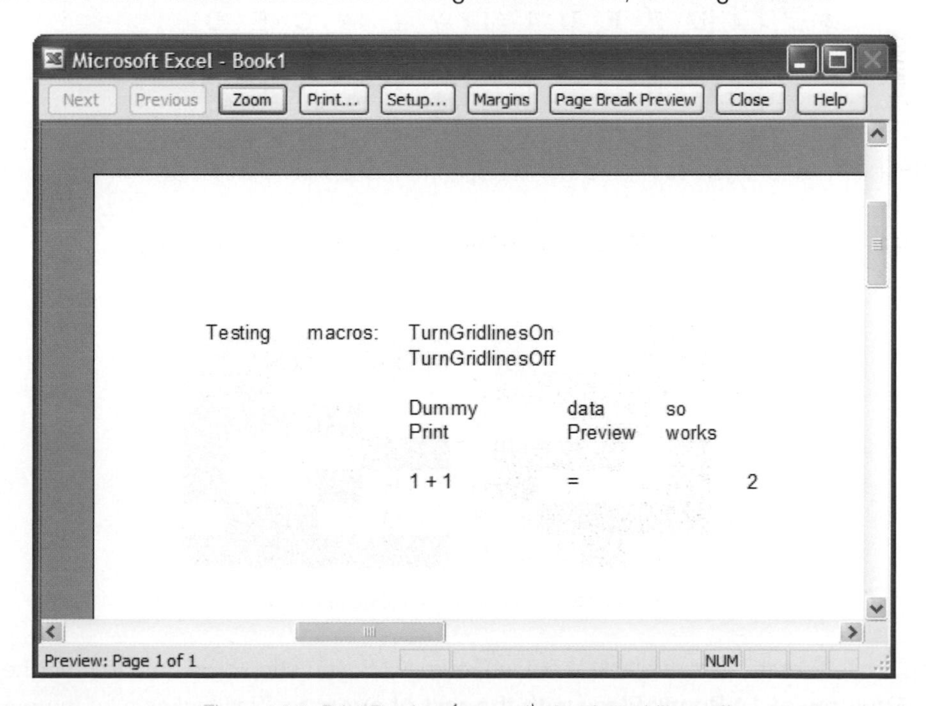

Figure 12.6: Print Preview (zoomed) showing gridlines off

Scenario 2: sending coded messages

As a more entertaining example of what you can do with macros, we'll set up macros to reveal and hide secret messages sent in code.

The technique we will use is to hide the real message in between filler words and letters, and then use a mask to extract the message.

Suppose you received the following message. To anyone else intercepting it, it might seem like complete nonsense!

Time we put them away!

Eat 142 dry loony shrimp, fully laced.

Switch their old chest of flour.

I'm entranced!

The trick is to put it into a grid of squares, ignoring punctuation, as shown in Figure 12.7.

	A	B	C	D	E	F	G	H	I	J	K	L
1	T	I	M	E	W	E	P	U	T	T	H	E
2	M	A	W	A	Y	E	A	T	1	4	2	D
3	R	Y	L	O	O	N	E	Y	S	H	R	I
4	M	P	F	U	L	L	Y	L	A	C	E	D
5	S	W	I	T	C	H	T	H	I	E	R	O
6	L	D	C	H	E	S	T	O	F	F	L	O
7	U	R	I	M	E	N	R	A	N	C	E	D

Figure 12.7: The secret message, one character per grid square

Then, by applying a mask, the message is revealed!

	A	B	C	D	E	F	G	H	I	J	K	L
1			M	E		E			T			
2	M					E	A	T	1	4		
3	R			O	O	N	E	Y				
4		P				L			A	C	E	
5		W	I	T		H	T	H		E	R	
6					E	S	T	O	F			O
7	U	R		M	E	N						

Figure 12.8: Revealing the hidden message

By reading the letters that aren't blacked-out in Figure 12.8, you should be able to read the hidden message: **Meet me at 14 Roony Place with the rest of our men**. This makes a lot more sense!

Let's create two macros: one to black-out the squares and reveal the message, and a second one to hide the message again.

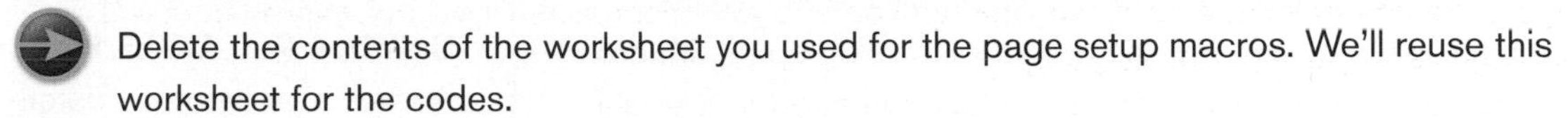

- Delete the contents of the worksheet you used for the page setup macros. We'll reuse this worksheet for the codes.
- Resize columns **A** to **I** so that they are roughly square (you can select them all, and then resize any one of them). Fill in the letters from the secret message, as shown in Figure 12.7.
- From the menu, select **Tools**, **Macro**, **Record New Macro**. The **Record Macro** dialogue appears.
- Fill in the **Macro name** and **Description** shown in Figure 12.9, then press **OK**.

Figure 12.9: Preparing to record the ShowSecretMessage macro

- Referring to Figure 12.8, hold down the **Ctrl** key and click in turn on each of the cells to be blacked out. This will select them all.
- With the cells still selected, use the **Fill Color** control on the **Formatting** toolbar to make the cells black.

Fill Color

- Click in any other cell, so that the black cells are no longer selected.
- Click the **Stop Recording** icon on the **Stop Recording** toolbar (see Figure 12.2 on page 142).
- Record a macro called **HideSecretMessage** that sets the fill colour for these cells back to **No Fill**.
- Try running these macros to check that they work.

Assigning a macro to a custom button on a toolbar

The whole point of using macros is to simplify repetitive tasks, but it still takes quite a few mouse clicks to bring up the **Macro** dialogue and run a macro. We can reduce the effort to a single click by adding our macros to custom buttons on a toolbar.

Syllabus Ref: AM4.5.1.3
Assign a macro to a custom button on a toolbar.

Right-click on any of the toolbars and choose **Customize** (the bottom option) from the resultant menu. The **Customize** dialogue box appears.

With the **Toolbars** tab selected, press the **New** button. The **New Toolbar** dialogue box appears. Type the name **ECDL Macros: Cryptography**, as shown in Figure 12.10, and press **OK**. A new empty toolbar appears.

If you get a warning that a toolbar with this name already exists, then press **Cancel**, select the existing **ECDL Macros: Cryptography** toolbar in the **Customize** dialogue and press **Delete**. Then try the previous action again.

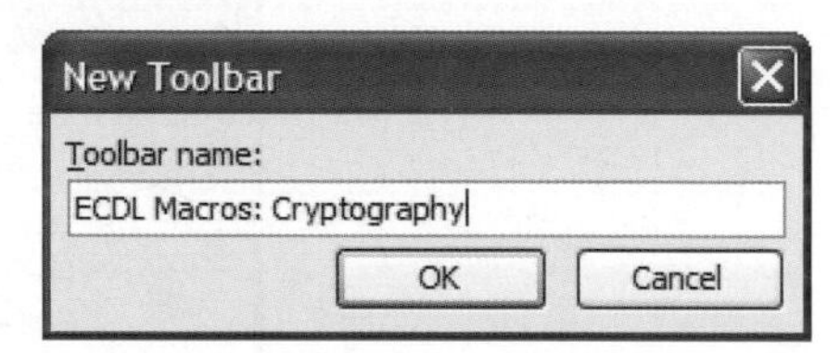

Figure 12.10: Naming a new toolbar

Back in the **Customize** dialogue box, switch to the **Commands** tab. Select **Macros** in the **Categories** list, then drag the **Custom Button** from the **Commands** list into the new toolbar, as shown in Figure 12.11.

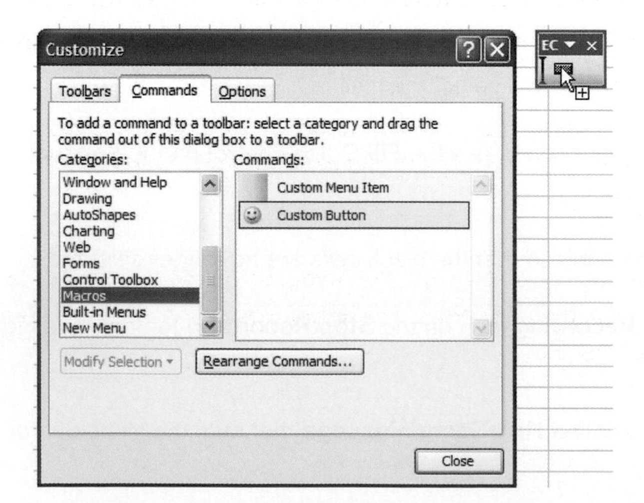

Figure 12.11: Adding a custom button to a toolbar

Right-click the new button and select **Assign Macro** (the bottom option) from the resultant menu. The **Assign Macro** dialogue box appears. Select **ShowSecretMessage** and then press **OK**.

Right-click the new button, select **Change Button Image**, then click on an appropriate icon, such as the eye, to represent the macro.

Right-click the button again and select **Image and Text**. This displays the text **Custom Button**, which is the default name it was given. Right-click again and change the name to **&Show Secret Message**.

The optional **&** symbol is used before the letter that you want to act as a shortcut for the command - in this case **S**. This shortcut key is underlined in the button text.

Add a second button. Assign the **HideSecretMessage** macro to it and change the image and text as appropriate. If you add a shortcut indicator (**&**), put it before one of the characters, such as **M**, that isn't already used for something else.

The new toolbar should look like Figure 12.12.

Figure 12.12: The new toolbar

When you create a new toolbar, it is saved to the general Excel workspace on your PC by default. In this case, we only want the toolbar to appear for this specific workbook, so we will attach the toolbar to the workbook.

In the **Customize** dialogue box, switch to the **Toolbars** tab. Highlight **ECDL Macros: Cryptography** in the list of **Toolbars** and press the **Attach** button. The **Attach Toolbars** dialogue box appears.

Select **ECDL Macros: Cryptography** from the list on the left and press the **Copy** button to copy it to the list on the right. Press **OK** to confirm the change, and to embed a copy of the toolbar in the workbook.

If you are asked to create a custom toolbar in the exam then you will probably have to attach it to a workbook, as you have just done, so that the examiner will be able to see the toolbar by opening the workbook. (Otherwise the toolbar would just exist in the Excel workspace on your PC.)

Attached toolbars work differently in Word and Excel. In Word, you can attach a toolbar to a document, and the toolbar will appear and disappear as that document is opened and closed. In Excel, once you open a workbook that has an attached toolbar, a copy of the toolbar is loaded into the Excel workspace; this toolbar will remain available even after you close the workbook.

There are two important points to remember. First, if you need to modify an attached toolbar then you must unattach it, modify it, and then reattach it – otherwise you will just be changing the copy of the toolbar in the Excel workspace, not the copy in the workbook itself. Second, you can delete a toolbar from the Excel workspace (see the following step), but it will reappear every time you load the document to which it is attached. If you are working on a shared computer, you should take care to tidy up after yourself by deleting the local copy of this toolbar after you have finished using this workbook.

Select **ECDL Macros: Cryptography** in the **Toolbars** tab of the **Customize** dialogue and press the **Delete** button. Press **OK** when asked if you are sure – we have saved a copy in the workbook itself. Don't worry that the new toolbar closes.

Click the **Close** button on the **Customize** dialogue box.

Because we have deleted the general instance of the new toolbar, Excel has closed it. Don't worry though, because we saved a copy in the workbook. We will have to close and reopen the workbook to reactivate the toolbar.

Save the workbook as **cryptography.xls**.

Close the workbook and then reopen it. The **ECDL Macros: Cryptography** toolbar should reappear, or be available via **View**, **Toolbars**.

If you see the error message shown in Figure 12.13 then just press the **Enable Macros** button.

If you see the error message shown in Figure 12.14 then perform the following steps. Press **OK** to close the dialogue. From the menu, select **Tools**, **Options**. On the **Security** tab, press the **Macro Security** button and change the **Security Level** to **Medium**. **OK** the dialogues and then close and reopen the worksheet. This time, you will be asked whether you trust the macros (Figure 12.13). Press the **Enable Macros** button.

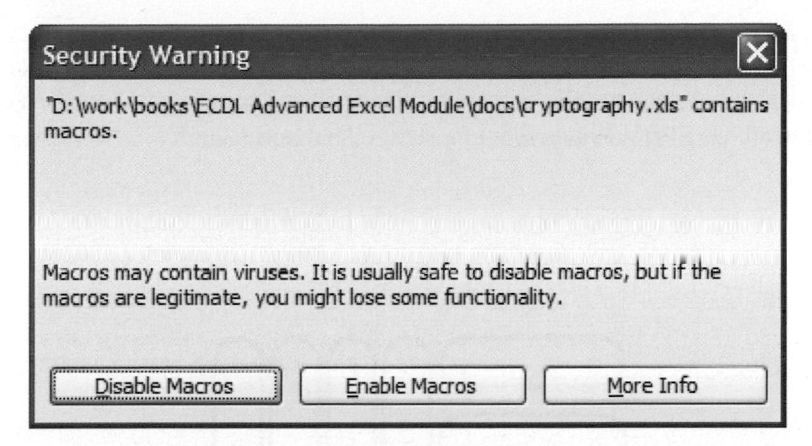

Figure 12.13: Warning that the document you are opening contains macros

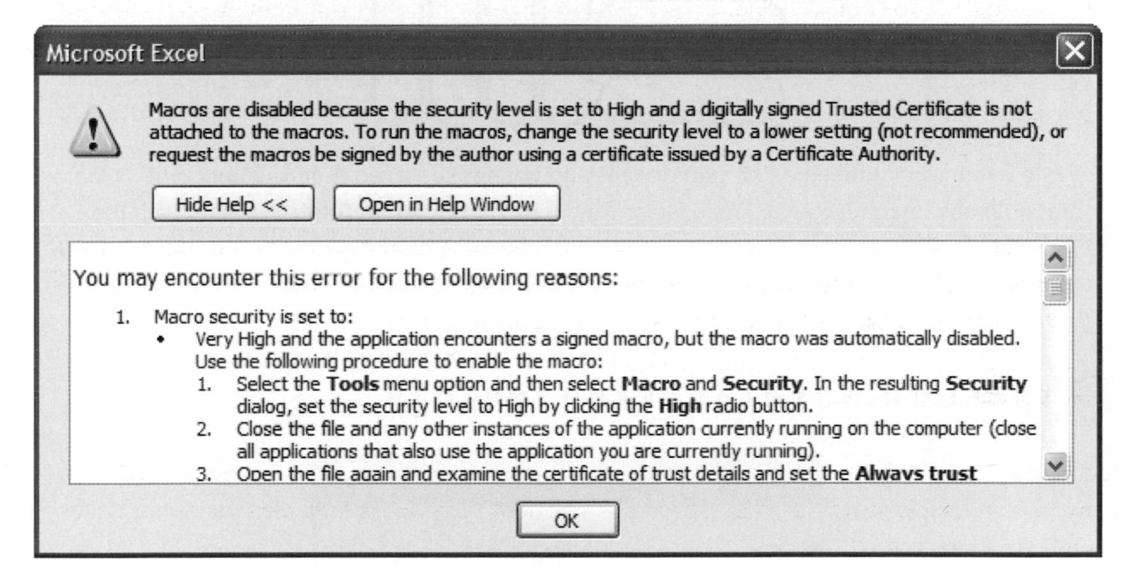

Figure 12.14: Warning that the document contains macros, and that the security level is too high for them to run

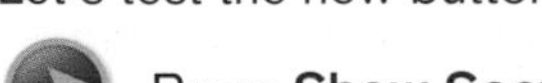

Let's test the new buttons.

Press **Show Secret Message.** The black cells should appear, and the secret message should be visible.

Press **Hide Secret Message.** All of the cells should be shown again.

You should now be able to decode the following secret message.

Just take your car to Lea Road for the hotels inside Seoul.

At wet area, fly the plunderer.

Wait! Chill! Stay!

Test yourself

1. Record a macro that changes the page orientation to **Landscape**, and another that changes it back to **Portrait**. Use **Print Preview** to check that the macros work.

2. Another way to encode messages is to write them in a grid, and then to read down the columns instead of across the rows. For example, using a 4x4 grid to code the message 'Meet me in Brighton' results in 'M M B H E E R T E I I O T N G N'.

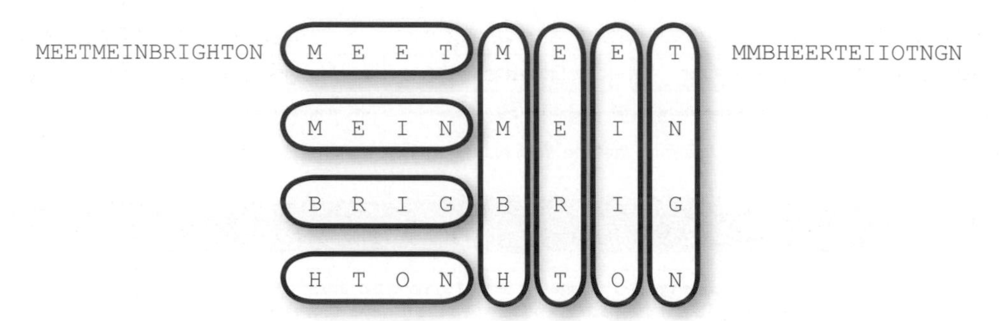

Write a macro that takes a 7x7 grid of cells and transposes it (so that rows become columns and columns become rows). The easiest way to do this is to use **Paste Special** with the **Transpose** box ticked, as shown in Figure 12.15 (see Chapter 1, page 10 for details). Note that you will have to paste the answer into another area of the worksheet.

Use your macro to solve the code **C U S E D R G, O L Y C T E O, N A O R H T O, G T U A E C D, R I H C S O J, A O A K E D O, T N V E C E B.**

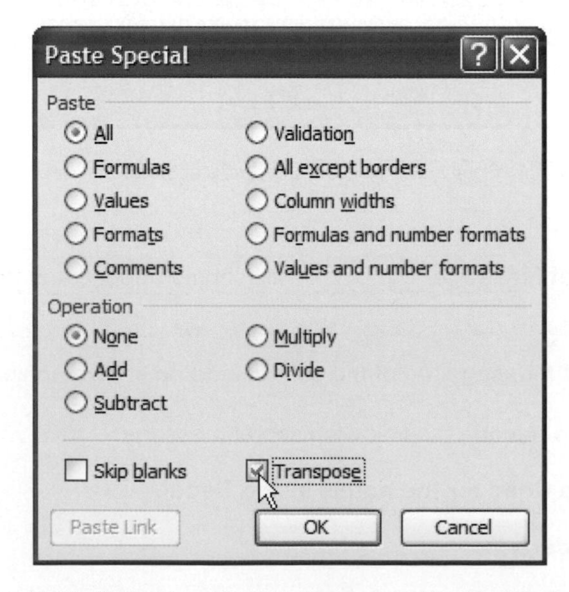

Figure 12.15: Using Paste Special to transpose cells and solve the code

3. Add to your toolbar a button that runs the new macro. Delete your result from Question 2 (select the solution grid cells and press the **Delete** key), then test the new button. Use the **Customize** dialogue's **Attach** button to make sure that the copy of the toolbar embedded in your workbook is kept up to date.

After you have finished the exercises and saved and closed the workbook, do the following step to tidy up.

Right-click on any of Excel's toolbars, and select **Customize** from the menu that appears. Delete the **ECDL Macros: Cryptography** toolbar from your workspace (it is still safely saved in **cryptography.xls**), as shown in Figure 12.16.

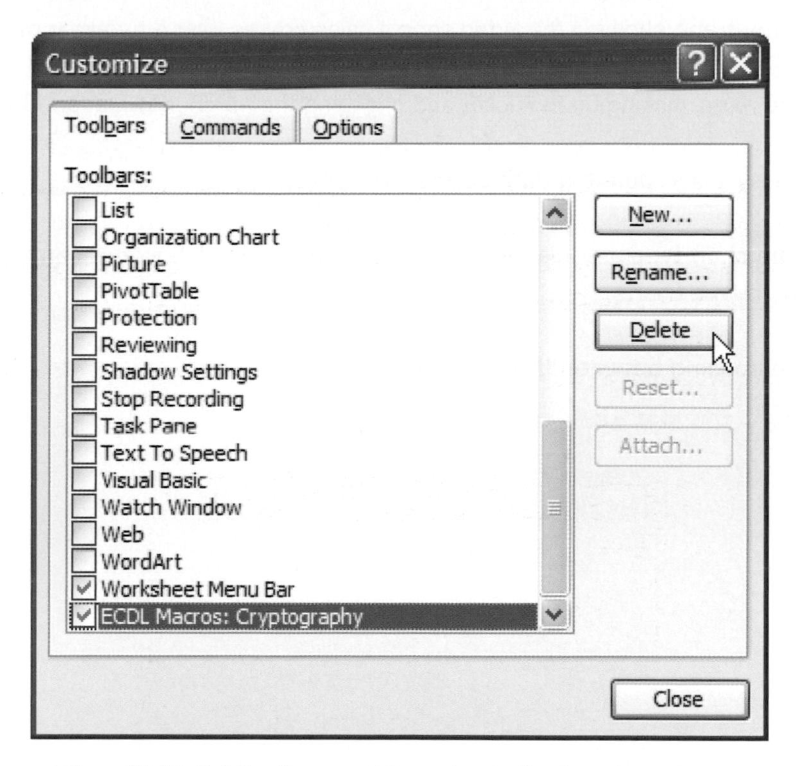

Figure 12.16: Deleting the copy of the custom toolbar from the workspace

13 Graphs

Introduction

It's quite straightforward to create graphs from Excel data, using the default settings.
The **Charts & Graphs** section of the **Advanced ECDL Spreadsheets** course is concerned with how to modify existing graphs or charts to improve their clarity or visual appeal.

This chapter covers graphs with axes; Chapter 14 goes into detail about pie charts.

In this chapter you will

- create a **line graph** showing the video shop's sales figures over a two-year period
- **modify the axes**, making them thicker and changing the number format and font they use
- see how easy it is to **delete a data series** from a graph
- **change the chart type** associated with a data series, and see how this can be used to create mixed-type charts
- **adjust the spacing between the columns** of a column graph.

Graphs

In this chapter, we're going to create a graph that shows the sales of new and ex-rental goods made by the video shop.

Open the file **videoshop.xls** and switch to the **Sales** worksheet. It should look like Figure 13.1.

	A	B	C	D	E	F
1	**Quarter**	**Video Sales**	**DVD Sales**	**Game Sales**	**Quarterly Sales Total**	**Sales Running Total**
2	Q1 2003	£9,068.70	£0.00	£2,178.30	£11,247.00	£11,247.00
3	Q2 2003	£7,996.95	£0.00	£3,061.20	£11,058.15	£22,305.15
4	Q3 2003	£7,403.10	£506.30	£3,837.45	£11,746.85	£34,052.00
5	Q4 2003	£6,132.50	£954.90	£5,014.40	£12,101.80	£46,153.80
6	Q1 2004	£5,110.35	£2,368.45	£5,616.35	£13,095.15	£59,248.95
7	Q2 2004	£4,012.25	£5,104.35	£6,351.50	£15,468.10	£74,717.05
8	Q3 2004	£2,611.10	£9,080.00	£8,795.70	£20,486.80	£95,203.85
9	Q4 2004	£1,335.30	£12,872.55	£8,710.90	£22,918.75	£118,122.60

Figure 13.1: Two years' sales figures

We are going to create a graph with three data series: one each for video, DVD and game sales.

Select cells **A1:D9** and from the menu choose **Insert**, **Chart**. The **Chart Wizard** appears. Set the **Chart type** to **Line**, leave the **Chart sub-type** at its default value, and press the button entitled **Press and Hold to View Sample**. The preview should look like that shown in Figure 13.2.

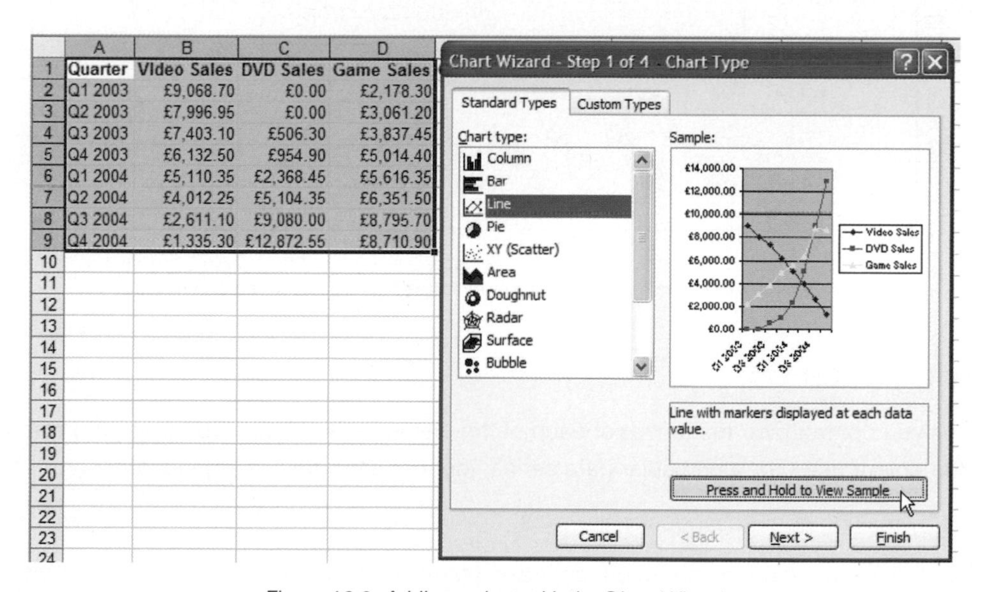

Figure 13.2: Adding a chart with the Chart Wizard

Click **Finish**.

Excel inserts an initial version of the graph into the worksheet. This is a good start, but there is some tidying up to do.

Move and resize the graph so that it looks like the one in Figure 13.3 – click and drag the graph to move it; use the black handles to resize it.

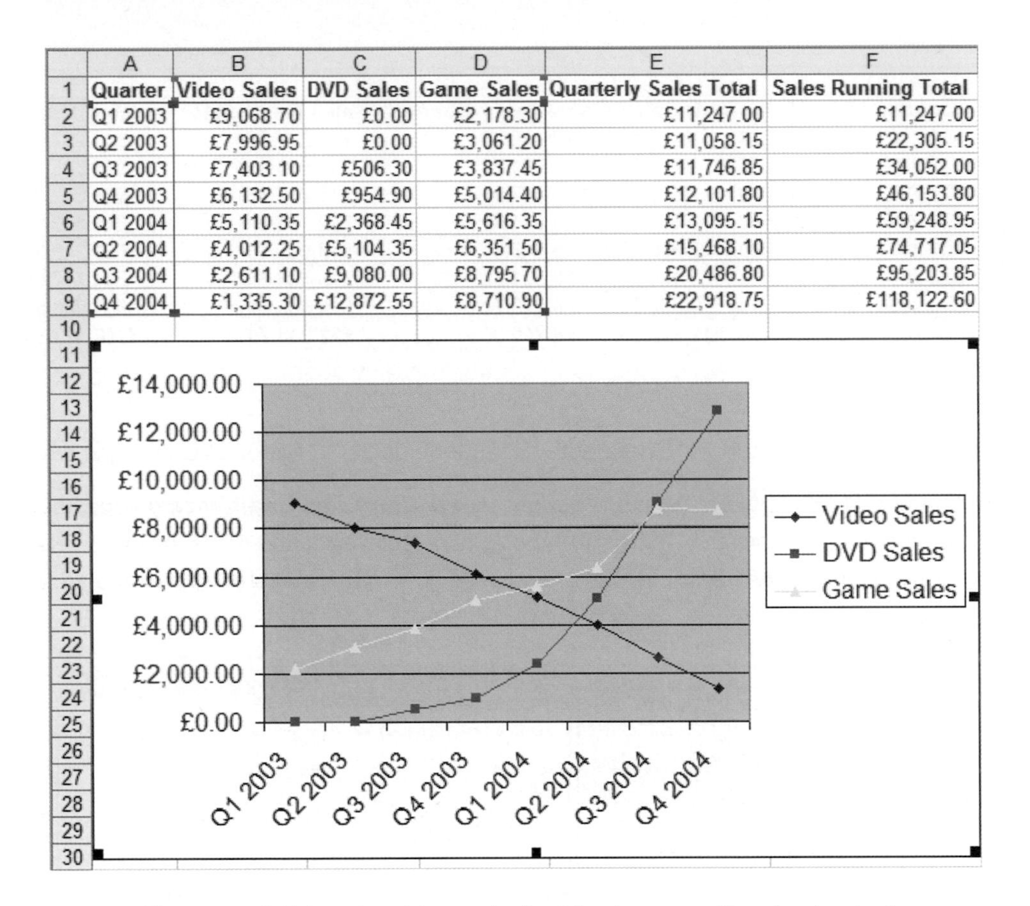

	A	B	C	D	E	F
1	Quarter	Video Sales	DVD Sales	Game Sales	Quarterly Sales Total	Sales Running Total
2	Q1 2003	£9,068.70	£0.00	£2,178.30	£11,247.00	£11,247.00
3	Q2 2003	£7,996.95	£0.00	£3,061.20	£11,058.15	£22,305.15
4	Q3 2003	£7,403.10	£506.30	£3,837.45	£11,746.85	£34,052.00
5	Q4 2003	£6,132.50	£954.90	£5,014.40	£12,101.80	£46,153.80
6	Q1 2004	£5,110.35	£2,368.45	£5,616.35	£13,095.15	£59,248.95
7	Q2 2004	£4,012.25	£5,104.35	£6,351.50	£15,468.10	£74,717.05
8	Q3 2004	£2,611.10	£9,080.00	£8,795.70	£20,486.80	£95,203.85
9	Q4 2004	£1,335.30	£12,872.55	£8,710.90	£22,918.75	£118,122.60

Figure 13.3: Initial version of the graph, after it has been repositioned and resized

Modifying axes

Excel gives you control over the format of each of the elements that make up the graph; you can change the colour used for a particular data series, the font used for the legend, and so on.

We'll start by making some changes to the axes.

Right-click any of the numbers on the Y-axis (vertical). A menu should appear with the option **Format Axis**; select this.

The **Format Axis** dialogue appears. Let's make the axis line thicker.

Switch to the **Patterns** tab. Choose a thicker line from the **Weight** drop-down list, as shown in Figure 13.4, and press **OK**.

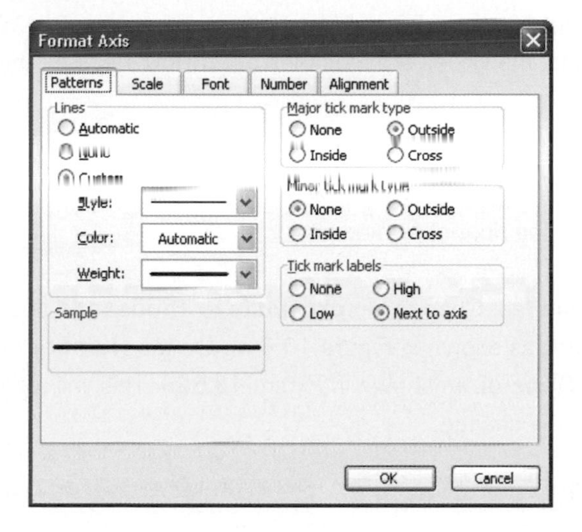

Figure 13.4: Increasing the weight of the Y-axis

Click the X-axis (horizontal) to select it (it will show square black selection handles at both ends). From the menu, select **Edit**, **Repeat Format Axis** (or press **Ctrl+Y**). The X-axis becomes thicker. This is a useful tip to remember – it's quicker than making the same change twice via the **Format Axis** dialogue.

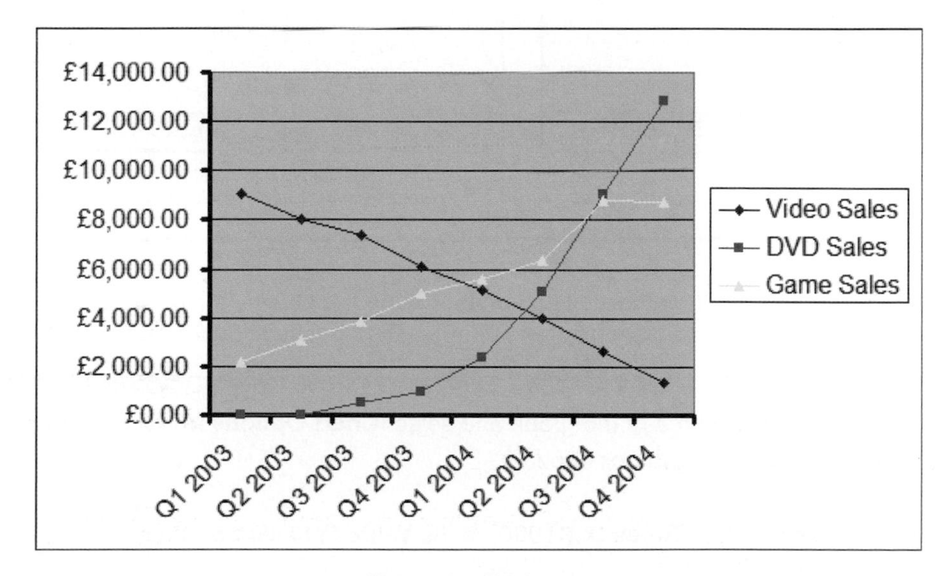

Figure 13.5: Thicker axes

Let's look at some of the other options available on the **Format Axis** dialogue.

Excel has automatically chosen a sensible step size of £2,000 for the values marked against the Y-axis, but they take up a lot of space. It would be better to just show 2, 4, 6, and so on, and to add a description explaining that the values are multiples of £1,000. Let's try this.

Double-click anywhere along the Y-axis. This is a quicker way of bringing up the **Format Axis** dialogue than using the right-click menu.

Syllabus Ref: AM4.2.5.2
Format chart axes numbers or text.

Change to the **Scale** tab. Change **Display units** to **Thousands** and untick **Show display units label on chart**, as shown in Figure 13.6(a). On the **Number** tab, change the **Category** from **Currency** to **General**, as shown in Figure 13.6(b). This will remove the pound signs. Press **OK** to make the change.

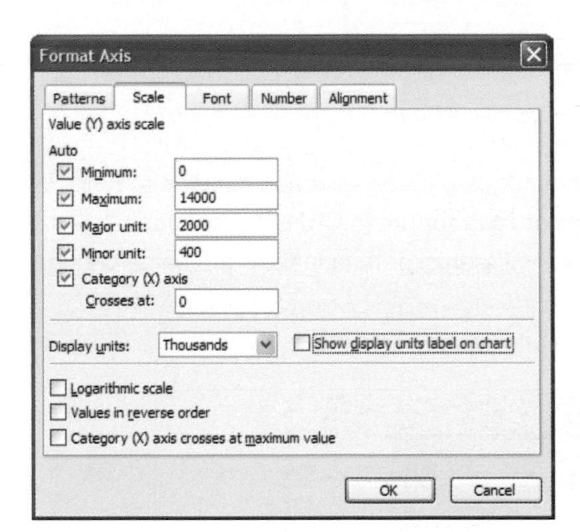

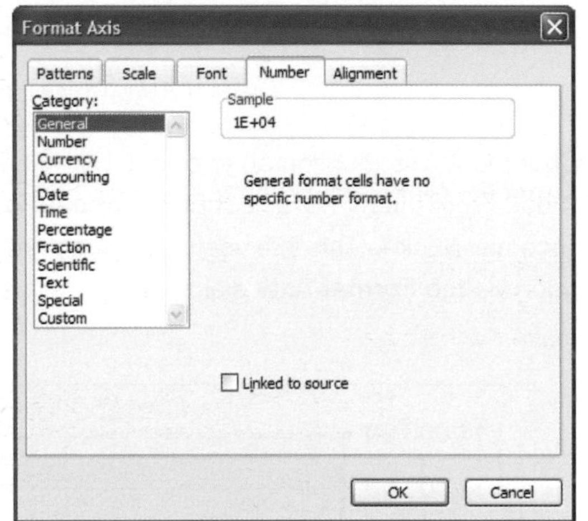

Figure 13.6: Overriding the format of the Y-axis (a) Scale and (b) Number

TIP

Notice that you could use the other options on the **Scale** tab shown in Figure 13.6(a) to change the maximum and minimum numbers and the jump between successive labels.

Right-click in any blank area of the graph and select **Chart Options** from the resultant menu. The **Chart Options** dialogue box appears.

Click the **Titles** tab. Type **Sales (x £1000)** in the **Value (Y) axis** box, then press **OK**.

The graph should now look like Figure 13.7.

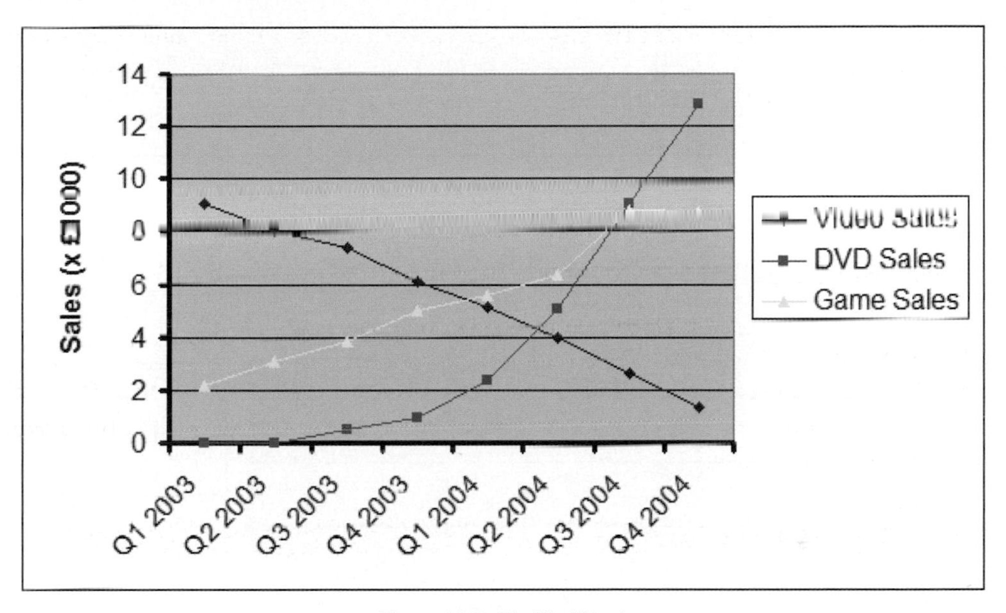

Figure 13.7: Modified Y-axis

Let's change the font used for the quarter names along the X-axis.

Bring up the **Format Axis** dialogue for the X-axis. Change the **Font** to **Georgia** (or some other font if you prefer) and change the **Size** to **9**, as shown in Figure 13.8. Press **OK** to make the change.

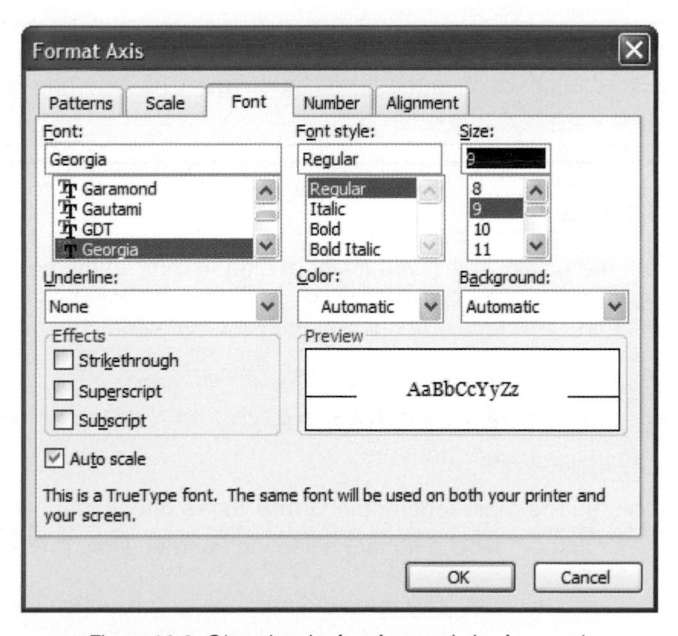

Figure 13.8: Changing the font face and size for an axis

Apply the same change to the Y-axis (remember the shortcut; you don't need to use the **Format Axis** dialogue).

The graph should now look like Figure 13.9.

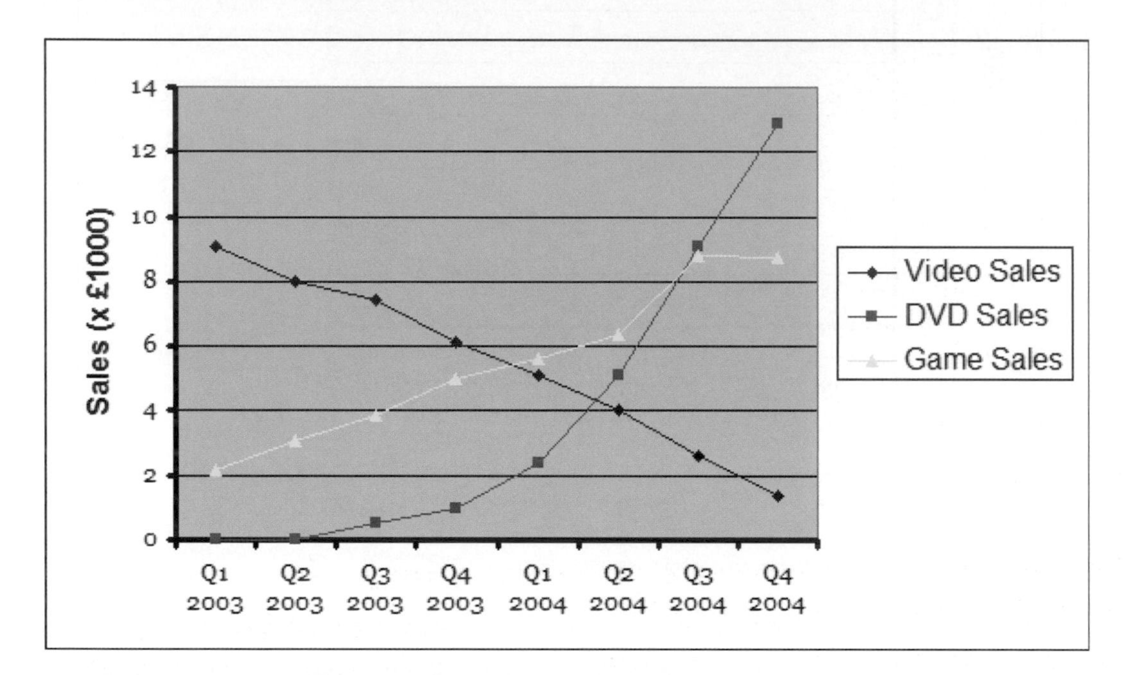

Figure 13.9: Graph after changing the format of the axes

Notice that the X-axis labels have changed from tilted (Figure 13.7) to horizontal (Figure 13.9) as a result of reducing the size of the font.

Deleting data series

If you wanted to concentrate on film sales, you might decide to remove the game sales line from the graph. This is easy to do.

Syllabus Ref: AM4.2.5.5
Delete a data series in a chart.

Click anywhere on the line representing the **Game Sales** data series. This selects it (each of its data points should get a solid square selection handle). Now press the **Delete** key.

The **Games Sales** data series is completely removed from the graph, which should now look like Figure 13.10.

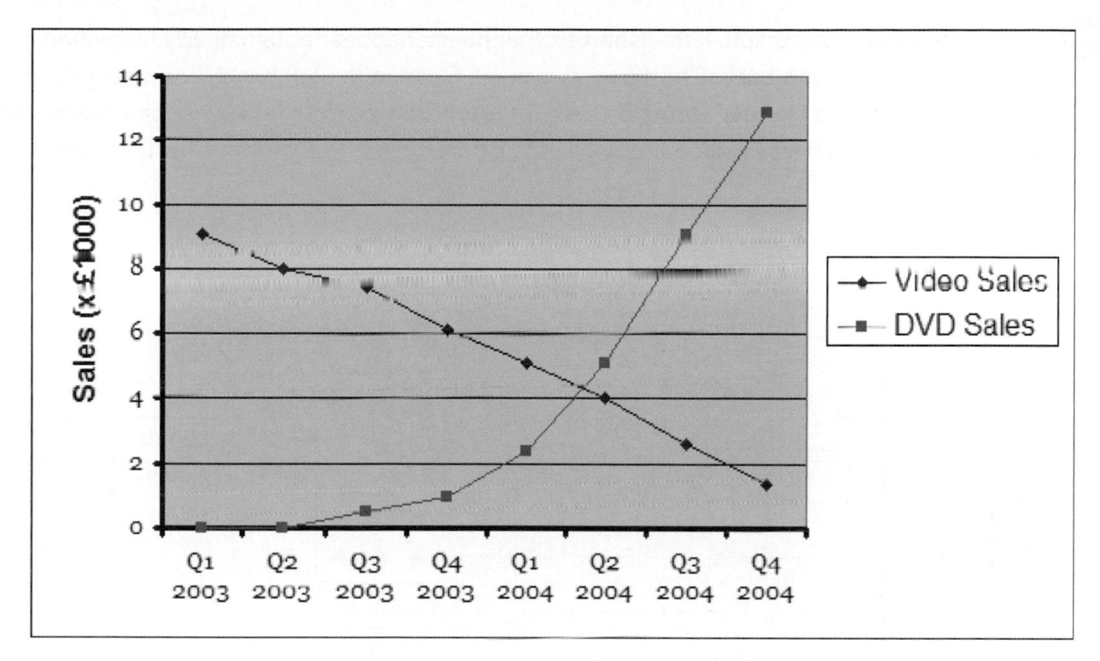

Figure 13.10: Graph after deleting one of the data series

This couldn't be easier! However, we don't really want to delete the data series, so we'll undo the deletion.

From the menu, select **Edit**, **Undo Clear** (or press **Ctrl+Z**).

The graph now looks like it did before (Figure 13.9).

If you delete a data series that contains very large or very small values, then Excel will rescale the Y-axis to fit the data series that remain.

Changing the chart type

Syllabus Ref: AM4.2.5.6
Modify the chart type for a defined data series.

Perhaps this information would look better as a column graph. Thankfully, we don't have to throw away our line graph and build a column graph from scratch. Instead, we can change the graph type associated with the data series themselves.

You might expect that the chart type would be a property of the chart itself. However, it is, in effect, a property of the data series (although, when you create a new chart of a particular type, that type is applied as the default chart type to all of the series). The advantage of this arrangement is that you can mix and match chart types for different data series on the same chart, as we shall see in the next example.

Let's change the **Game Sales** data series from a line graph to a column graph. We'll use the **Chart** toolbar to do this.

Click anywhere in the graph. If the **Chart** toolbar doesn't appear automatically then open it by selecting **View**, **Toolbars**, **Chart** from the menu. Change the left-hand drop-down list in the **Chart** toolbar to **Series "Game Sales"**; the **Game Sales** data series becomes selected. Now, change the **Chart Type** drop-down in the **Chart** toolbar to **Column Chart**, as shown in Figure 13.11.

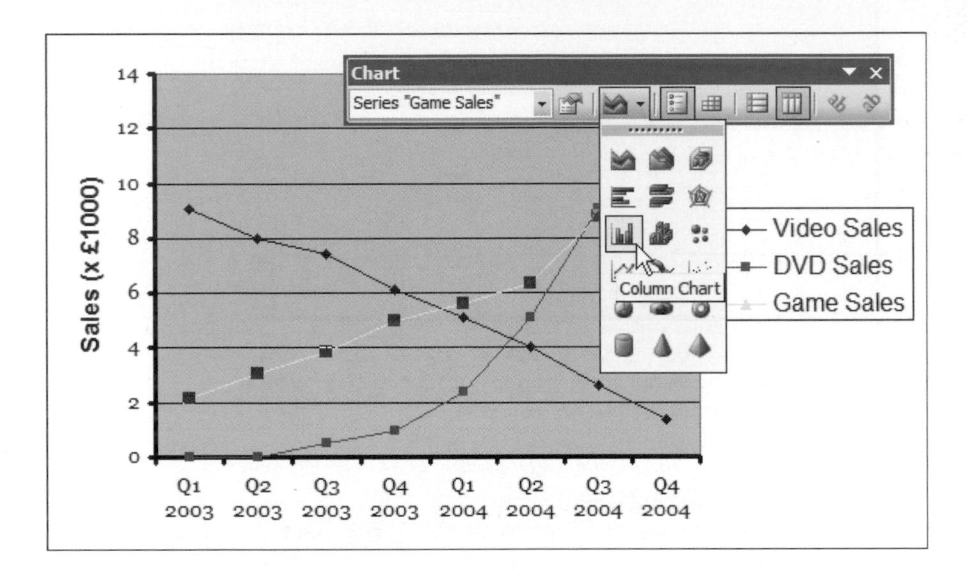

Figure 13.11: Changing the chart type associated with a data series

The line representing the **Game Sales** data series is replaced by a set of columns, so that we get the mixed-type graph shown in Figure 13.12. Note that not all of the chart types can be combined in this way – for example, you cannot combine 2D and 3D chart types on the same chart – but you are likely to find that any combination you actually want to use is possible.

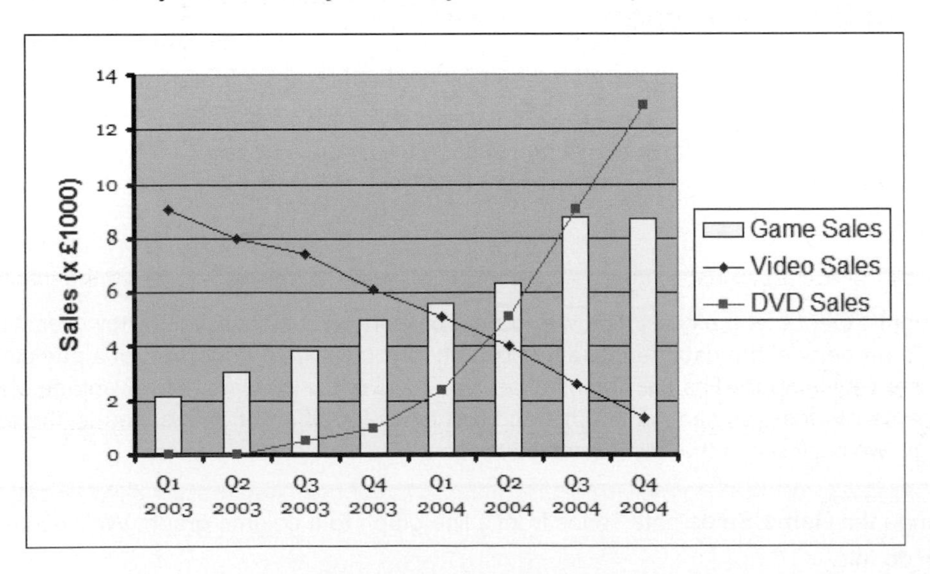

Figure 13.12: Mixed-type chart

We want to change the type of the other two series as well; for the sake of variety, we'll use a slightly different method.

Right-click the line representing the **Video Sales** data series (which will select it) and choose **Chart Type** from the menu that appears. The **Chart Type** dialogue appears.

This is the method you should use if you want to choose a specific **sub-type** for your chart, or you want to choose one of the more unusual chart types. The **Chart Type** dialogue has lots more options than the **Chart Type** drop-down list on the **Chart** toolbar.

Select **Column** as the **Chart type** and check that the first of the **sub-types** is selected, as shown in Figure 13.13. Press **OK**.

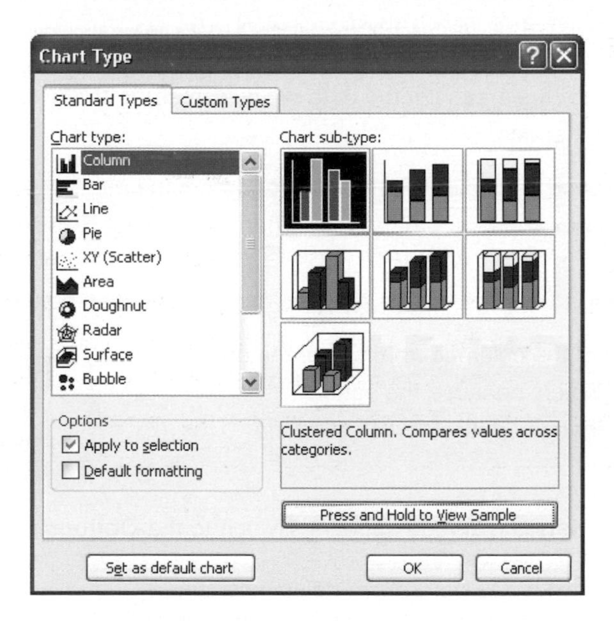

Figure 13.13: Changing the chart type using the Chart Type dialogue

Click the line representing the **DVD Sales** data series; this selects it. From the menu, select **Edit**, **Repeat Chart Type**.

The result of changing the data series to columns can be seen in Figure 13.14. This is what we would have had if we had chosen a column graph as the graph type when originally creating the graph.

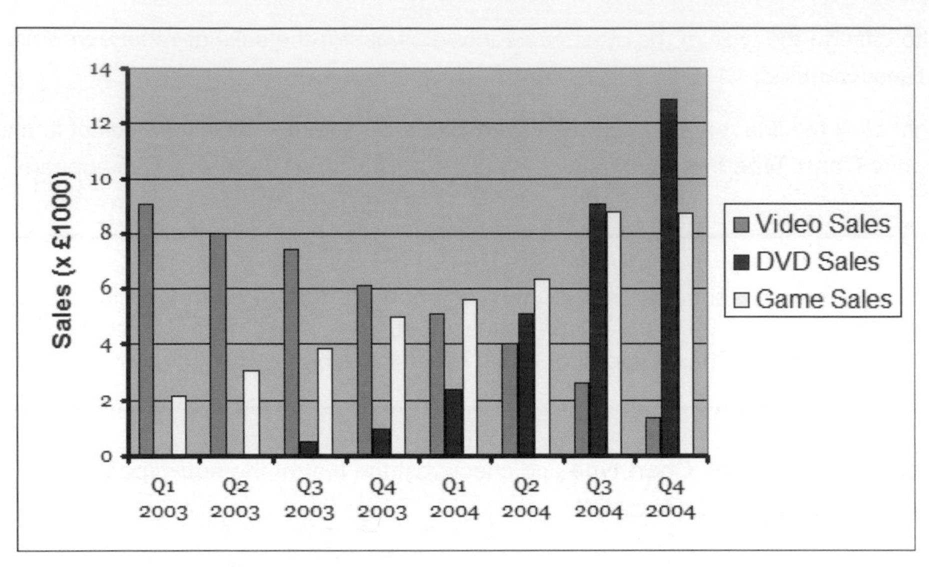

Figure 13.14: The graph after changing the data series to columns

Let's also move the legend (the area with the data series names) to the bottom of the graph. This will give the columns more space.

Right-click the legend and select **Format Legend** from the menu that appears. The **Format Legend** dialogue box appears. On the **Placement** tab, select **Bottom** and then press **OK**.

The last thing we're going to change on this graph is the gap between columns.

Double-click one of the columns from any of the data series; it doesn't matter which, because the setting we are going to change applies across all of the series in a graph.

Syllabus Ref: AM4.2.5.7

Widen the gap between columns/bars in a 2D chart.

The **Format Data Series** dialogue appears. Switch to the **Options** tab.

The **Overlap** and **Gap width** boxes control the column spacing.

Overlap controls the degree to which the columns of consecutive series overlap with one another. It is expressed as a percentage of the column width: a value of **50** would cause each column in a group to overlap the next by half its width. A negative number can be used to add space between the columns of consecutive series, again expressed as a percentage of the column width. The default value of **0** makes the columns touch.

Gap width controls the gap between each group of columns; for example, between the three **Q4 2003** columns and the three **Q1 2004** columns. This is also set as a percentage relative to the column width, so that the default of **150** means that the gap between each column group is one and a half times the width of a column.

Change **Overlap** to **-20**: this will create a gap of one-fifth the column width between each pair of **Video Sales**, **DVD Sales** and **Game Sales** columns. Change **Gap width** to **140**, which will reduce the gap between each group of columns to just under one and a half times the width of a single column. Press **OK** to make the changes.

The technique for changing the gaps is identical for column graphs and bar graphs.

Try to avoid spacing columns exactly one column-width apart, since this makes it harder to see the separate groups. This is why we set the **Gap width** to **140** instead of **100**.

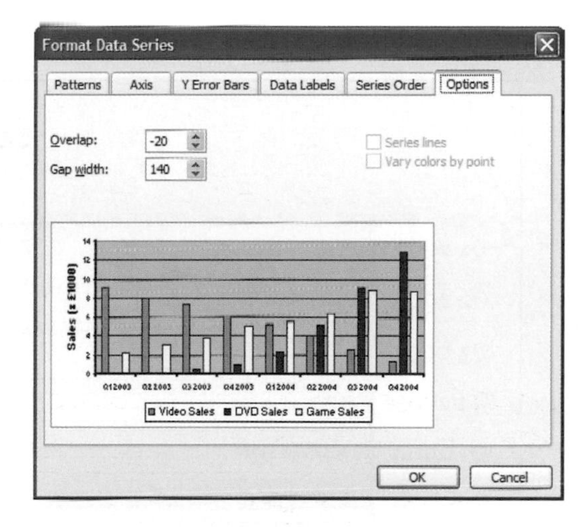

Figure 13.15: Changing the gap between columns

The final graph should look like Figure 13.16.

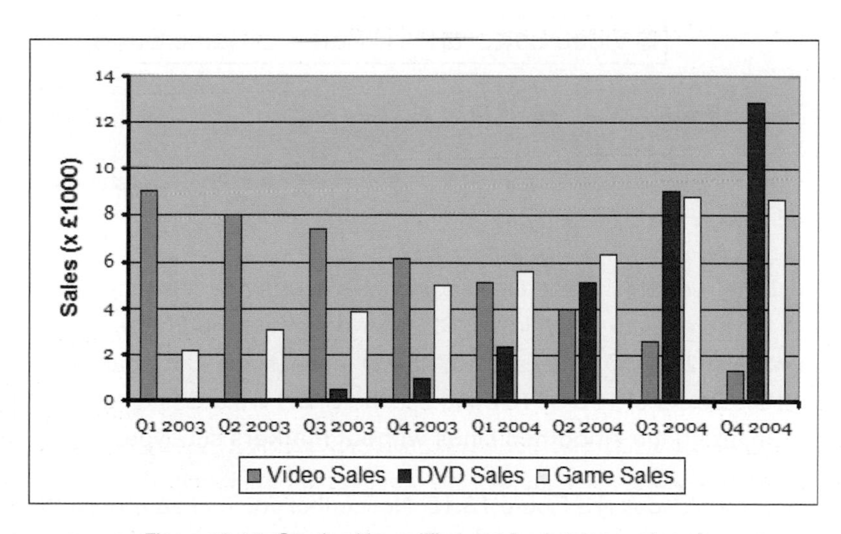

Figure 13.16: Graph with modified spacing between columns

Save the workbook.

Test yourself

1. Still on the **Sales** tab of the **videoshop.xls** workbook, change the graph type from a **Column Chart** to a **Bar Chart**. [Hint: do this for the graph as a whole, rather than for the three data series in turn]. Use the **Alignment** tab of the **Format Axis** dialogue to make the **Sales (x £1000)** title horizontal. Give the bars a **20%** overlap and reduce the gap width to **40%**. Bring up the **Format Axis** dialogue for the Y-axis and set the **Categories in reverse order** option in the **Scale** tab.

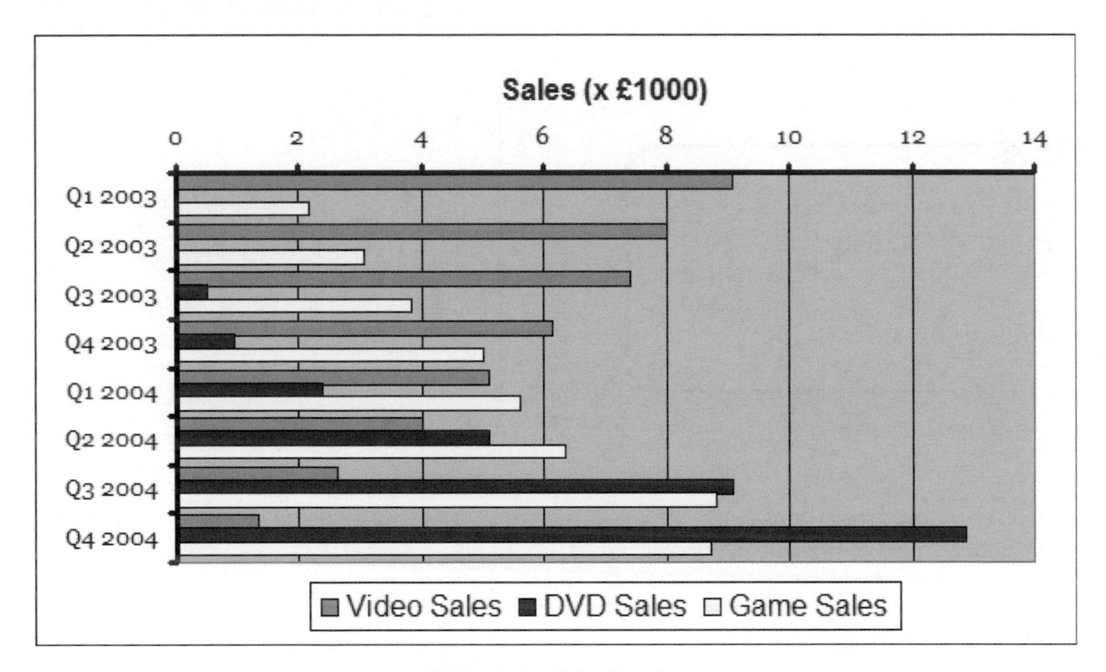

Figure 13.17: Sales bar chart

2. Don't let the following example intimidate you – you don't need to understand any of the maths, just how to edit the graph!

   Create a new blank workbook. Type the headings **x**, **sin**, **cos** and **tan** in cells **B1:E1**. Fill cells **A2:A101** with the numbers **0** to **99**. In cell **B2**, type the formula **=A2*PI()/50**. Give cells **C2:E2** the formulas **=SIN(B2)**, **=COS(B2)** and **=TAN(B2)** respectively. Copy each of these formulas down to row **101**. Select cells **B1:E101** and use the **Chart Wizard** to create an **XY (Scatter)** graph from them, using the **smoothed Lines without markers** sub-type.

   The initial graph should look like Figure 13.18. Notice that you can barely see the lines for **sin** or **cos** because the values for **tan** are so big. (**1.8E+16** is scientific notation meaning **18 000 000 000 000 000**.

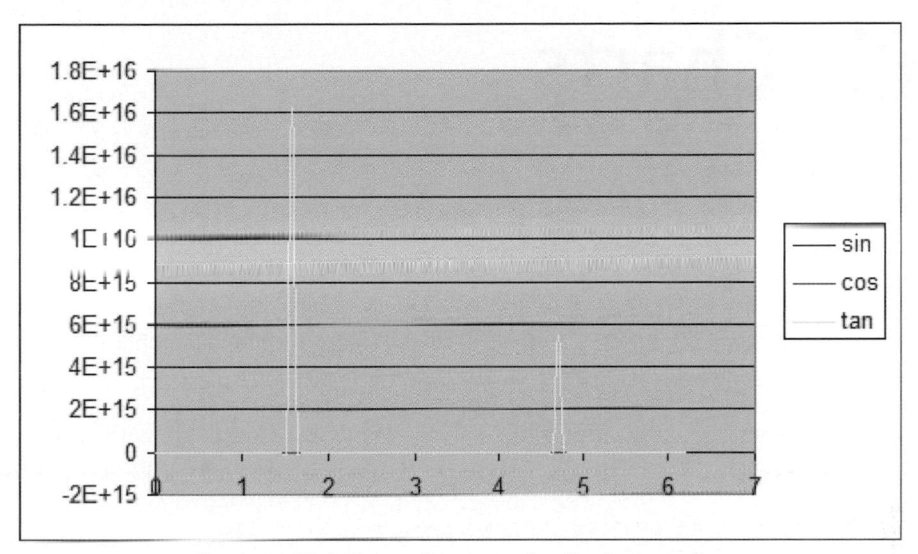

Figure 13.18: Initial graph – the tan function is dominating

Delete the **tan** data series. Notice how the values for **sin** and **cos** are bounded by **+1** and **-1**: no wonder they were invisible when **tan** was plotted too. Undo the deletion and change the **Minimum** and **Maximum** values of the Y-axis to **-1.5** and **1.5**, with a **Major unit** of **0.5** and a **Minor unit** of **0.1**. (The **Major unit** controls the frequency of the numbered labels and the major gridlines, and the **Minor unit** controls the frequency of the minor tick marks.) On the **Patterns** tab, set the **Minor tick mark type** to **Outside** (so the ticks fall outside the axis instead of overlapping the graph area). Increase the line weight of both axes. Give the X-axis a **Maximum** of **6.28** and a **Major unit** of **1.57**.

Your final graph should look like Figure 13.19.

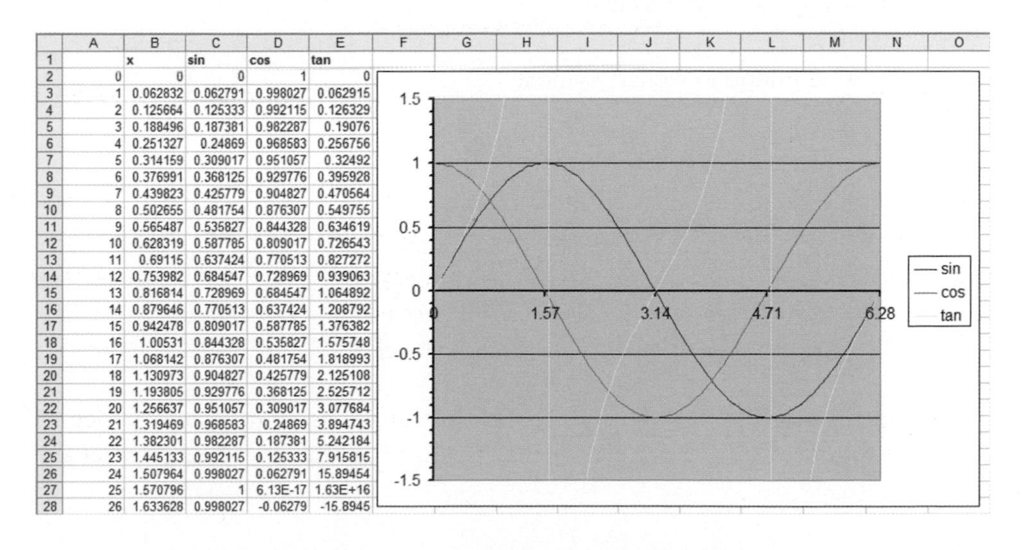

	A	B	C	D	E
1		x	sin	cos	tan
2	0	0	0	1	0
3	1	0.062832	0.062791	0.998027	0.062915
4	2	0.125664	0.125333	0.992115	0.126329
5	3	0.188496	0.187381	0.982287	0.19076
6	4	0.251327	0.24869	0.968583	0.256756
7	5	0.314159	0.309017	0.951057	0.32492
8	6	0.376991	0.368125	0.929776	0.395928
9	7	0.439823	0.425779	0.904827	0.470564
10	8	0.502655	0.481754	0.876307	0.549755
11	9	0.565487	0.535827	0.844328	0.634619
12	10	0.628319	0.587785	0.809017	0.726543
13	11	0.69115	0.637424	0.770513	0.827272
14	12	0.753982	0.684547	0.728969	0.939063
15	13	0.816814	0.728969	0.684547	1.064892
16	14	0.879646	0.770513	0.637424	1.208792
17	15	0.942478	0.809017	0.587785	1.376382
18	16	1.00531	0.844328	0.535827	1.575748
19	17	1.068142	0.876307	0.481754	1.818993
20	18	1.130973	0.904827	0.425779	2.125108
21	19	1.193805	0.929776	0.368125	2.525712
22	20	1.256637	0.951057	0.309017	3.077684
23	21	1.319469	0.968583	0.24869	3.894743
24	22	1.382301	0.982287	0.187381	5.242184
25	23	1.445133	0.992115	0.125333	7.915815
26	24	1.507964	0.998027	0.062791	15.89454
27	25	1.570796	1	6.13E-17	1.63E+16
28	26	1.633628	0.998027	-0.06279	-15.8945

Figure 13.19: Completed graph with customised axes

14 Pie Charts

Introduction

This chapter will continue to explore charts. While the previous chapter dealt with various graph types with axes, this chapter concentrates on **pie charts**. As before, the emphasis is on modifying existing charts, so I have kept the steps you need to follow to create the initial charts as simple as possible.

We continue with the example of the video shop's sales, this time looking at how the proportion of sales made up by videos, DVDs and games has changed over the two years 2003 and 2004.

In this chapter you will

- **create a pie chart** representing the Q4 2004 sales
- learn how to **'explode the pie'** and see how segments can be moved relative to one another
- learn how to rotate a pie chart by changing the **angle of the first slice**
- learn how to **reposition** the different chart elements: title, legend and data labels
- learn how to **edit the data labels**
- **insert clip art** and group it with a chart
- add a **background image** to a chart element.

Pie charts

Open the file **videoshop.xls** and change to the **Sales** worksheet. This should show the column graph you created in the previous chapter (or the bar chart if you have already done the **Test yourself** section).

Let's create a simple pie chart to show the relative contributions made by video sales, DVD sales and game sales in Q4 2004.

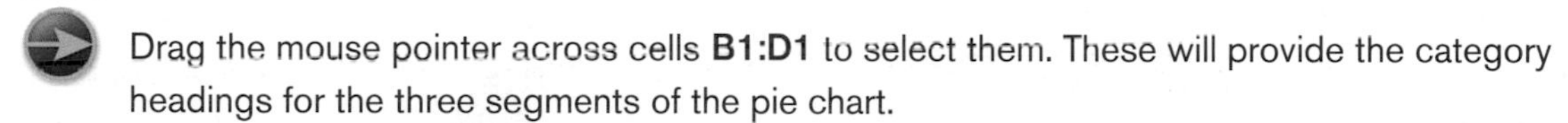

Drag the mouse pointer across cells **B1:D1** to select them. These will provide the category headings for the three segments of the pie chart.

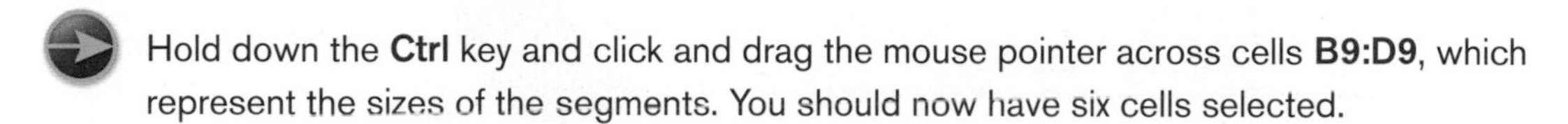

Hold down the **Ctrl** key and click and drag the mouse pointer across cells **B9:D9**, which represent the sizes of the segments. You should now have six cells selected.

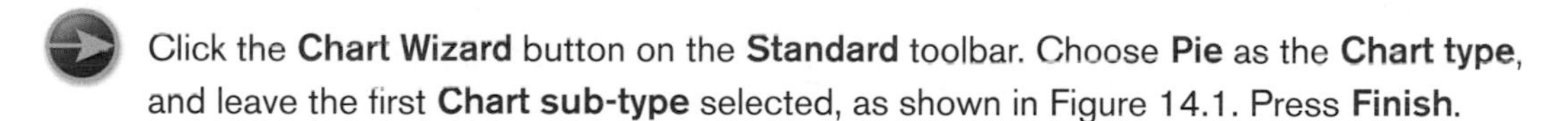

Click the **Chart Wizard** button on the **Standard** toolbar. Choose **Pie** as the **Chart type**, and leave the first **Chart sub-type** selected, as shown in Figure 14.1. Press **Finish**.

Chart Wizard

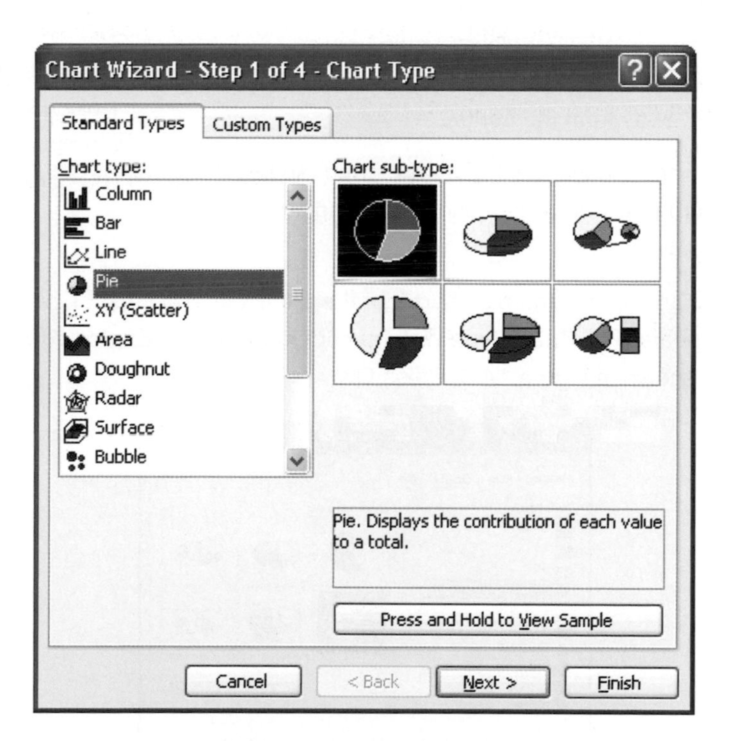

Figure 14.1: Creating a pie chart

Click in a blank area of the pie chart and drag it to the right of the graph.

Your worksheet should now look like Figure 14.2. From the new pie chart you can see at a glance that in Q4 2004 **DVD Sales** are the most significant, followed by **Game Sales**. **Video Sales** make up only a small part of the total sales.

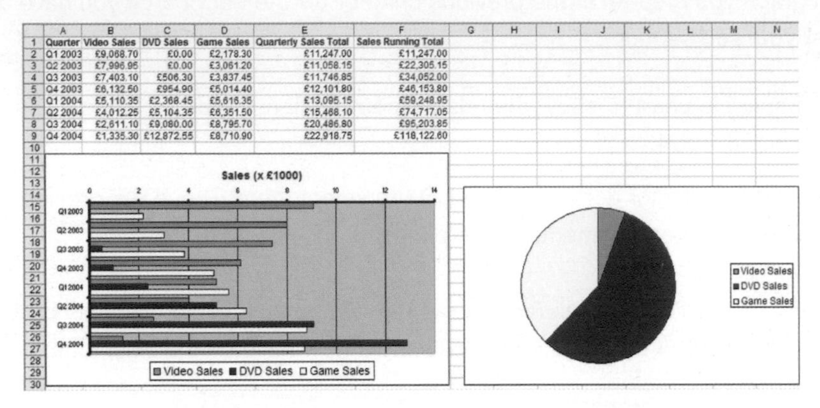

Quarter	Video Sales	DVD Sales	Game Sales	Quarterly Sales Total	Sales Running Total
Q1 2003	£9,068.70	£0.00	£2,178.30	£11,247.00	£11,247.00
Q2 2003	£7,996.95	£0.00	£3,061.20	£11,058.15	£22,305.15
Q3 2003	£7,403.10	£506.30	£3,837.45	£11,746.85	£34,052.00
Q4 2003	£6,132.50	£954.90	£5,014.40	£12,101.80	£46,153.80
Q1 2004	£5,110.35	£2,368.45	£5,616.35	£13,095.15	£59,248.95
Q2 2004	£4,012.25	£5,104.35	£6,351.50	£15,468.10	£74,717.05
Q3 2004	£2,611.10	£9,080.00	£8,795.70	£20,486.80	£95,203.85
Q4 2004	£1,335.30	£12,872.55	£8,710.90	£22,918.75	£118,122.60

Figure 14.2: Sales worksheet showing the new pie chart

Exploding pie!

Although it sounds like something a clown would use, an **exploded pie** is a pie chart in which each segment can be moved independently away from the centre.

Syllabus Ref: AM4.2.5.4

'Explode' all the segments in a pie chart.

We can change this normal pie chart into an exploded pie by changing the chart sub-type, as we did when changing lines to columns in Chapter 13.

Right-click a blank area in the pie chart (not the pie itself) and select **Chart Type** from the menu that appears. The **Chart Type** dialogue appears. Select **Exploded Pie** for the **Chart sub-type**, as shown in Figure 14.3. Press **OK**.

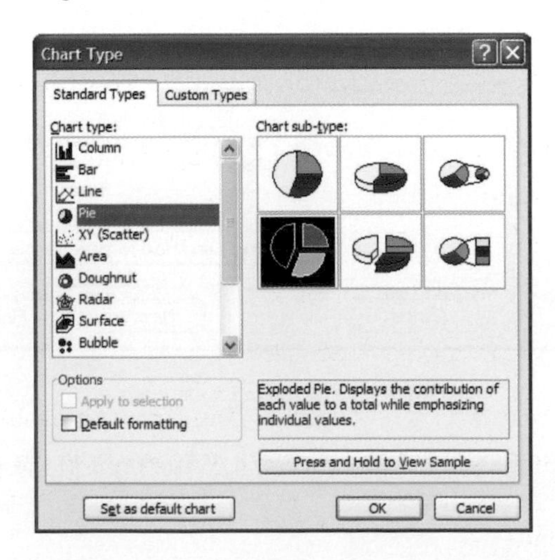

Figure 14.3: Changing an ordinary pie chart into an exploded pie

The pie chart changes so that each of the segments is separated from the others.

Excel 2003 is more forgiving than earlier versions and lets you explode a normal pie chart by dragging its segments, without requiring you to change the chart type. However, changing the chart type is still probably safer in terms of compatibility with other versions of Excel and other spreadsheet programs.

With the whole data series selected (click once on any segment of the pie), click and drag one of the segments. Two guide lines appear (see Figure 14.4) during the drag: a segment-shaped area shows where the segment you are dragging will be placed, and a circle shows the area the exploded pie will cover. Drop the segment when you have 'exploded the pie' by roughly the amount shown in Figure 14.4.

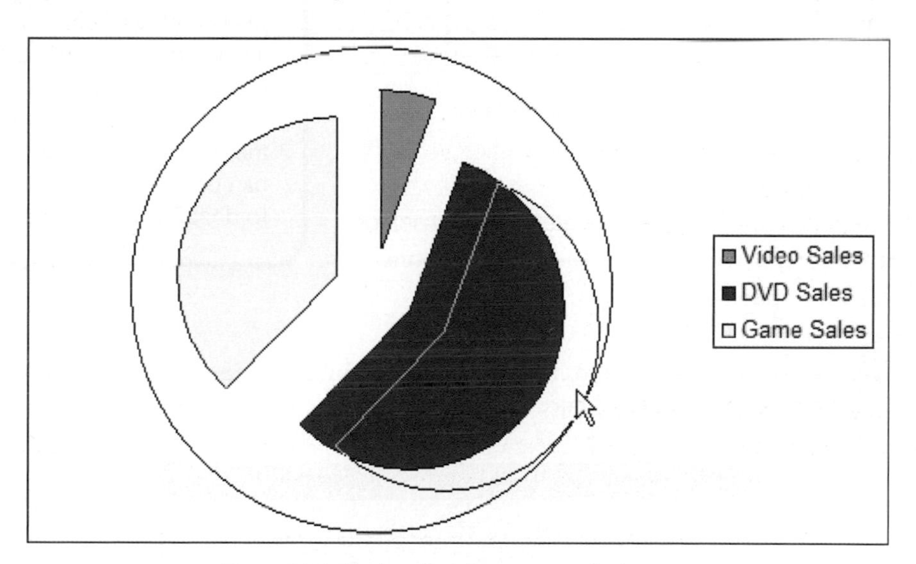

Figure 14.4: Moving all of the segments further apart

Because the whole data series was selected, all of the segments have been moved, in this case slightly further out from the centre.

Click and drag any one of the segments back to the middle, and then drop it. This should return the pie chart to its original state, without any gaps between the segments.

It is also possible to move a single segment, as follows.

Click on the small blue **Video Sales** segment. The selection handles should change to show that just this segment is now selected, not the whole pie. Drag this segment outwards slightly. This emphasises the **Video Sales** segment by moving it on its own away from the other segments.

Click away from the chart to deselect it, then right-click the chart and select **Format Data Series** from the menu that appears. Experiment with adjusting the **Angle of first slice** control on the **Options** tab, as shown in Figure 14.5. Press **Cancel** to discard the change – we'll keep the small slice at the top.

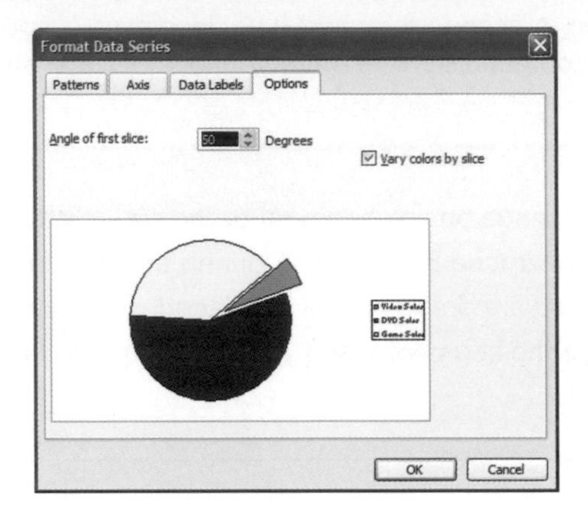

Figure 14.5: Changing the angle of the first slice

Syllabus Ref: AM4.2.5.1
Change angle of pie chart slices

If you click on a pie chart when it is already selected, you change the selection to the segment of pie you clicked on.
If you click on a pie chart when neither it nor a segment of it is already selected then you select the whole pie data series. You can click outside the chart area to deselect everything.

Let's add a title to the pie chart.

Right-click in a blank area of the pie chart and select **Chart Options** from the menu. The **Chart Options** dialogue box appears.

Click on the **Titles** tab, then enter the **Chart title** as **Sales by category (Q4 2004)**, as shown in Figure 14.6. Press **OK**.

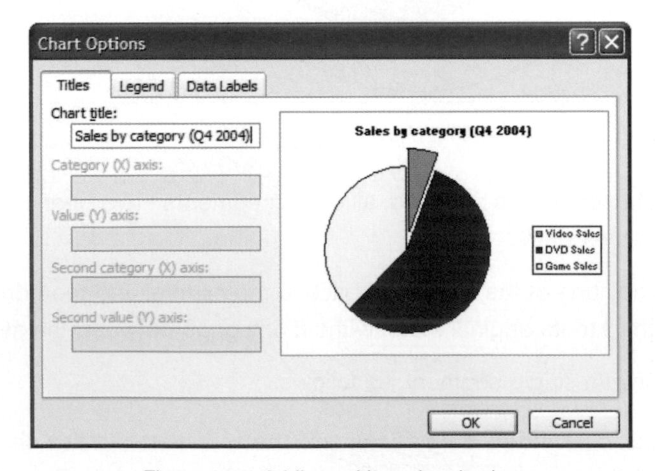

Figure 14.6: Adding a title to the pie chart

Repositioning chart elements

Syllabus Ref: AM4.2.5.3

Reposition title, legend, or data labels in a chart.

You can move other parts of the chart in much the same way as you have just moved the pie segment.

The **legend** (the box that tells you which colour corresponds to which category) is special because it has some default positions that it can snap to. We'll look at these first, before showing that you can drag it anywhere else you want too.

Double-click the legend, to display the **Format Legend** dialogue. Switch to the **Placement** tab. The options here are self-explanatory, apart from **Corner**, so select this one to see what it does (see Figure 14.7). Press **OK**.

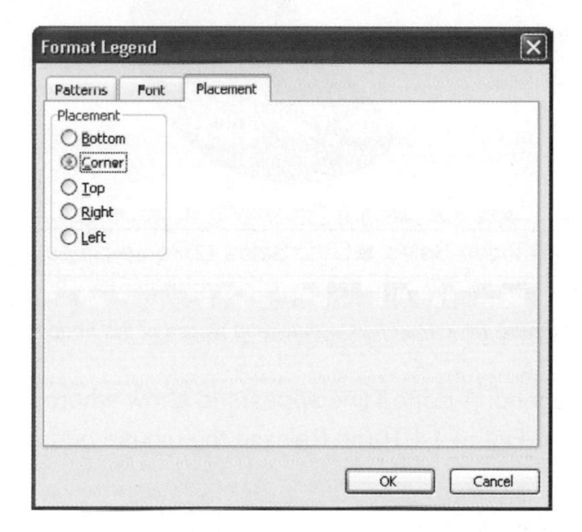

Figure 14.7: Changing the placement of the legend

It turns out that this means the top-right corner. Unfortunately, the pie chart gets squashed up into the bottom-left corner (see Figure 14.8), so this isn't very satisfactory.

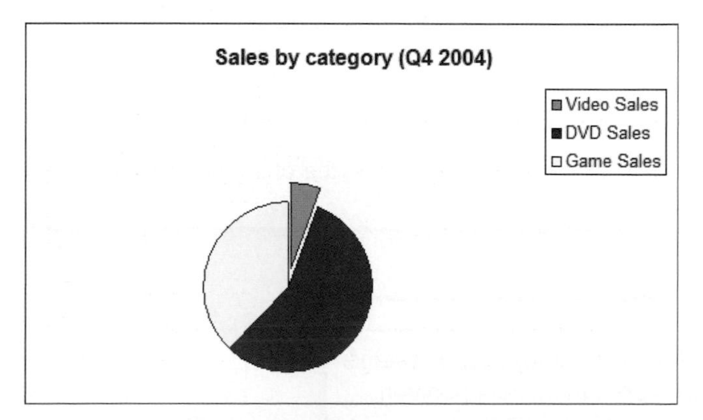

Figure 14.8: Pie chart with legend placed in the corner

Change the legend placement to **Bottom**. Notice how the legend has been changed to have a horizontal layout, and the pie has been re-enlarged, as shown in Figure 14.9.

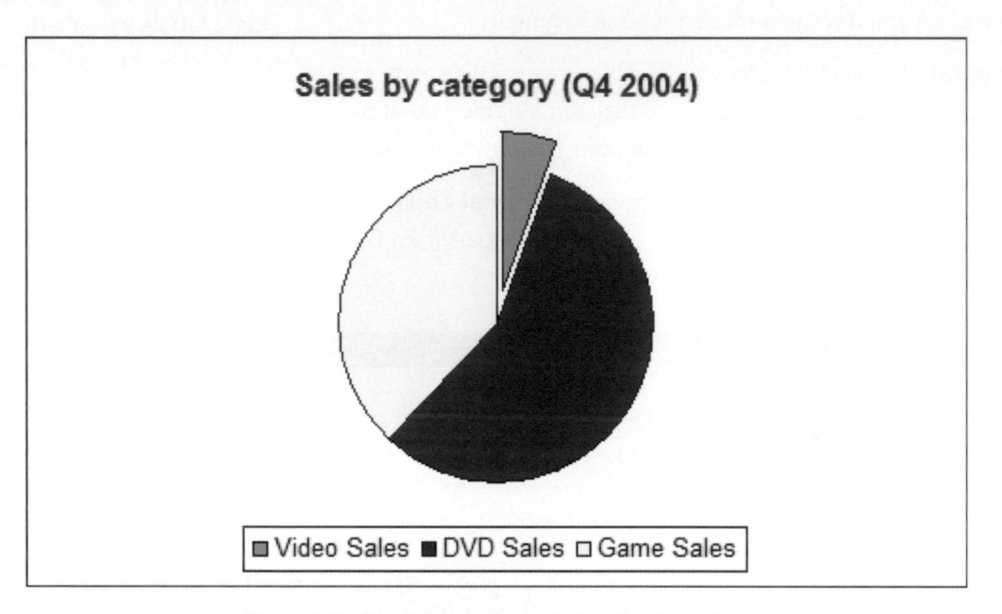

Figure 14.9: Pie chart with legend placed at the bottom

Click and drag the legend. A dotted line appears to show where the legend will be moved to, as shown in Figure 14.10(a). Release the mouse button to drop the legend in its new position.

Resize the legend by dragging its bottom-right selection handle, as shown in Figure 14.10(b). Notice how Excel chooses a horizontal or vertical layout based on the legend's new shape.

The moved and resized legend should now look like it does in Figure 14.10(c).

When you move a chart element by dragging it, the chart will **not** be resized to compensate.

You can move a chart's title in exactly the same way: just click and drag it to its new position.

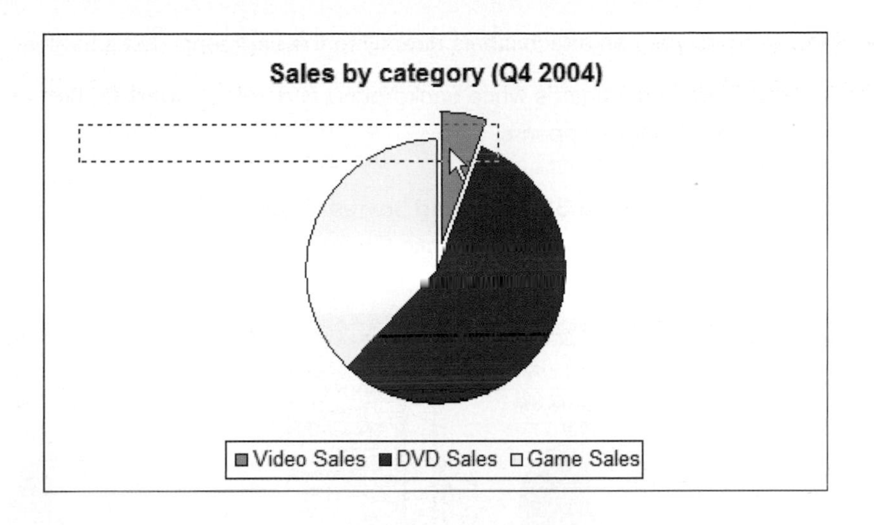

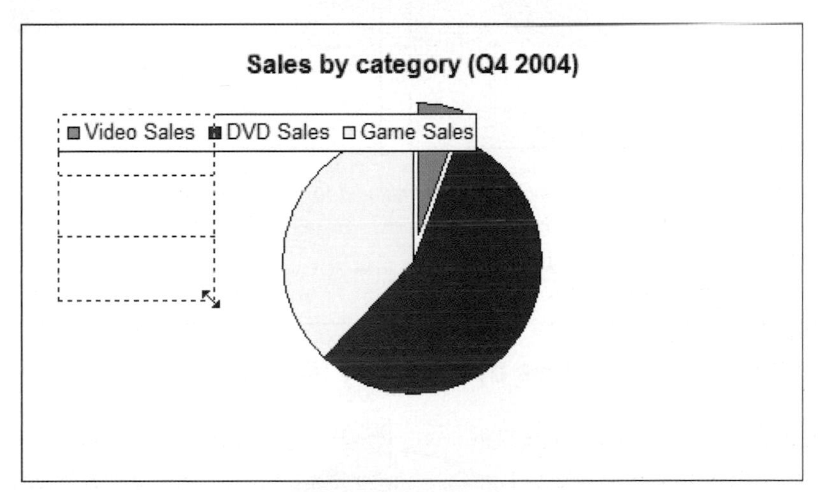

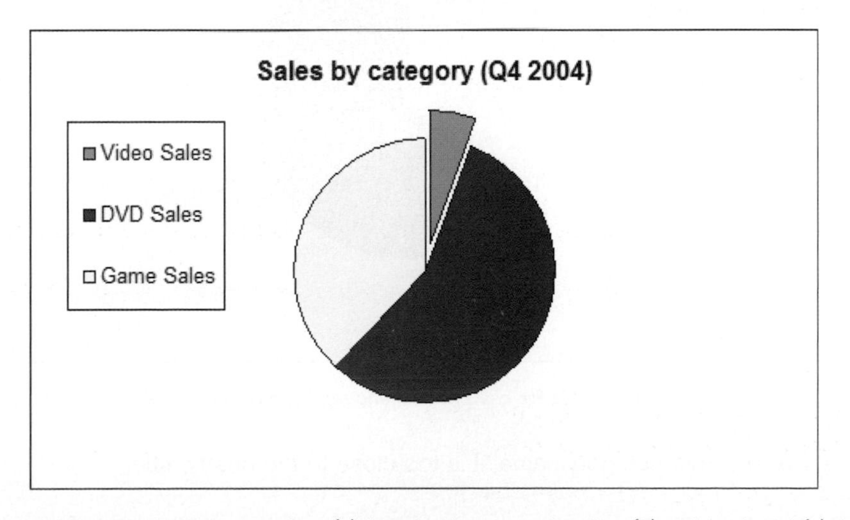

Figure 14.10: Moving a legend manually – (a) dragging it to a new location, (b) resizing it and (c) the result

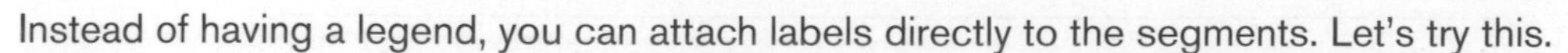

Instead of having a legend, you can attach labels directly to the segments. Let's try this.

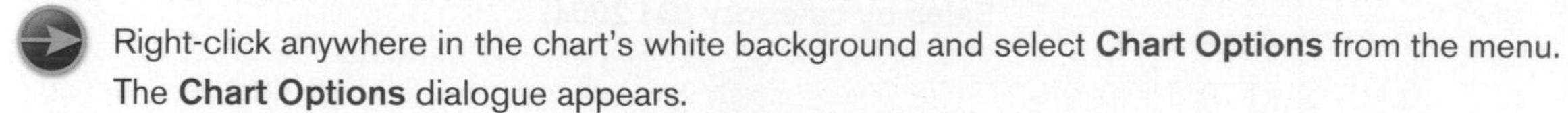

Right-click anywhere in the chart's white background and select **Chart Options** from the menu. The **Chart Options** dialogue appears.

On the **Legend** tab, untick the **Show legend** box, as shown in Figure 14.11(a). On the **Data Labels** tab, tick the **Category name** box, as in Figure 14.11(b). Press **OK**.

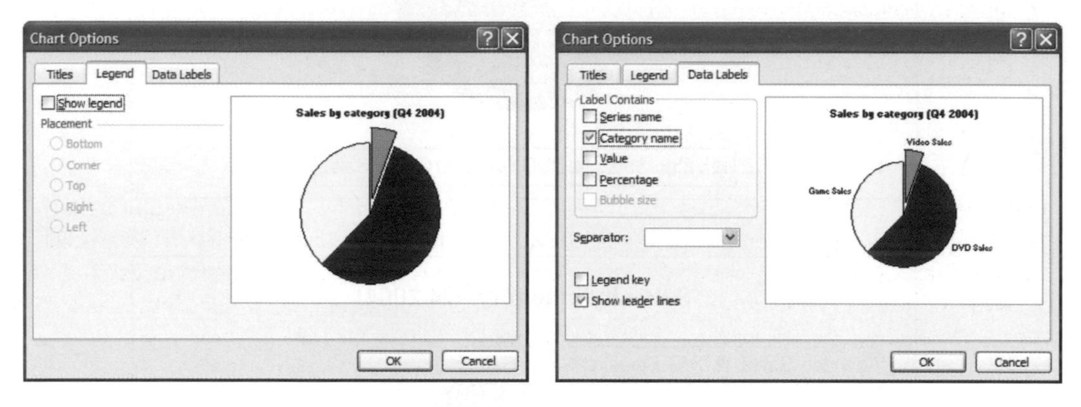

Figure 14.11: (a) Removing the legend, and (b) replacing it with data labels

The resultant pie chart is shown in Figure 14.12.

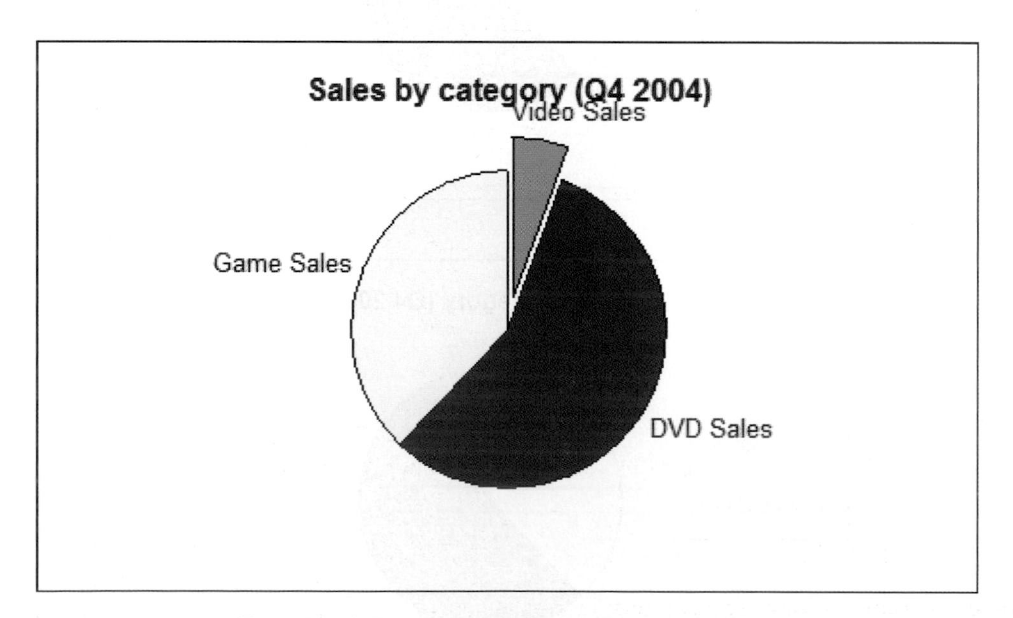

Figure 14.12: Pie chart with legend replaced by data labels

Let's move the **Video Sales** category name; it is too close to the chart's title.

Click on the label **Video Sales**. This first click will select the data series – all of the labels will have selection handles. Now click and drag the label **Video Sales** slightly down and to the right. When you drop it, it should move to its new location and be joined by a line to its data segment.

With the **Video Sales** label still selected, click in it. A flashing **text insertion point** should appear. Change the text to **Videos** (we know from the title that the pie chart is about sales); do not press **Enter** (which will just add a new line) – instead, click anywhere outside the label to complete the change.

Change the two other labels to **DVDs** and **Games** respectively.

If you have difficulty getting the labels into 'text edit' mode, click away from the pie chart to deselect everything, and then click three times on the label, with a gap between each click. The first click selects the labels data series (in effect, the cells **B1:D1**, which we used to originally create the chart); the second click selects an individual label in the data series, and surrounds it with a box to show that it is selected; the third click tells Excel that you want to edit the text.

You can use the same technique to edit the chart's title.

Your pie chart should now look something like Figure 14.13.

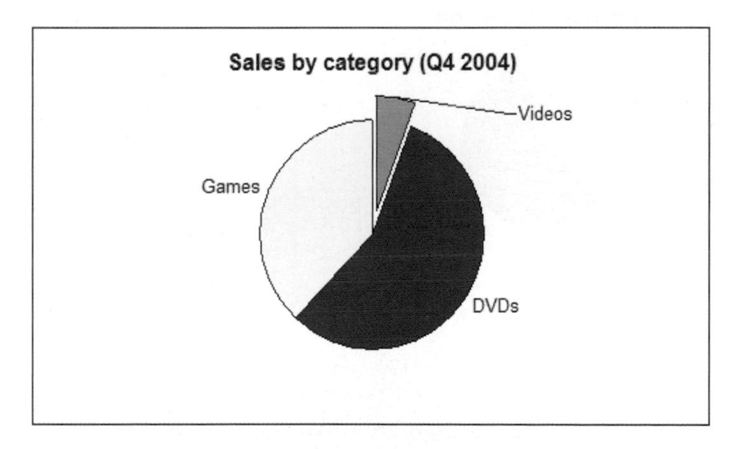

Figure 14.13: Pie chart with customised labels

Inserting images

Syllabus Ref: AM4.2.5.8
Insert an image in a 2D chart.

There are a couple of ways you can use images in your charts. You can add clip art, and you can use an image to fill a chart element, such as a pie-chart slice or the whole chart background. We will look at both of these options.

First, we'll insert some clip art.

 Click away from the pie chart so that it is not selected.

 From the menu, select **Insert**, **Picture**, **Clip Art**. The **Clip Art** task pane is displayed.

 Under **Search for**, type **film** and press **Go**. Click on the film-strip image to insert it into the spreadsheet. Move and resize it so that it sits on the left of the chart, taking up half of its height. Copy the same clip art below it, as shown in Figure 14.14.

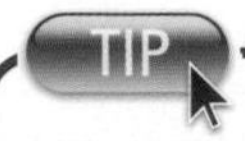

Hold down the **Shift** key when resizing clip art to prevent it from being stretched. You can copy the first film strip by dragging it with the **Ctrl** key held down – in this way, you end up with two identically sized pictures.

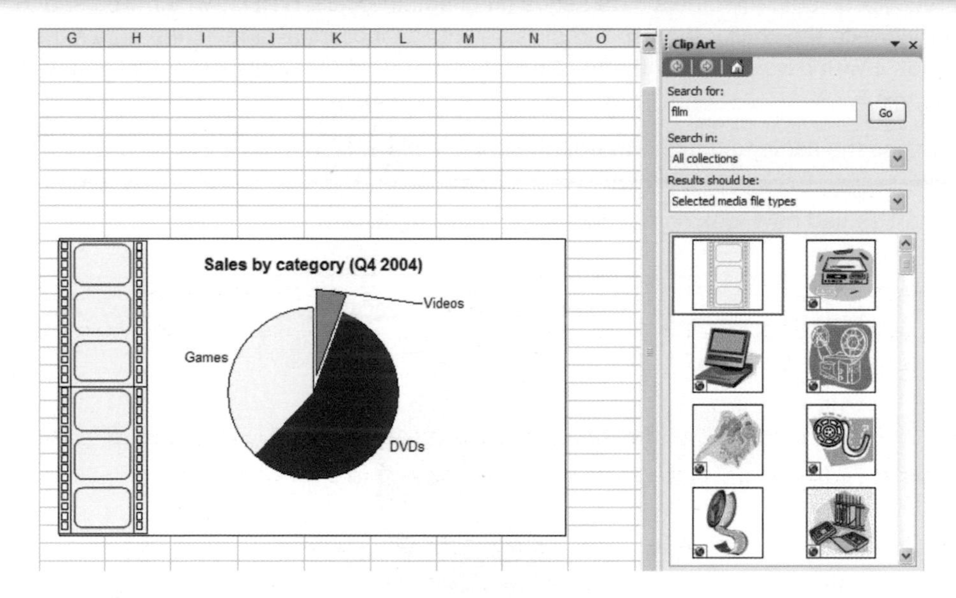

Figure 14.14: Inserting clip art into a chart

Now we'll add a background image to the chart area. We will need to browse for an image that has been saved to disk. Normally, you would download an image from the Internet or create one with a graphics package; instead, we'll use one of the image files that Microsoft Office uses for its clip art.

 In the **Clip Art** task pane, do a search for **backgrounds**. Hover your mouse pointer over the image that looks like a stylised TV set, but don't click it (this would insert the image directly into the worksheet). Instead, click the arrow that appears on the right of the image, and then choose **Copy** from the menu that appears, as shown in Figure 14.15.

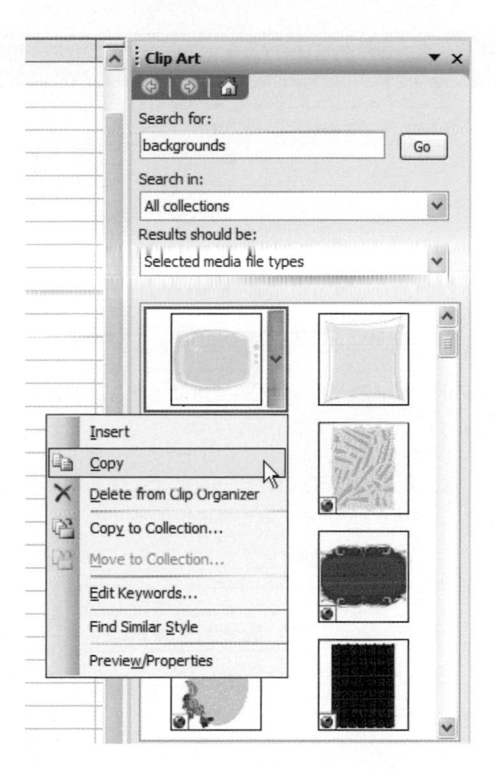

Figure 14.15: Copying a clip-art file

Open **Windows Explorer** (**+E** is a convenient shortcut for this, where is the **Start button** in the bottom-left of the keyboard). Browse to the location where you are saving your worksheets, then select **Edit**, **Paste** from the menu.

A file named **J0229385.WMF** should appear. This file contains the clip-art picture of the stylised TV, and it is this file that we will be inserting as the background of the chart.

Double-click anywhere in the white space in the chart area to display the **Format Chart Area** dialogue. On the **Patterns** tab, click the **Fill Effects** button; the **Fill Effects** dialogue appears. Switch to the **Picture** tab and press the **Select Picture** button. Navigate to the **J0229385.WMF** file, select it and click **Insert**.

The **Fill Effects** dialogue should now look like Figure 14.16.

If you are asked to insert an image in the ECDL exam then one will be provided for you. The previous two steps are only necessary if you want to use a clip-art image for the background of a chart element.

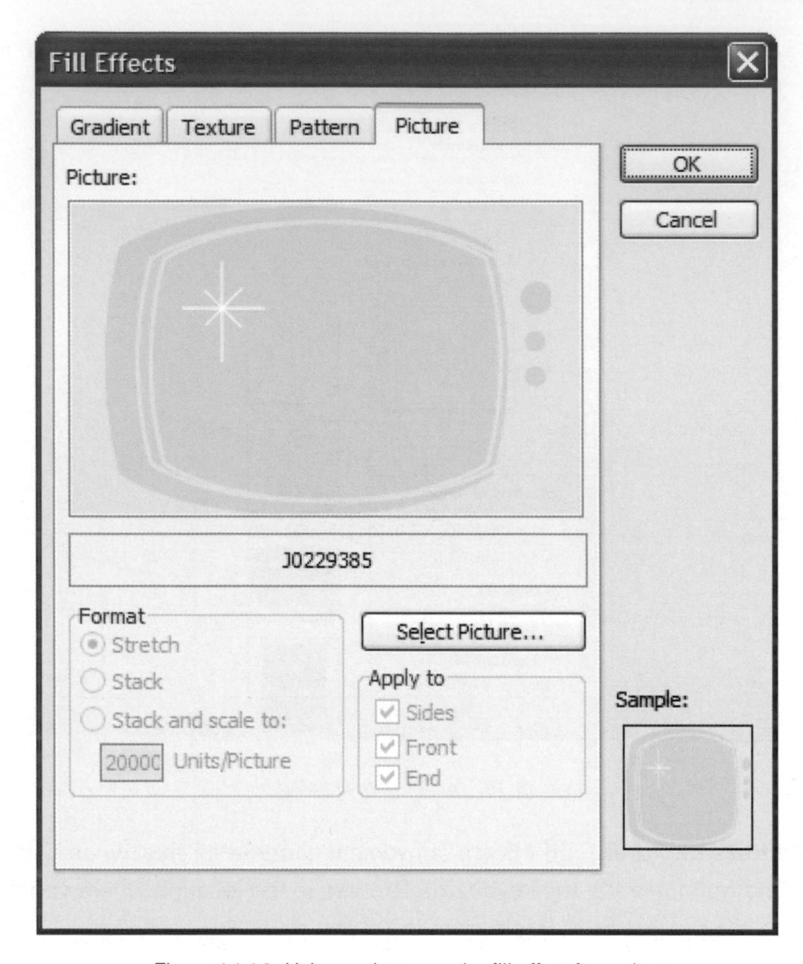

Figure 14.16: Using a picture as the fill effect for a chart

 Press **OK** on the **Fill Effects** dialogue to close it.

 Press **OK** on the **Format Chart Area** dialogue to apply the new background image.

If you click away from the chart, so that the film strips reappear in front of it, it should look like Figure 14.17.

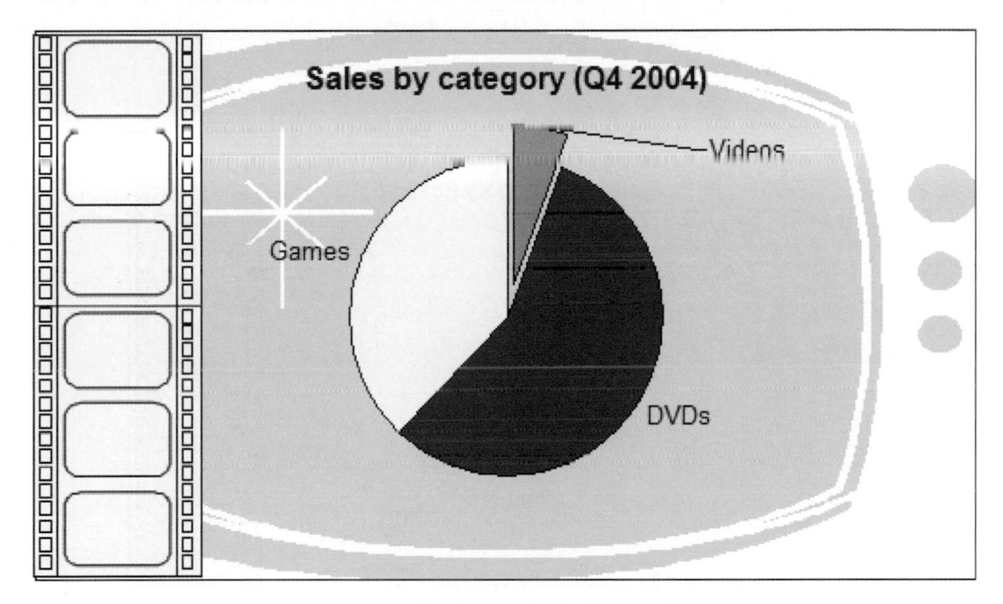

Figure 14.17: Pie chart with a background image

You can use a similar method to add an image as the background to a data segment.

If the **Drawing** toolbar isn't on display (it is usually at the bottom of the screen) then select **View**, **Toolbars**, **Drawing** from the menu.

Hold down the **Shift** key and click on each of the two film strips and the pie chart in turn, to select all three. From the drawing toolbar, select **Draw**, **Group**.

The two clip-art film strips are now treated as part of the pie chart. You can move and resize them as a single object – try it!

After grouping a chart with another object, you will need to click once on the chart to select the whole grouped object (white selection handles), click again to select the pie chart part of the group (grey selection handles), then right-click the chart and select **Edit Chart Object** in order to edit it.

Save the changes you have made to **videoshop.xls**.

Test yourself

1. Create a second pie chart, showing the values for Q1 2003 (cells **B2:D2**). Make it look like Figure 14.18 – you will need to manually delete the **DVDs** label. Group all of the elements together when you have finished.

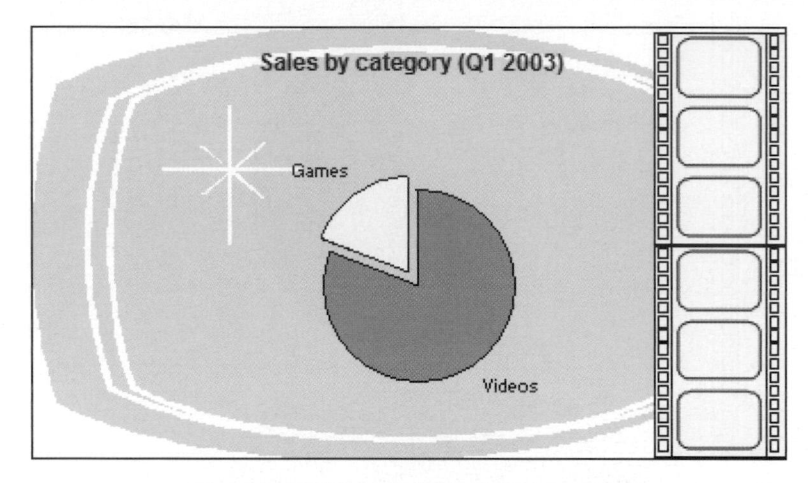

Figure 14.18: Pie chart for the first sales period

2. Resize and rearrange the three graphs so that they look something like Figure 14.19.

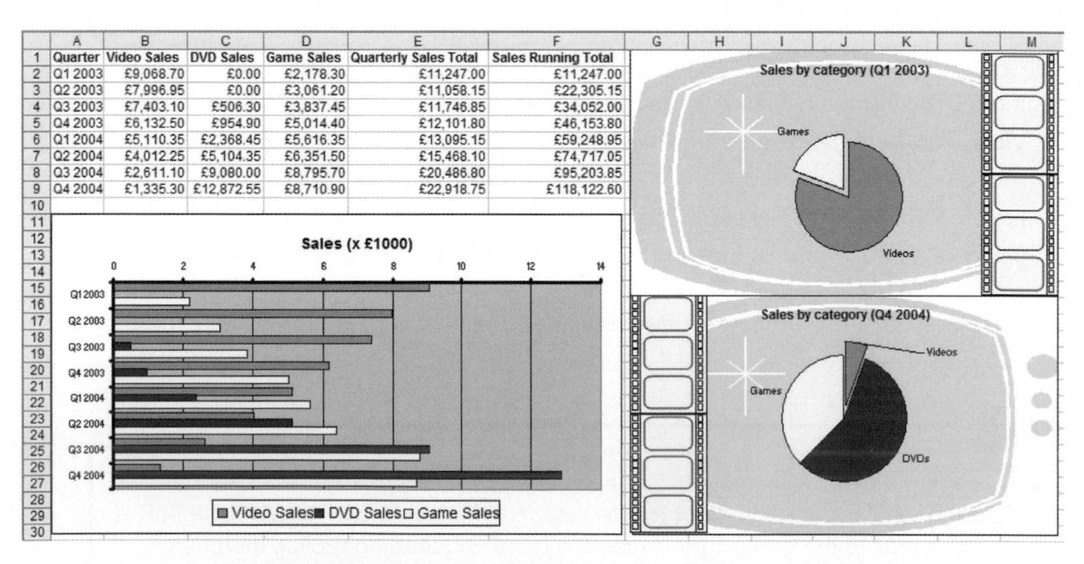

Quarter	Video Sales	DVD Sales	Game Sales	Quarterly Sales Total	Sales Running Total
Q1 2003	£9,068.70	£0.00	£2,178.30	£11,247.00	£11,247.00
Q2 2003	£7,996.95	£0.00	£3,061.20	£11,058.15	£22,305.15
Q3 2003	£7,403.10	£506.30	£3,837.45	£11,746.85	£34,052.00
Q4 2003	£6,132.50	£954.90	£5,014.40	£12,101.80	£46,153.80
Q1 2004	£5,110.35	£2,368.45	£5,616.35	£13,095.15	£59,248.95
Q2 2004	£4,012.25	£5,104.35	£6,351.50	£15,468.10	£74,717.05
Q3 2004	£2,611.10	£9,080.00	£8,795.70	£20,486.80	£95,203.85
Q4 2004	£1,335.30	£12,872.55	£8,710.90	£22,918.75	£118,122.60

Figure 14.19: Sales worksheet showing the three graphs

3. Try to recreate the worksheet shown in Figure 14.20. This worksheet shows the world population in 1950, 1975 and 2005, split up into major areas of the world. The pie chart shows the 2005 values. The pie chart has been rotated using the **Angle of first slice** control on the **Options** tab of the **Format Data Series** dialogue box. To make the title blue, double-click it to bring up the **Format Chart Title** dialogue, and use the **Color** control on the **Font** tab. To select the 3D pie itself (to resize or move it relative to the other elements of the pie chart), click in a blank area just outside the pie (within the smallest rectangle that could enclose its shape).

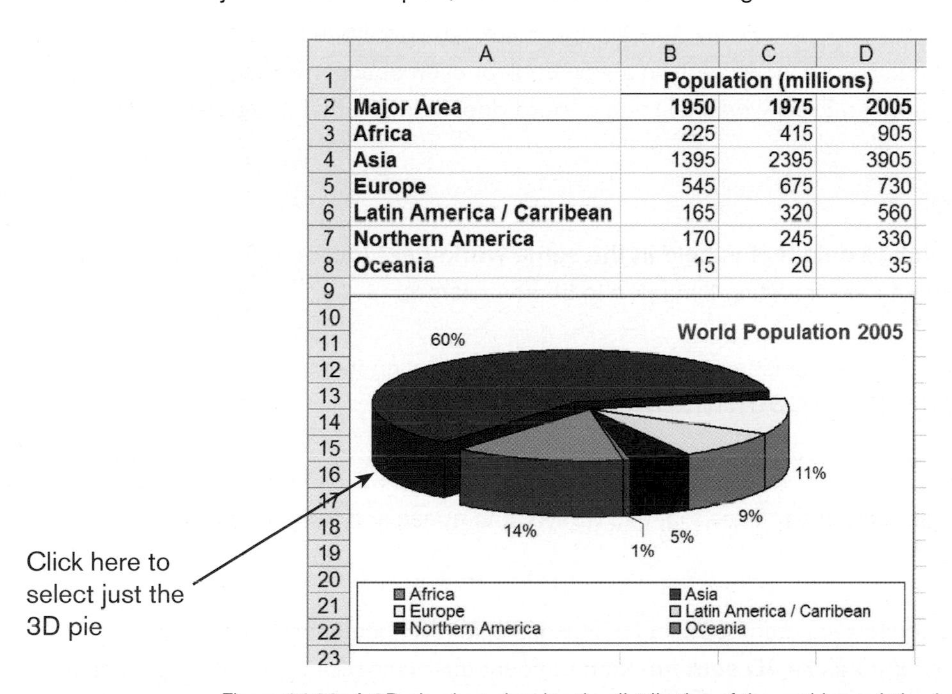

	A	B	C	D
1		**Population (millions)**		
2	**Major Area**	**1950**	**1975**	**2005**
3	**Africa**	225	415	905
4	**Asia**	1395	2395	3905
5	**Europe**	545	675	730
6	**Latin America / Carribean**	165	320	560
7	**Northern America**	170	245	330
8	**Oceania**	15	20	35

Figure 14.20: A 3D pie chart showing the distribution of the world population in 2005

15 Linking

Introduction

In this chapter, we will create a pair of Excel worksheets that would let two people play battleships against one another. In the process, we will look at how to link data from one place to another, be it on the same worksheet, across worksheets in a workbook or even between separate workbooks. We will also pull data from an Excel worksheet into a Word document, so that it updates automatically.

In this chapter you will

- look at how to **link to data that is held in the same worksheet** (this is simple, but there are some issues about cell formatting that need to be considered)
- set up the battleships spreadsheet, and look at how the counting functions – **COUNT**, **COUNTA**, **COUNTIF** and **COUNTBLANK** – work
- create a second workbook, for Player 2, based on the first; this will use **linking between workbooks** to set up the game, so that each player can guess and see straight away whether it was a hit or a miss
- set up a workbook to record an opponent's previous ship arrangements, using **linking between workbooks** and a **3D sum function** to count the number of times each grid square has been occupied (this will give us a hint about where the opponent is likely to place ships in the future)
- set up a battleships league table in Excel, and create a **Word document that links to the spreadsheet data** so that it is automatically updated whenever the spreadsheet changes.

Linking data within a worksheet

We have already used linking, without giving a name to it: when you write a formula such as **=SUM(A1:A10)**, you are, in effect, linking to cells **A1:A10**. If any of the values in cells **A1:A10** change then your calculated linked value will be updated accordingly.

The simplest form of link simply copies the value from one cell to another. Before we get started on writing the game, we'll take a quick look at linking data.

> **Syllabus Ref: AM4.2.3.1**
> Link data/chart within a worksheet.

Create a new blank workbook.

In cell **A2**, enter the formula **=A1**.

> **Note!**
> To link a chart within a worksheet you simply copy and paste it.

The formula evaluates to **0**. This is because the result of a calculation (in this case =) cannot be empty – it must have a value. We could cheat and change the formula to **=IF(ISBLANK(A1), "", A1)**, which would evaluate to the empty string "" whenever cell **A1** were blank; however, there is a subtle difference between a blank cell and one containing an empty string, as we will see when we look at the counting functions later in the chapter. For now, just remember that a direct link to an empty cell will yield a value of **0**.

Give cell **A1** a value of **ABC**; cell **A2** changes to match (notice that both cells are formatted as strings; that is, their contents are left-aligned).

Give cell **A1** a value of **123**; cell **A2** changes to match (notice that both cells are formatted as numbers; that is, their contents are right-aligned).

Type the formula **=TODAY()** into cell **A1**.

Notice how cell **A1** has been automatically reformatted as a date, whereas cell **A2** remains as a number (remember that Excel represents dates internally as numbers), as shown in Figure 15.1.

A2 ▾ fx =A1

	A	B	C
1	15/02/2006		
2	38763		
3			

Figure 15.1: Linking to a date without setting a date format for the cell

In practice, this is rarely a problem, since you usually know the type of value you are linking to and can just set the format of the linking cell appropriately.

Try out some other types of value in cell **A1** (for example, times), and look at what you get in cell **A2**. You might have to reset the cell format for cell **A1** to **General** in between these changes.

Select rows **1** and **2** by clicking and dragging the mouse pointer down the row headings on the left-hand side. Right-click and select **Delete** from the menu that appears. This gives us a clean worksheet, which we can use to start building the battleships game.

Battleships – a brief introduction

Just in case you have never played the game battleships, I'll explain how to play. Each player has a grid that represents an area of ocean and has to place an agreed number of ships on that grid. The ships are of different sizes (that is, they take up different numbers of consecutive squares on the grid), and they may be placed horizontally or vertically, but not diagonally.

When both players have arranged their ships, they take it in turns to guess a square in their opponent's grid that contains part of a ship, and they are told whether or not they have scored a hit. The first player to 'sink' all of his or her opponent's ships is the winner.

Setting up the game area

First, we will create the workbook to be used by Player 1. This will have two worksheets: one with the grid showing where Player 1's ships are located; and one that shows Player 1's guesses for the locations of Player 2's ships, and whether each of those guesses is a hit or a miss.

We want a ten-by-ten grid of squares to act as the ocean:

Select columns **A** to **J** by clicking and dragging the mouse pointer across their column headings. Notice that the **tooltip** helpfully shows how many columns you have selected as you go along, ending up as **10C** (10 columns). Reduce the width of any of the selected columns until its cells are approximately square: when you release the mouse, all of the selected columns will resize to this new width.

Now select only cells **A1:J10**. Give this group of cells the name **SHIPS**, and use the **Borders** button on the **Formatting** toolbar to cover them with a grid. Your worksheet should now look like Figure 15.2.

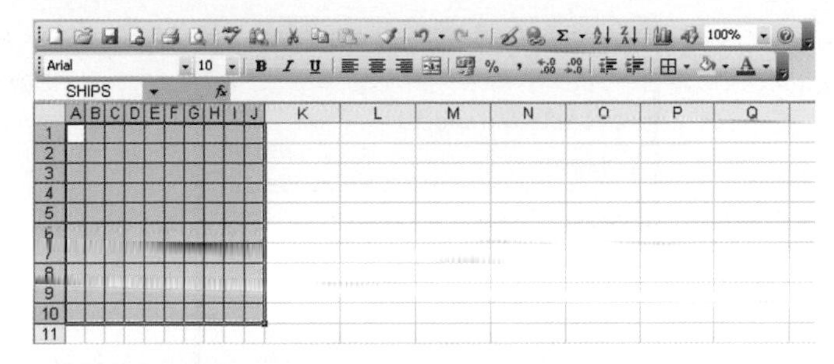

Figure 15.2: Resizing columns to create a ten-by-ten grid of squares

As a reminder to the players, we'll create an area to the right of the grid that lists the sizes of the ships and how many of each there should be.

The ships will be as follows:

One **battleship**, length **4**, represented by B;

Two **destroyers**, length **3**, represented by D;

Three **cruisers**, length **2**, represented by C;

Three **submarines**, length **1**, represented by S.

Add the following labels, working down column **L**: **1 x BBBB**, **2 x DDD**, **3 x CC** and **3 x S**. Similarly, in column **M**, add their descriptions: **Battleship**, **Destroyer**, **Cruiser**, **Submarine**.

Rename **Sheet1** to **My Fleet** (right-click on the tab at the bottom and select **Rename** from the menu).

We want a second worksheet that will contain this player's guesses. Since this will need a similar grid structure, and reminders about the ship types and numbers, we can create a copy of this worksheet as a starting point.

Right-click the **My Fleet** worksheet tab and select **Move or Copy** from the menu. The **Move or Copy** dialogue appears.

Keep the default **To book** value; this should be the current workbook, which will be called **Book*n*** (for some number ***n***) if you haven't saved it yet. Set **Before sheet** to **Sheet 2**. Make sure **Create a copy** is ticked, as shown in Figure 15.3, otherwise we would only move the worksheet. Press **OK** to create the new worksheet.

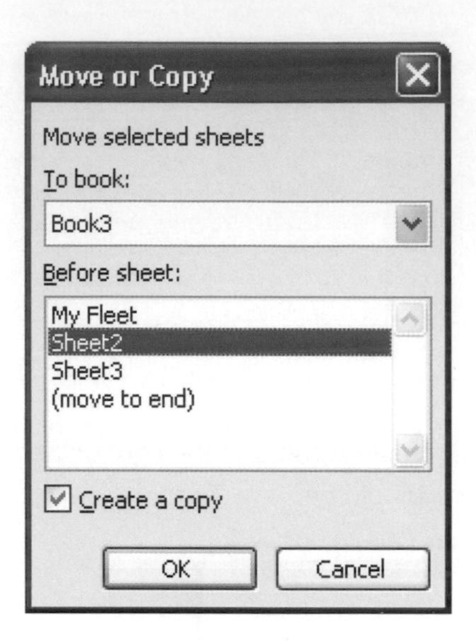

Figure 15.3: Creating a copy of a worksheet

 Rename this new worksheet as **My Guesses**, and delete worksheets **Sheet2** and **Sheet3**.

Your workbook should now look like Figure 15.4.

Book3

	A	B	C	D	E	F	G	H	I	J	K	L	M	N
1												1 x BBBB	Battleship	
2												2 x DDD	Destroyer	
3												3 x CC	Cruiser	
4												3 x S	Submarine	
5														
6														
7														
8														
9														
10														
11														

My Fleet | My Guesses

Figure 15.4: Battleships game after initial set-up

 On the **My Guesses** worksheet, select cells **A1:J10**. Notice how these are named **SHIPS**, just as in the original worksheet. Rename the selection as **GUESSES** by entering the new name over the original one.

If you check the drop-down menu to the right of the **Name Area**, you will see that **SHIPS** is still in the list. We have not actually renamed **SHIPS** to **GUESSES**, but we have instead added **GUESSES** as a second name for the same group of cells.

Let's tidy up by deleting **SHIPS**.

From the menu, select **Insert**, **Name**, **Define**. The **Define Name** dialogue appears. Notice the qualifier **My Guesses** on the right of the **SHIPS** line, which shows that the name **SHIPS** on this worksheet clashes with a more general name **SHIPS** defined elsewhere.

Select **SHIPS** and press the **Delete** button **only once**, as shown in Figure 15.5. The **My Guesses** qualifier disappears, although **SHIPS** is still shown (and now refers to the range defined on the **My Fleet** worksheet, which we want to keep). Press **OK** to dismiss the **Define Name** dialogue.

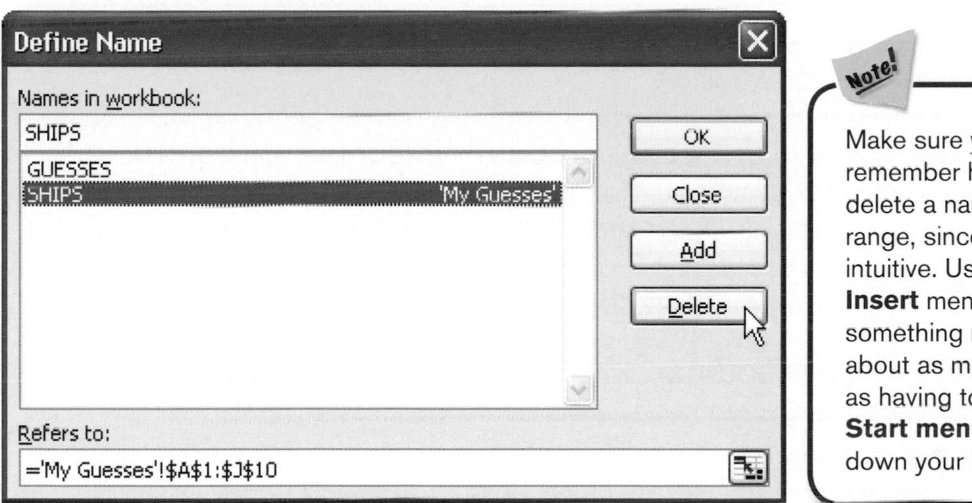

Figure 15.5: Deleting a name

Note!

Make sure you remember how to delete a named range, since it is not intuitive. Using the **Insert** menu to delete something makes about as much sense as having to use the **Start menu** to shut down your PC!

Select cells **A12:J21** and give them grid-style borders.

The player will use the top grid to make a guess, and the bottom grid (which you have just created) will show whether the guess was a hit. It would be useful to show the number of guesses that the player has made so far – we can extend this later to also show the number of guesses that the opponent has made, which will help to keep the game in sync.

Functions for counting

Whatever marker we decide to use in the top grid, we need a way of counting how many of them the player has used. Excel has various functions that count non-empty cells, so this is a good opportunity to examine the differences between them, so that we can choose the most appropriate one for our game.

Syllabus Ref: AM4.3.1.3
Use statistical functions: COUNT; PURECOUNT; COUNTA; COUNTIF.

In cell **L7** on the **My Guesses** worksheet, type the label **COUNT=**. In cell **M7**, type the formula **=COUNT(GUESSES)**.

The **COUNT** function counts the number of cells in the supplied range that contain numbers. Blank cells and text labels are ignored.

Although the ECDL syllabus names the functions **COUNT**, **PURECOUNT** and **COUNTA**, no spreadsheet application provides all three. The two Excel functions **COUNT** and **COUNTA** are equivalent to the **Lotus 1-2-3** functions **@PURECOUNT** and **@COUNT** respectively. Therefore, if you are learning and being tested in Excel (and, if you're not, then you are reading the wrong book!) then you can ignore the reference to **PURECOUNT**.

In cell **L8**, type the label **COUNTA=**. In cell **M8**, type the formula **=COUNTA(GUESSES)**.

The **COUNTA** function counts the number of cells in the supplied range that are not blank. Any cells containing numbers, strings (even the **empty string ""**), or any other value, are counted.

There is a third, related, function: **COUNTBLANK**. This returns the number of truly blank cells (although, unlike for **COUNTA**, **empty strings** also count as blank) in the supplied range. It is not mentioned in the exam syllabus, but it is worth examining here for the sake of completeness. For easier comparison with **COUNT** and **COUNTA**, we will look at **100** (the number of cells in the ten by ten grid) **minus the number of blank cells**.

In cell **L9**, type the label **100 - COUNTBLANK=**. In cell **M9**, type the formula **=100 - COUNTBLANK(GUESSES)**.

We start with nothing in any of the top grid's cells, so we get three counts of zero. Let's see how this changes as we add different types of values to the grid.

In cell **A1**, type **99**. All three counts change to **1**: both **COUNT** and **COUNTA** include numbers, and cell **A1** is no longer blank.

In cell **B1**, type **X**. The **COUNT** value stays as **1**, because **COUNT** includes only numbers. The other two values increase to **2**.

In cell **C1**, type a **space**. The values for **COUNTA** and **100 - COUNTBLANK** both increase to **3**: even though you can't see it, a **space** is still a string.

 In cell **D1**, type =" " to set the cell to the **empty string**. The value of **COUNTA** increases to **4**, but **100 - COUNTBLANK** stays at **3**. This shows the difference between the two functions' treatment of the empty string: **COUNTBLANK** treats it as a blank, whereas **COUNTA** doesn't.

Your worksheet should now look like Figure 15.6. I have added comments to the cells containing the **space** and the **empty string**, but you don't need to do this.

	A	B	C	D	E	F	G	H	I	J	K	L	M	N
1	1	X										1 x BBBB	Battleship	
2												2 x DDD	Destroyer	
3												3 x CC	Cruiser	
4												3 x S	Submarine	
5														
6														
7												COUNT=	1	
8												COUNTA=	4	
9												100-COUNTBLANK=	3	

Figure 15.6: Testing the counting functions with different values

We can summarise this information about which function is counting what as follows, where **YES** means that the value is treated as blank (that is, it is ignored by **COUNT** and **COUNTA**, and counted by **COUNTBLANK**), and **NO** means that the value is treated as not blank:

	Numbers	General Strings	Empty String	Blank Cell
COUNT	NO	YES	YES	YES
COUNTA	NO	NO	NO	YES
COUNTBLANK	NO	NO	YES	YES

For our purposes, players are likely to clear their guesses either by pressing the **Delete** key with cells selected (making them truly blank), or perhaps by pressing the **Space Bar**. We could use the **COUNT** function, and force users to enter a number to represent each of their guesses. Although that would work, I would prefer to use **G** for guess.

We can 'roll our own' count function to match only the letter **G**, using yet another counting function: **COUNTIF**.

> **COUNTIF(range, criteria)**
> Counts those cells in the supplied **range** for which the **criteria** (passed in as a string) evaluates to **true**.

 In cell **L10**, type the label **COUNTIF=**. In cell **M10**, type the formula **=COUNTIF(GUESSES, "G")**.

 Initially, this function evaluates to **0**, since there are no **G**s on the board. Type a few **G**s into the top grid and check that this new count detects them.

> The criteria you pass into the **COUNTIF** function can be only a very simple comparison, for example "**XYZ**", "**>3**" or "**=123**". You cannot get Excel to evaluate the result of passing each cell's value to a function.

 Create bold labels for a player statistics area, as shown in Figure 15.7.

 Copy the formula from cell **M10** to cell **M13**.

M13 =COUNTIF(GUESSES, "G")

Space — Empty string (="")

	A	B	C	D	E	F	G	H	I	J	K	L	M	N	O	P
1	1	X										1 x BBBB	Battleship			
2												2 x DDD	Destroyer			
3												3 x CC	Cruiser			
4												3 x S	Submarine			
5																
6			G													
7								G				COUNT=	1			
8												COUNTA=	7			
9						G						100-COUNTBLANK=	6			
10												COUNTIF=	3			
11																
12													**Guesses**	**Hits**	**Still to find**	
13												**You**	3			
14												**Your Opponent**				
15																
16																
17																
18																
19																
20																
21																
22																

Figure 15.7: Starting to add player statistics

 Tidy up by selecting cells **A1:J10** and pressing the **Delete** key. Do the same for cells **L7:M10**.

We can also use the **COUNTIF** function to help players to check that they have entered the correct number and type of ships into the grid for their own fleets.

Switch to the **My Fleet** worksheet. In cell **N1**, type the formula **=IF(COUNTIF(SHIPS, "B")=4, "<OK>", "<PENDING>")**.

This formula displays **<PENDING>** until exactly four **B**s have been added to the grid (that is, the battleship has been placed). It's not a perfect check – it doesn't care whether the four **B**s are next to each other – but it's better than nothing.

Place your battleship on the grid by entering a **B** in each of the squares **G4:G7**.

The label to the right of **Battleship** changes from **<PENDING>** to **<OK>**.

Enter the appropriate formulas in cells **N2:N4**, remembering that the letter you are checking for and the total count (number of ships multiplied by the size of each ship) will need to be adjusted for each. Finally, position your fleet as shown in Figure 15.8.

	A	B	C	D	E	F	G	H	I	J	K	L	M	N
1												1 x BBBB	Battleship	<OK>
2	D	D	D									2 x DDD	Destroyer	<OK>
3												3 x CC	Cruiser	<OK>
4		S		S			B					3 x S	Submarine	<OK>
5							B							
6	C	C					B							
7					C	C	B							
8		C												
9		C		S										
10						D	D	D						
11														

Figure 15.8: Arranging your fleet

Save the workbook as **battleships player 1.xls**.

Linking data between workbooks

We can't get much further without creating a similar workbook for Player 2 to use. We want to create the file **battleships player 2.xls** as a copy of **battleships player 1.xls**.

From the menu, select **File**, **Save As**. Save the workbook again, in the same folder as **battleships player 1.xls**, but this time call it **battleships player 2.xls**.

If you look at Excel's title bar, you will see that the open file has changed to the Player 2 version.

Reopen the file **battleships player 1.xls**.

Your **Window** menu should now list both files. We will edit them together, because the changes we are going to make need to be symmetric.

An example of this symmetry is the number of guesses that the other player has made. Look at the **My Guesses** worksheet for Player 1: cell **M14** needs the value held in cell **M13** on the other player's worksheet, and vice versa.

You can use **Ctrl+Tab** to switch quickly between open workbooks.

It will be easier to check that we are doing the right thing if the two players have made different numbers of guesses. Type a **G** in one of the cells in the top grid for Player 1. Type **G** in each of two different cells in the equivalent grid for Player 2.

Syllabus Ref: AM4.2.3.3
Link data/chart between spreadsheets
(e.g. combine and merge, using shared workbooks).

On Player 1's worksheet, select cell **M14**. Press the = key to show that you are entering a formula, then switch to Player 2's worksheet, click in cell **M13** and, finally, press **Enter**.

Excel sets the formula in cell **M14** to **='[battleships player 2.xls]My Guesses'!$M$13**, meaning that it is a direct copy of the value held in cell **M13** on the **My Guesses** worksheet in the **battleships player 2.xls** workbook. We could have typed this formula in, but it's usually quicker to use the mouse. Notice that single quotation marks are used around the worksheet and workbook names because they contain spaces.

If two or more people might need to edit your workbook at the same time then you can select **Tools**, **Share Workbook** from the main menu. Excel will then keep track of all the changes people make, and will merge these changes together to keep everyone in sync.

Player 1's worksheet **My Guesses** should now look like Figure 15.9.

M14 | fx | ='[battleships player 2.xls]My Guesses'!$M$13

	A	B	C	D	E	F	G	H	I	J	K	L	M	N	O	P
1												1 x BBBB	Battleship			
2												2 x DDD	Destroyer			
3												3 x CC	Cruiser			
4			G									3 x S	Submarine			
5																
6																
7																
8																
9																
10																
11																
12													**Guesses**	**Hits**	**Still to find**	
13												**You**	1			
14												**Your Opponent**	2			
15																
16																
17																
18																
19																
20																
21																
22																

Figure 15.9: Linking between workbooks

Give Player 2 a third guess. Notice how Player 1's **Your Opponent Guesses** cell is updated to hold the new value.

Add the reverse link from Player 2's cell **M14** to Player 1's cell **M13**.

We want to use the bottom grid to show whether the guesses were hits or misses. We'll represent a hit by **X** and a miss by **-**. For the moment, we'll ignore the top grid – let's just get the bottom grid looking up values in the opponent's workbook. For this we can use the **ISBLANK** function, which is equivalent to **COUNTBLANK** for a single cell.

In Player 1's worksheet **My Guesses**, select cell **A12**. Type the partial formula **=ISBLANK(** and then switch to Player 2's worksheet **My Fleet**; click in cell **A1**, and then press **Enter**.

This formula evaluates to **TRUE**, but shows up as one or more **#**s, because the cell is too small to show **TRUE**. If you hover your mouse pointer over the cell, you should get a tooltip saying **TRUE**. This is good, because Player 2's top-left **My Fleet** square is indeed blank, so this guess would count as a miss. (At present, both players have matching fleet arrangements, but they obviously wouldn't in a real game.)

We can wrap an **IF** function around this result to display **X** for a hit and **-** for a miss. At the same time, we'll remove the dollar signs from the cell reference, since we'll want to copy this formula to the other cells in the bottom grid and we want the location to be relative not absolute.

 Edit the formula in cell **A12** to
=IF(ISBLANK('[battleships player 2.xls]My Fleet'!A1), "-", "X").

This evaluates as the **-** character: a miss!

 Use the **fill handle** to copy the formula from cell **A12**, first to columns **B:J** and then to rows **13:21**.

You should end up with a copy of the whole of Player 2's fleet, as shown in Figure 15.10, with any part of any ship represented by an **X**.

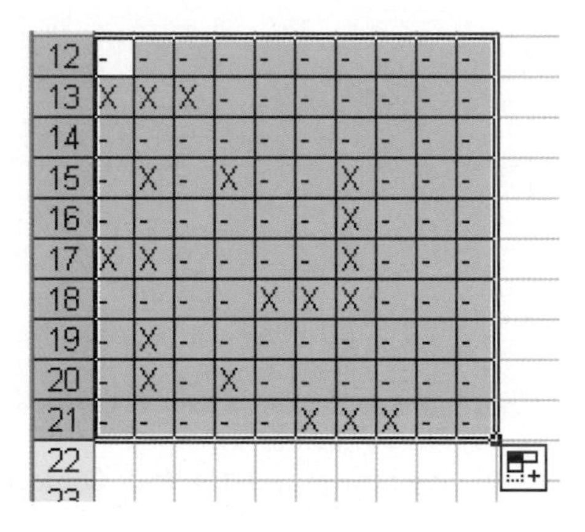

Figure 15.10: Bird's-eye view of the opponent's fleet

Of course, we want to limit this display according to the guesses that have been marked on the top grid. We can wrap an **IF** statement around our formula so that it displays nothing at all unless the corresponding cell in the top grid is set to **G**.

 Change cell **A12**'s formula to
=IF(A1="G", IF(ISBLANK('[battleships player 2.xls]My Fleet'!A1), "-" "X"), " ").

 Copy this formula across the rows and columns of the bottom grid.

 Put several **G**s into the top grid and check that the correct result (hit or miss) is shown in the bottom grid, as shown in Figure 15.11.

	A	B	C	D	E	F	G	H	I	J
1										
2										
3							G		G	
4			G							
5										
6					O					
7			O	O	O	O	O	O		
8							G			
9		G								
10										
11										
12										
13										
14							-		-	
15			-							
16										
17					-					
18			-	-	X	X	X	-		
19							-			
20		X								
21										

Figure 15.11: Result of 12 guesses at ship locations

Create the equivalent formulas in the bottom grid for Player 2, making sure that you reference **battleships player 1.xls**. You should be able to copy the formula text between the two cell **A12**s, change the **2** to a **1**, and copy the formula across the rows and columns of the grid. Make sure you copy the formula text (by clicking in cell **A12**, selecting the formula from the **formula bar** and pressing **Ctrl+C**) instead of copying the whole cell.

Now we can fill in the values for **Hits** and **Still to find**.

Back with Player 1, set cell **N13** to the formula **=COUNTIF(A12:J21, "X")**.

This counts the number of hits (**X**s) in the bottom grid. Since we know that there are (1x4 + 2x3 + 3x2 + 3x1 =) **19** hits to find in total, we can also put a formula in cells **O13** and **O14**.

In cell **O13**, type the formula **=19 - N13**. Copy this formula to cell **O14**.

Select cells **N13** and **O13** and press **Ctrl+C** to copy them. Click in cell **N13** of the equivalent worksheet for Player 2, then press **Ctrl+V** to paste the copied cells. Select cell **O13** on its own and use the **fill handle** to copy the formula to cell **O14**.

Back with Player 1, click in cell **N14** and type = to show that you are starting a formula. Switch to Player 2's workbook and click in cell **N13**, then press **Enter**. Make the equivalent change in the opposite direction.

The two workbooks are now in a state where you could try to play battleships. Figure 15.12 shows an example scenario where Player 1 has had **4** hits from **12** guesses and Player 2 has had **3** hits from **13** guesses.

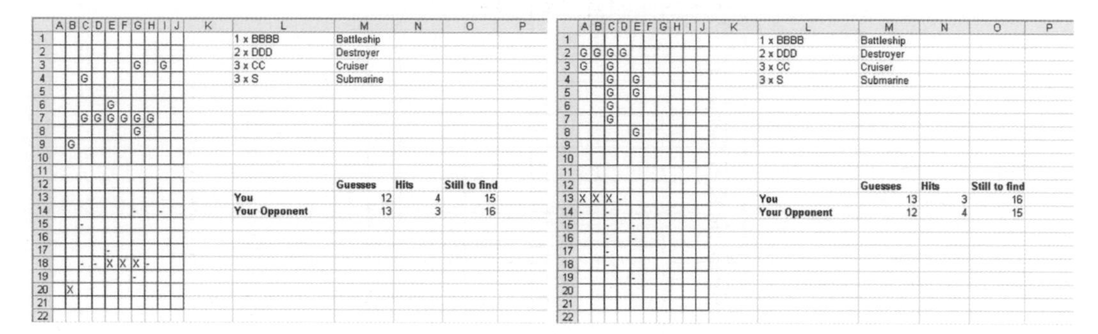

Figure 15.12: A game of battleships – (a) Player 1's worksheet and (b) Player 2's worksheet

Linking data between worksheets

Linking data between worksheets in the same workbook is done in exactly the same way as linking data between workbooks: either by typing a named reference, or by clicking on the target cell(s) with the mouse. In fact, you have already linked between worksheets when using **VLOOKUP** in Chapter 6.

There is another form of linking – **hyperlinking** – that may be more appropriate in certain circumstances. If you just want to provide a way for the user to jump quickly to a range of cells, then you can use a hyperlink. We'll look at this first.

Syllabus Ref: AM4.2.3.2
Link data/chart between worksheets.

Syllabus Ref: AM4.1.2.3 (2 of 2)
Understand how referencing can improve efficiency (e.g. using hyperlinks, naming of cells and ranges).

Using a hyperlink to link to a range of cells

Let's create a hyperlink to take Player 1 from the **My Guesses** worksheet to the fleet arrangement (cells **A1:J10**) on the **My Fleet** worksheet.

Select cell **L6** in Player 1's **My Guesses** worksheet.

From the menu, select **Insert**, **Hyperlink**. The **Insert Hyperlink** dialogue appears.

Click the **Place in This Document** button, then select **'My Fleet'** from the list and type the cell reference **A1:J10** into the **Type the cell reference** box, as shown in Figure 15.13. Press **OK**.

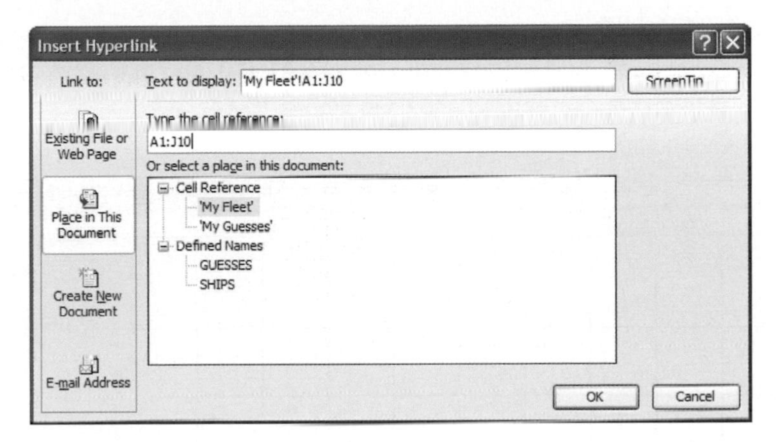

Figure 15.13: Inserting a hyperlink to cells A1:J10 on the My Fleet worksheet

We could equally well have linked to **SHIPS** under **Defined Names** in the list, since this refers to the same range. In this case, we wouldn't have needed to specify the cell reference.

Click the new hyperlink. You should jump to the **My Fleet** worksheet with the grid of ships selected.

Change back to the **My Guesses** worksheet. Right-click the hyperlink and select **Edit Hyperlink** from the menu. The **Edit Hyperlink** dialogue appears (apart from the title and the **Remove Link** button, this is identical to the **Insert Hyperlink** dialogue).

Change the **Text to display** to **Show My Fleet** and press **OK**.

Check that the link still works. After you click on it for the first time, it changes from blue to purple.

Create an equivalent hyperlink for Player 2.

This shows how hyperlinks can improve the efficiency of your workbook by taking people quickly to the information they require.

Linking data values between worksheets

Suppose you want to keep a record of where your battleships opponent has placed ships in the past, so that you can predict where he is likely to have ships when you play him again. Let's create another workbook to record this.

Create a new workbook. Add a grid border to cells **A1:J10**, and make the cells square and as large as will fit on your screen, as shown in Figure 15.14.

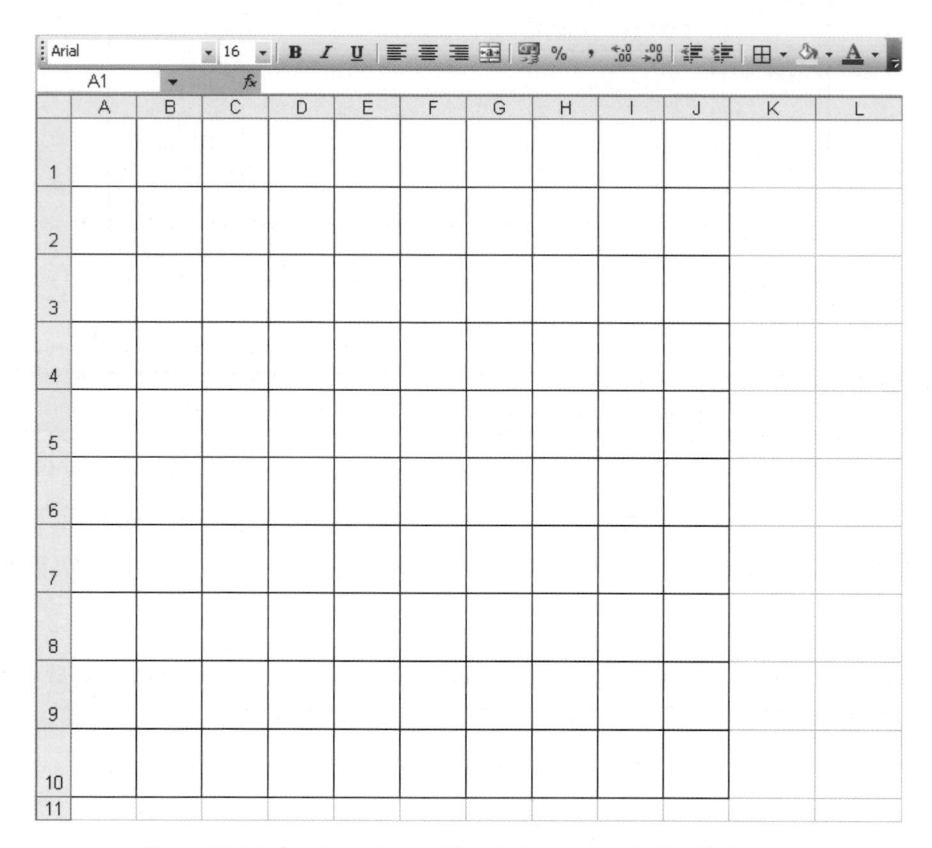

Figure 15.14: Creating a big grid for storing previous battleship layouts

Rename **Sheet1** to **Overview** and delete **Sheet2** and **Sheet3**. Create three copies of the **Overview** worksheet, and name them **Game 1**, **Game 2** and **Game 3**.

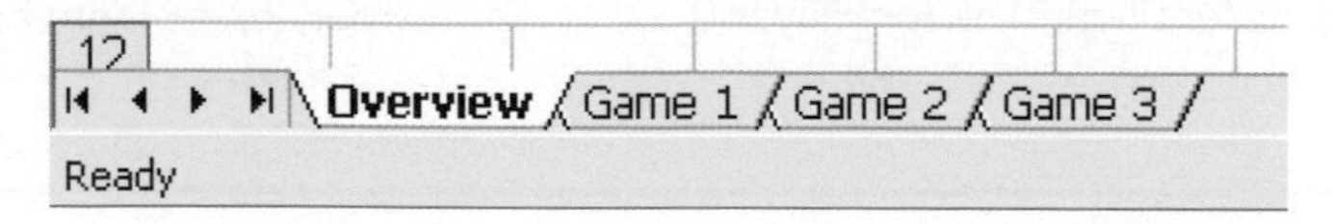

Figure 15.15: The four worksheets in the new workbook

Using **1** to represent the presence of a ship, copy the three game layouts shown in Figure 15.16 into the worksheets **Game 1**, **Game 2** and **Game 3** respectively.

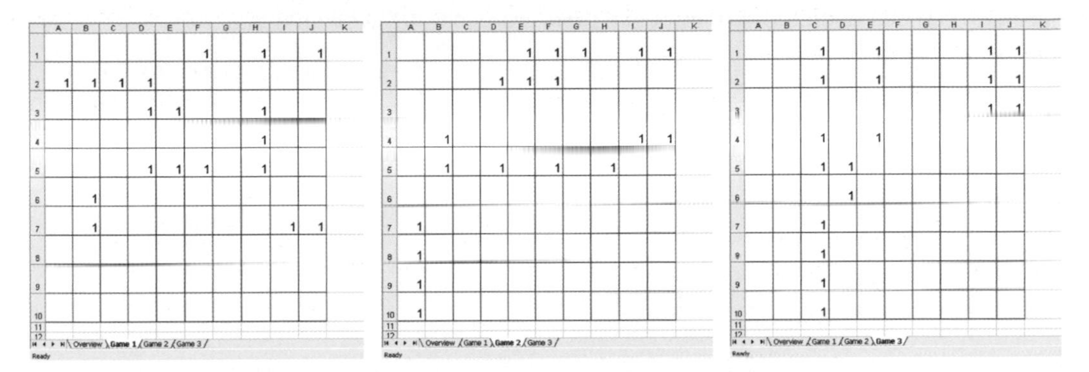

Figure 15.16: History of previous games – (a) Game 1, (b) Game 2 and (c) Game 3

We want to sum these numbers together on the **Overview** worksheet, to see if any patterns emerge.

First, we'll use the method you're used to: **linking data between worksheets.** Shortly, we'll see how to use a **3D sum** function to achieve the same thing.

As a quick check that you haven't missed any 1s, select cells **A1:J10** and check that the **Status bar** says **Sum=19**.

Switch to the **Overview** worksheet and select cell **A1**. Type =, then switch to **Game 1** and click in cell **A1**. Type +, then switch to **Game 2** and click in cell **A1**. Type +, then switch to **Game 3** and click in cell **A1**. Finally, press **Enter**.

The formula in cell **A1** becomes **='Game 1'!A1+'Game 2'!A1+'Game 3'!A1**, which evaluates to **0** because there are no ships in cell **A1** in any of the three recorded games.

Use the **fill handle** to copy this formula to all of the cells in the **Overview** grid.

The overview should now look like Figure 15.17.

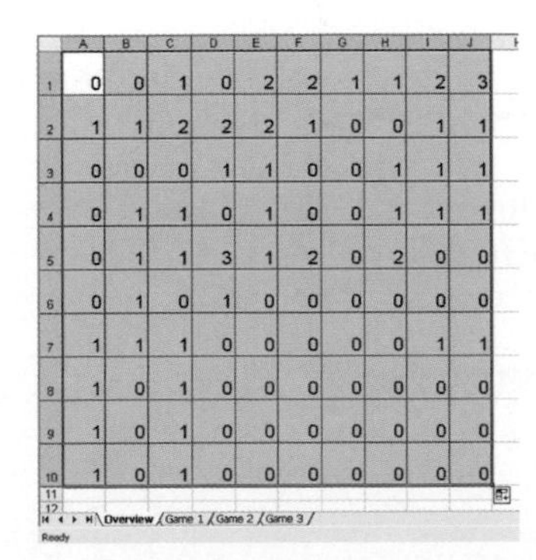

Figure 15.17: Overview created by summing individual cells

To link a chart between worksheets, simply open them both and use cut and paste.

3D sums

The method we have used works when there are only a few worksheets to sum across, but it would be incredibly tedious to create this formula if there were, say, 25 worksheets.

Just as we can use the formula **=SUM(A1:A5)** as shorthand for **=A1+A2+A3+A4+A5**, we can use Excel's **SUM** function in 3D to add together values that are in the same cell in different worksheets.

Syllabus Ref: AM4.2.3.5
Consolidate data in adjacent worksheets using a 3D sum function.

In the **Overview** worksheet, select cells **A1:J10** and then press the **Delete** key. We will replace these formulas with 3D sum functions.

In cell **A1**, type **=SUM(**. Change to the **Game 1** worksheet and click on cell **A1**. Hold down the **Shift** key and click on the **Game 3** tab (this selects all of the worksheets **Game 1**, **Game 2** and **Game 3**). Press **Enter** to show that you have finished choosing worksheets.

Cell **A1** should now have the formula **=SUM('Game 1:Game 3'!A1)**, which evaluates to **0**, as before.

Again, use the **fill handle** to copy the formula to the rest of the grid.

The grid of totals should once again look like it did in Figure 15.17, only this time using 3D functions.

Save the worksheet as **battleships history.xls**, and save both **battleships player 1.xls** and **battleships player 2.xls**.

From our overview, we can see that the opponent tends not to place ships in the bottom right-hand corner; this will be useful information for future games!

You can use 3D references with only the following functions: **AVERAGE**, **COUNT**, **COUNTA**, **MAX**, **MIN**, **PRODUCT**, **STDEV**, **STDEVP**, **SUM**, **VAR** and **VARP**.

Using Excel data from Word

One of the advantages of an office suite, such as **Microsoft Office 2003**, over a 'pick and mix' selection of office tools from different companies, is that you are encouraged to link information between the applications. You can embed spreadsheet figures into a document, charts into a presentation, and so on.

We'll create a **Battleships League Table** worksheet, and then use Word's **Paste Special** command to embed selected cells into a document.

Syllabus Ref: AM4.2.3.4
Link data/chart into a word processing document.

Close all of your open workbooks, then create a new blank workbook. Name its first worksheet **League Table** and delete its other worksheets.

Type in the current league table, as shown in Figure 15.18. Notice that cells **B3:F3** have been right-aligned.

Book1

	A	B	C	D	E	F
1	**Battleships League**					
2						
3	**Player**	**Played**	**Won**	**Lost**	**Abandoned**	**Points**
4	Luca		3	0	1	
5	Penny		3	1	0	
6	Mark		2	3	1	
7	Terry		2	3	0	
8	Jane		1	4	0	
9						

League Table

Figure 15.18: League table of battleship games

Add the appropriate **SUM** formula to cell **B4**, and then use the **fill handle** to copy it down to cell **B8**. If players get **3** points for a win, and **1** point each if both agree to abandon the match, then fill in the appropriate formula in cell **F4**, and copy it down to cell **F8**.

Select cells **A3:F8** and copy them to the clipboard (**Edit**, **Copy** or **Ctrl+C**). Your worksheet should now look like Figure 15.19.

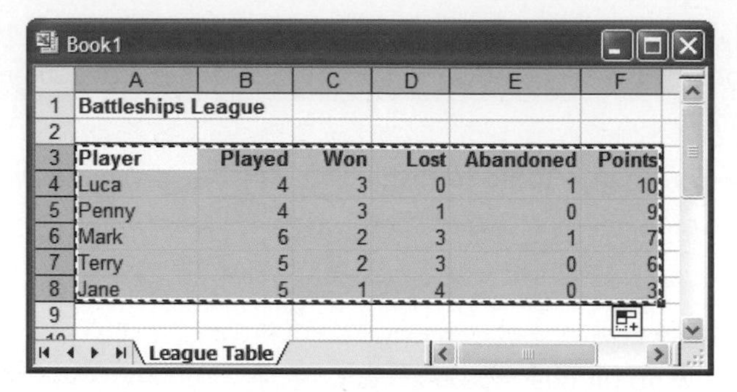

	A	B	C	D	E	F
1	Battleships League					
2						
3	Player	Played	Won	Lost	Abandoned	Points
4	Luca	4	3	0	1	10
5	Penny	4	3	1	0	9
6	Mark	6	2	3	1	7
7	Terry	5	2	3	0	6
8	Jane	5	1	4	0	3
9						

Figure 15.19: Copying the league table to the clipboard

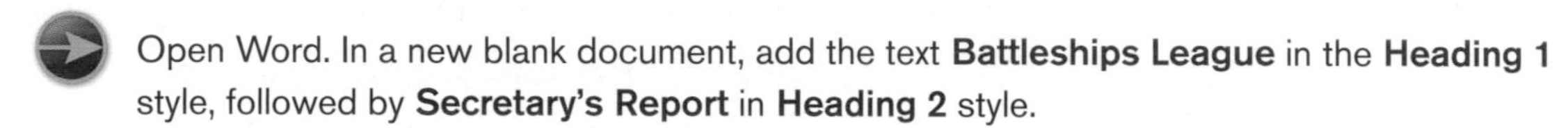

Open Word. In a new blank document, add the text **Battleships League** in the **Heading 1** style, followed by **Secretary's Report** in **Heading 2** style.

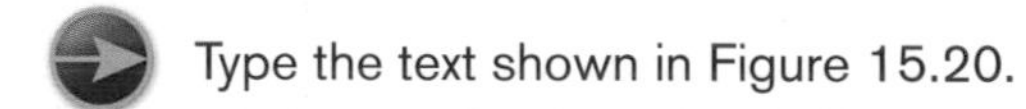

Type the text shown in Figure 15.20.

Battleships·League¶

Secretary's·Report¶

Here·is·the·latest·league·table.·Remember,·you·get·three·points·for·a·win,·and·each·player·gets·a·point·if·you·agree·to·abandon·a·game.¶
¶

Figure 15.20: Start of a document that will contain embedded spreadsheet cells

With the text insertion point on a blank line at the end of the document, select **Edit**, **Paste Special** from Word's menu. The **Paste Special** dialogue appears.

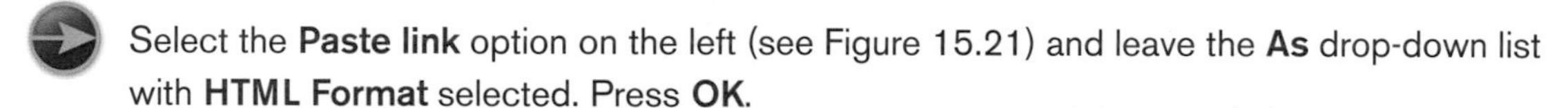

Select the **Paste link** option on the left (see Figure 15.21) and leave the **As** drop-down list with **HTML Format** selected. Press **OK**.

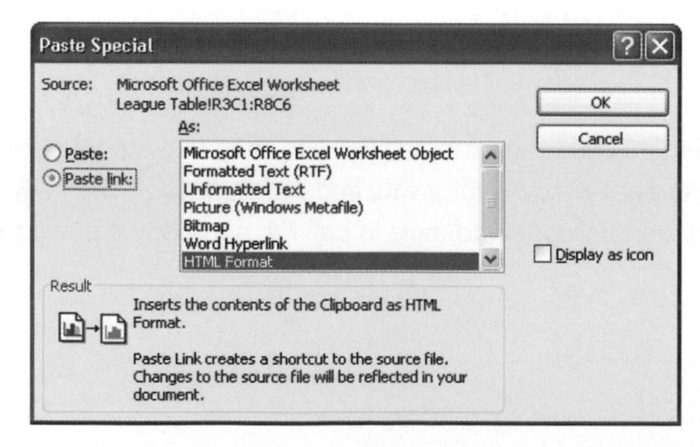

Figure 15.21: Pasting a link to spreadsheet information into a document

Switch back to the spreadsheet. Select and copy cell **A4**, which contains the name of the player in the lead.

In your Word document, after the pasted table, type **Congratulations to**, followed by a **space**. Again, choose **Edit**, **Paste Special** and make sure **Paste link** is selected, but this time specify **Unformatted Text** as the type. Press **OK** to paste the link. Finish off the sentence by typing **, who is at the top of the leader board!**

If the **Paste** option is selected then only a snapshot of the information that was copied will be pasted; if **Paste link** is used then the pasted information will be updated whenever the original spreadsheet is modified, as we shall demonstrate shortly.
You have a wide choice of formats in which to paste copied spreadsheet data:

Microsoft Office Excel Worksheet Object embeds the whole worksheet into the document. You can edit the embedded worksheet from inside Word – Excel takes over Word's menus and toolbars.

Formatted Text (RTF) embeds the copied data as text and tries to preserve the formatting. In general, **HTML Format** is likely to give better results.

Unformatted Text or **Unformatted Unicode Text** embeds the copied data but strips out any formatting that was applied in Excel.

Picture (Windows Metafile) and **Bitmap** both embed what amounts to a screen capture of the copied information. This can be useful when you want an exact replica of the copied cells, but results in larger document files.

Word Hyperlink simply inserts a hyperlink (like you would find on a Web page). Clicking the hyperlink opens the information you linked to.

HTML Format is the default. It pastes the data as text and tries to preserve the formatting.

Battleships League¶

Secretary's Report¶

Here is the latest league table. Remember, you get three points for a win, and each player gets a point if you agree to abandon a game.¶

¶

Player	Played	Won	Lost	Abandoned	Points
Luca	4	3	0	1	10
Penny	4	3	1	0	9
Mark	6	2	3	1	7
Terry	5	2	3	0	6
Jane	5	1	4	0	3

¶

Congratulations to Luca, who is at the top of the leader board!¶

Figure 15.22: Word document containing two sets of linked spreadsheet cells

Click in any cell of the table in Word then from the menu choose **Table**, **Select**, **Table**. Change the font size to **18**, using the drop-down on the **Formatting** toolbar. Select just the top row of the table, by clicking in the margin to its left, and make the text **underlined**.

Select the last sentence in the document and make the font **red**, size **16** and **italic**.

Battleships·League¶

Secretary's·Report¶

Here·is·the·latest·league·table.·Remember,·you·get·three·points·for·a·win,·and·each·player·gets·a·point·if·you·agree·to·abandon·a·game.¶

¶

Player	Played	Won	Lost	Abandoned	Points
Luca	4	3	0	1	10
Penny	4	3	1	0	9
Mark	6	2	3	1	7
Terry	5	2	3	0	6
Jane	5	1	4	0	3

¶

Congratulations·to·Luca,·who·is·at·the·top·of·the·leader·board!¶

Figure 15.23: League table after formatting has been applied

Now imagine you are the secretary of the Battleships League, and that you are just about to print out your report. You get an email from Penny, telling you that she has just beaten Jane in a league game. So you decide to update the table.

In the spreadsheet, update Penny's **Won** total from **3** to **4**, and Jane's **Lost** total from **4** to **5**. Sort the table in descending order of **Points**.

Book1

	A	B	C	D	E	F
1	Battleships League					
2						
3	Player	Played	Won	Lost	Abandoned	Points
4	Luca	4	3	0	1	10
5	Penny	4	3	1	0	9
6	Mark	6	2	3	1	7
7	Terry	5	2	3	0	6
8	Jane	5	1	4	0	3
9						

League Table

Figure 15.24: Spreadsheet updated with last-minute result

Now switch to your Word document. As if by magic, it has been updated, as shown in Figure 15.25. The new league table is displayed, and congratulations are being offered to Penny instead of Luca, since she is the new head of the leader board. Notice also that the formatting has been kept intact, even though the underlying values have changed.

Battleships League

Secretary's Report

Here is the latest league table. Remember, you get three points for a win, and each player gets a point if you agree to abandon a game.

Player	**Played**	**Won**	**Lost**	**Abandoned**	**Points**
Penny	5	4	1	0	12
Luca	4	3	0	1	10
Mark	6	2	3	1	7
Terry	5	2	3	0	6
Jane	6	1	5	0	3

Congratulations to Penny, who is at the top of the leader board!

Figure 15.25: The document has been automatically updated, but the formatting has been left intact

Save the new worksheet as **battleships league table.xls**. Save the Word document as **battleships report.doc**.

The method for linking a chart from a spreadsheet into a word processed document is the same as for linking data: copy the chart in Excel, use **Paste Special** in Word and select the **Paste Link** option. Exercise 5 gives you the chance to try this out.

Test yourself

1. Change the **Overview** worksheet (**battleships history.xls**) so that the zeros are displayed as blanks – use an **IF** function for this. Type the label **Hot cells:** in cell **L1**. In cell **M1**, create a formula that gives the count of values in the grid that are greater than **2**. Use conditional formatting to make these cells red in the grid. [Hint: because "">**0** evaluates to **TRUE**, you can't just do a simple comparison in the **Conditional Formatting** dialogue; this would highlight all the cells containing empty strings too. Instead, use the formula **=AND(ISNUMBER(A1), A1>2)**.]

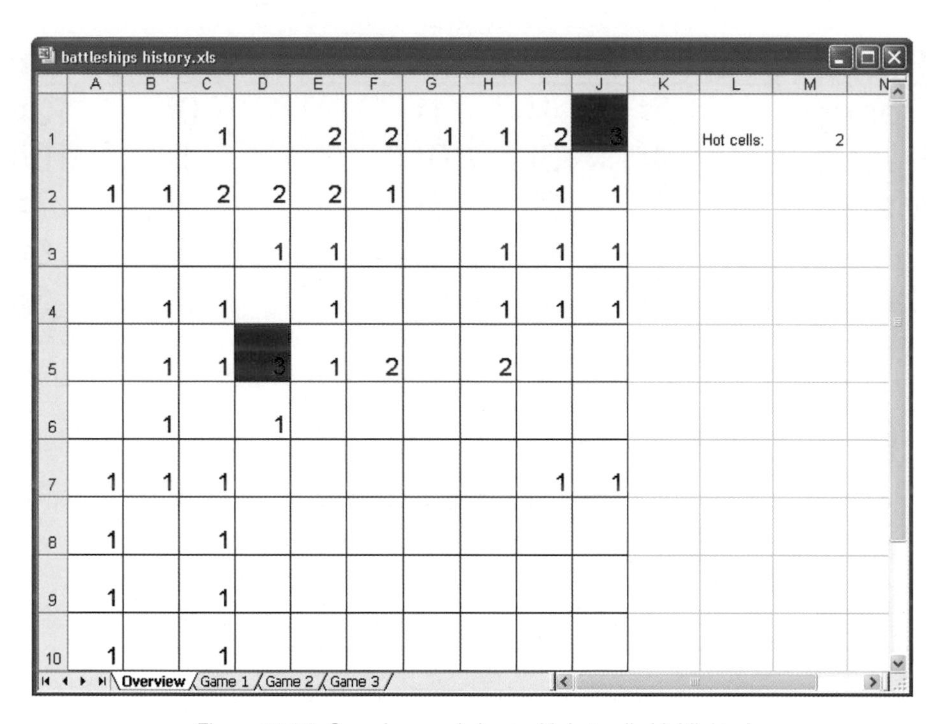

battleships history.xls

	A	B	C	D	E	F	G	H	I	J	K	L	M
1			1		2	2	1	1	2	3		Hot cells:	2
2	1	1	2	2	2	1			1	1			
3				1	1			1	1	1			
4		1	1		1			1	1	1			
5		1	1	3	1	2		2					
6		1		1									
7	1	1	1						1	1			
8	1		1										
9	1		1										
10	1		1										

Overview / Game 1 / Game 2 / Game 3

Figure 15.26: Overview worksheet with hot cells highlighted

2. With **battleships report.doc** open in Word, check that **Tools**, **Options**, **General**, **Update automatic links at Open** is ticked. Now close the document. Open the **battleships league table.xls** workbook if it isn't already open. Suppose Jane wins her next two games, beating Mark and Terry. Update the table to show this, sorting it as before. Now save and close **battleships league table.xls** and reopen **battleships report.doc**. What happens?

3. Add **protection** (without a password) to **battleships player 1.xls** and **battleships player 2.xls** so that the only cells a player can edit are the grid in **My Fleet** and the top grid in **My Guesses**.

4. In a new blank workbook, enter the opening, closing, high and low prices for each of four stock markets, as shown in Figure 15.27. Use a separate worksheet for each day of the week, naming it appropriately. (Alternatively, you can download the partially completed worksheet from www.payne-gallway.co.uk/ecdl.)

Monday

	A	B	C	D	E
1	Market	Open	Close	High	Low
2	FTSE 100	6039	6043	6061	6026
3	FTSE 250	7274	7302	7309	7272
4	FTSE SmallCap	2886	2889	2892	2886
5	FTSE All-Share	2524	2527	2530	2520

Tuesday

	A	B	C	D	E
1	Market	Open	Close	High	Low
2	FTSE 100	5048	5048	5054	5038
3	FTSE 250	7309	7309	7312	7290
4	FTSE SmallCap	2894	2897	2897	2893
5	FTSE All-Share	2529	2529	2532	2525

Wednesday

	A	B	C	D	E
1	Market	Open	Close	High	Low
2	FTSE 100	5058	5018	5058	5013
3	FTSE 250	7285	7273	7294	7259
4	FTSE SmallCap	2896	2899	2900	2895
5	FTSE All-Share	2532	2515	2532	2513

Thursday

	A	B	C	D	E
1	Market	Open	Close	High	Low
2	FTSE 100	5035	5040	5046	503
3	FTSE 250	7272	7313	7320	727
4	FTSE SmallCap	2899	2907	2907	289
5	FTSE All-Share	2522	2527	2529	252

Friday

	A	B	C	D	E
1	Market	Open	Close	High	Low
2	FTSE 100	5049	5078	5099	5049
3	FTSE 250	7325	7355	7360	7320
4	FTSE SmallCap	2905	2916	2916	2904
5	FTSE All-Share	2531	2545	2553	2531

Figure 15.27: Stock market data for each day of the week

Create another worksheet, called **Overview**, as shown in Figure 15.28. Each of the numbers on this worksheet should use formulas – don't just type in the numbers. Some of them are simple links to another worksheet, and some are calculations using the other figures on the same worksheet. The **Low** and **High** values should be 3D **MIN** and **MAX** formulas.

	A	B	C	D	E	F
1	Stock market weekly overview					
2		Start of week	End of week	Change	Low	High
3	FTSE 100	5039	5078	0.8%	5013	5099
4	FTSE 250	7274	7355	1.1%	7259	7360
5	FTSE SmallCap	2886	2916	1.0%	2886	2916
6	FTSE All-Share	2524	2545	0.8%	2513	2553
7						
8	Closing Prices	Mon	Tue	Wed	Thu	Fri
9	FTSE 100	5043	5048	5018	5040	5078
10	FTSE 250	7302	7309	7273	7313	7355
11	FTSE SmallCap	2889	2897	2899	2907	2916
12	FTSE All-Share	2527	2529	2515	2527	2545

Figure 15.28: The Overview worksheet

5. On the **Overview** worksheet, create a chart of the weekly change in the FTSE 100 (see Figure 15.29). Open a new blank Word document that you could update weekly from the spreadsheet. Design it as shown in Figure 15.29 (we'll only complete the FTSE 100 section, but the real report would have a section for each stock market). The three values and the chart should all be pasted as links, so that they update whenever the workbook changes. Modify Friday's closing price for the FTSE 100 in the **Friday** workbook, and check that the document updates appropriately.

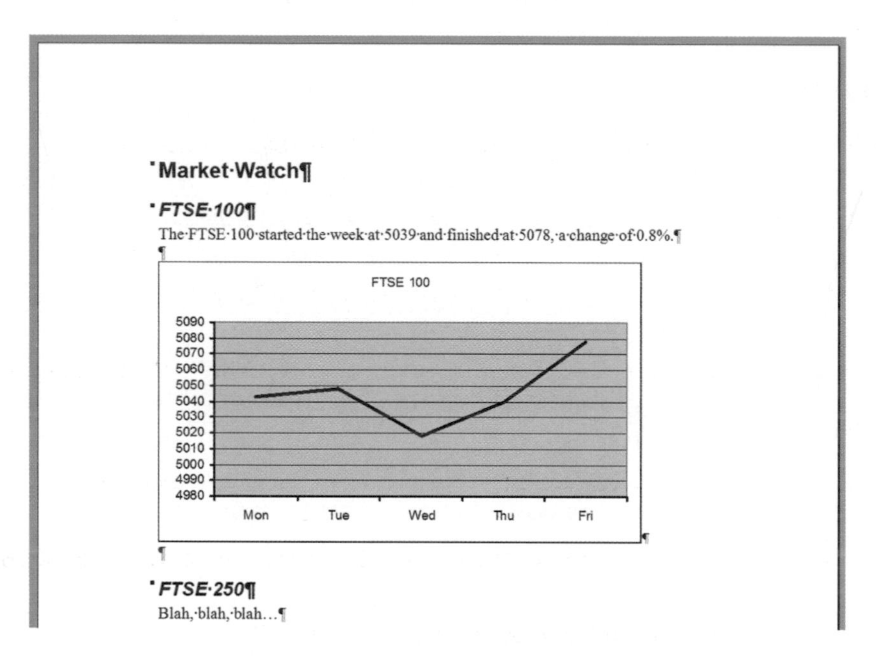

Figure 15.29: Embedding market data in a Word document

6. Create a new workbook somewhere that can be accessed from several accounts (such as on a network drive, or in the top level of your **C:** drive if your **PC** has several accounts). Use **Tools**, **Share Workbook** and then experiment with making changes to the data from two different acounts.

16 Pivot Tables

Introduction

This chapter shows you how to examine a set of data by extracting and grouping information with a **pivot table**. A pivot table summarises information from a data source (typically a worksheet) and allows you to rearrange your view of the information.

In this chapter you will

- **create a pivot table** showing information about the video shop's stock
- learn how to **change the function** used for the pivot table's data
- learn how to **add multiple fields** to a single area of a pivot table
- use **grouping** in the pivot table to provide information on subsets of the data, and learn how to **add subtotals** for these groups
- learn how to **refresh** a pivot table when the data on which it is based changes
- see how to '**drill down**' to discover the information behind any value in a pivot table
- use **AutoFormat** to change the appearance of a pivot table.

Pivot tables

A pivot table is an interactive grid that lets you investigate particular aspects of a large dataset. Once you understand pivot tables, you will find that they provide you with a very powerful tool for 'getting a handle' on large sets of data.

We'll be using the video shop's stock as the data behind our pivot table.

Open the **videoshop.xls** workbook and switch to the **Stock** worksheet.

Creating a pivot table

Syllabus Ref: AM4.4.1.1

Create a pivot table or a dynamic crosstab using defined field names.

The terms **pivot table** and **dynamic crosstab** mean the same. Modern versions of Excel use **pivot table**.

Select cell **A1** (or any other cell in the body of the data) and from the menu choose **Data**, **PivotTable and PivotChart Report**. The **PivotTable and PivotChart Wizard** appears.

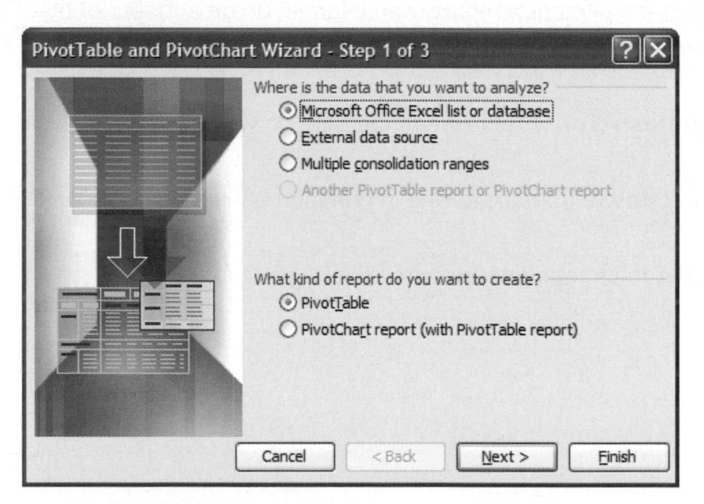

Figure 16.1: Creating a pivot table – Step 1 of 3

As you can see from Figure 16.1, you have a choice of data sources. We will be using the first option, since the source data is coming from the same worksheet. Choosing **External data source** instead allows you to import data, typically from another Excel spreadsheet or from an Access database.

You also have the option to create a **PivotChart report**, which is a chart based on a pivot table. You should experiment with this option, but it is not part of the ECDL Advanced Spreadsheets syllabus.

Make sure that the first option is selected in each group, as shown in Figure 16.1, then press **Next**.

The next step of the Wizard asks you to choose a range for the source data. It should automatically detect the correct range of **$A$1:$G$100**, as shown in Figure 16.2.

Figure 16.2: Creating a pivot table – Step 2 of 3

Press **Next** to go to the final step of the wizard.

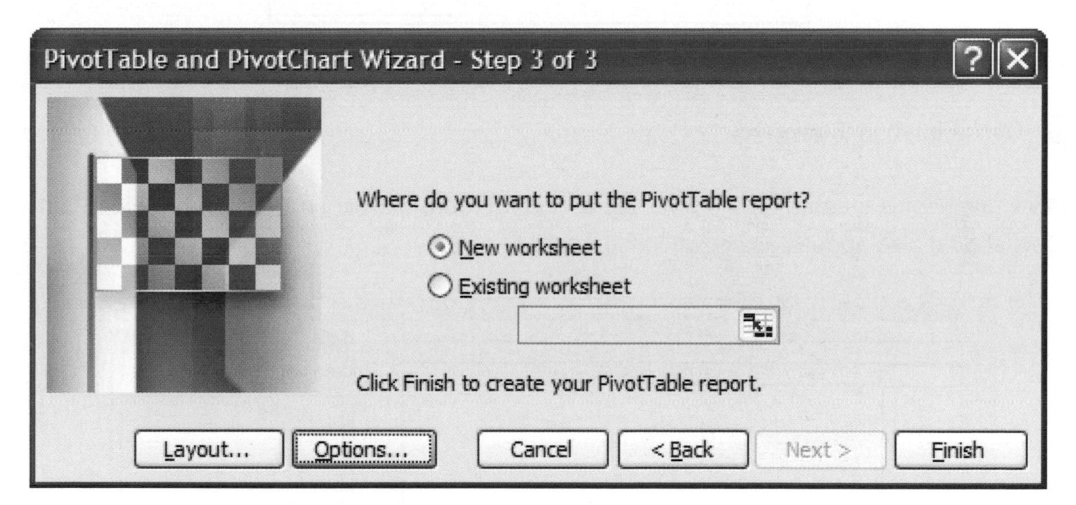

Figure 16.3: Creating a pivot table – Step 3 of 3

Press the **Options** button. The **PivotTable Options** dialogue appears. We won't be changing any of these options for this example, but you may find them useful in real workbooks that you create. Click **Cancel** to close the **PivotTable Options** dialogue without making any changes.

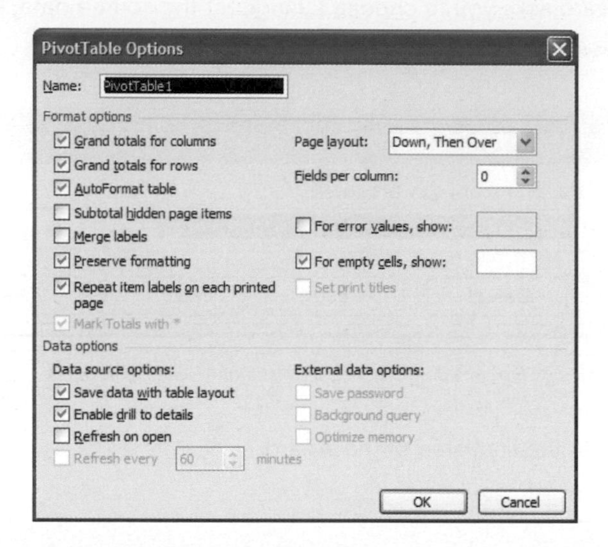

Figure 16.4: PivotTable Options dialogue

Click **Finish** in the wizard.

A new worksheet is created for the pivot table. A **PivotTable** toolbar and **PivotTable Field List** window should also appear, as shown in Figure 16.5.

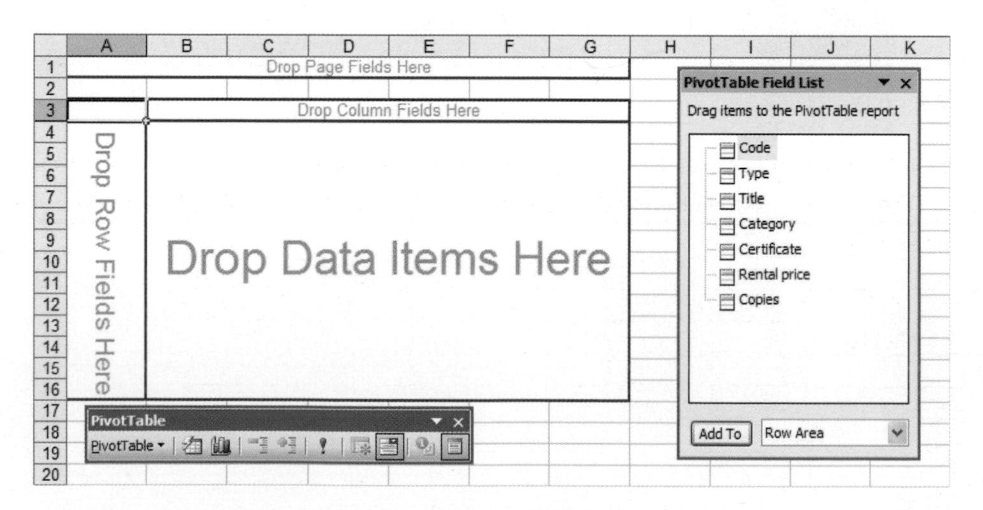

Figure 16.5: The blank pivot table

Now we need to choose which fields we want to compare. Suppose we want to know the distribution of rental prices among the different types of stock item.

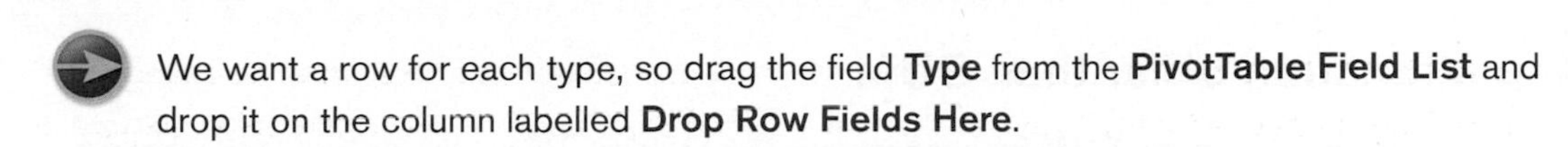

We want a row for each type, so drag the field **Type** from the **PivotTable Field List** and drop it on the column labelled **Drop Row Fields Here**.

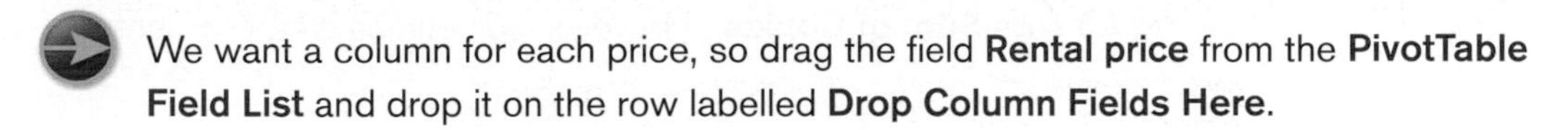

We want a column for each price, so drag the field **Rental price** from the **PivotTable Field List** and drop it on the row labelled **Drop Column Fields Here**.

We are interested in the number of copies, so drag the field **Copies** to the area labelled **Drop Data Items Here**.

Your pivot table should now look like Figure 16.6.

	A	B	C	D	E	F	G
1	Drop Page Fields Here						
2							
3	Sum of Copies	Rental price ▾					
4	Type ▾	£2.00	£3.00	£4.00	£5.00	Grand Total	
5	DVD		389	181		570	
6	Game				197	197	
7	Video	177	12			189	
8	Grand Total	177	401	181	197	956	
9							

Figure 16.6: First attempt at a pivot table

This tells us quite a lot about the video shop's pricing scheme for rentals. For example, all of the games are £5, and the only items that are £2 are videos.

Drag the field **Certificate** to the area labelled **Drop Page Fields Here**.

A drop-down list appears in cell **B1**. Click the arrow to its right and select **U**, and then press **OK**.

This restricts the pivot table so that it displays only those results where the **Certificate** field matches **U**. There are no games certified U, so this row disappears completely. Your pivot table should look like Figure 16.7.

	A	B	C	D	E	F
1	Certificate	U ▾				
2						
3	Sum of Copies	Rental price ▾				
4	Type ▾	£2.00	£3.00	£4.00	Grand Total	
5	DVD		61	11	72	
6	Video	53			53	
7	Grand Total	53	61	11	125	
8						

Figure 16.7: Adding page fields to a pivot table

Using a function other than SUM

Usually you will want to use the **SUM** function in your pivot tables. This is the default, and what we have used so far (notice that cell **A3** says **Sum of Copies**). However, sometimes it can be useful to pick a different function.

Let's find out the average rental price for each type of stock item.

Removing a pivot element

To remove an element of a pivot table, simply click it and drag it out of the table until your mouse pointer looks like the one shown in the margin. Drag **Certificate** out of cell **A1**, **Sum of Copies** out of cell **A3** and **Rental Price** out of cell **B3**. Now drag **Rental price** from the **PivotTable Field List** and drop it in the **Drop Data Items Here** area.

This gives a pivot table showing the sums of the rental prices. Let's change this to show the average rental prices instead.

Right-click cell **B5** and select **Field Settings** from the menu. The **PivotTable Field** dialogue box appears.

Change the **Summarize by** option from **Sum** to **Average**, as shown in Figure 16.8.

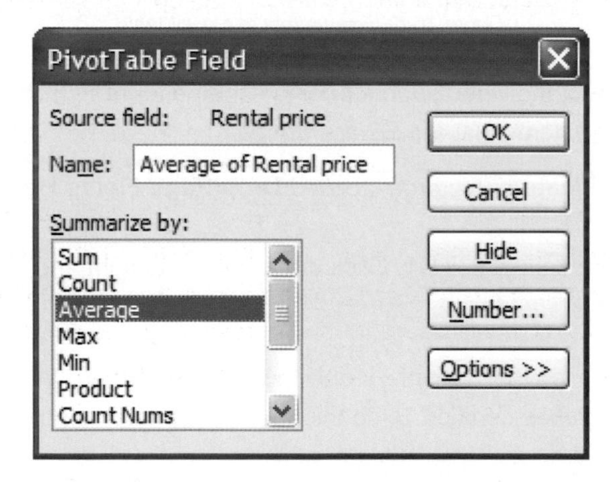

Figure 16.8: Changing the data in the pivot table from a Sum to an Average

Press **OK** to close the **PivotTable Field** dialogue box.

The pivot table now contains the average prices across the three types, as shown in Figure 16.9. So the average rental price is £3.31 for a DVD, £5.00 for a game and £2.05 for a video. The average price for any item is £3.48.

	A	B
1	Drop Page Fields Here	
2		
3	Average of Rental price	
4	Type	Total
5	DVD	3.314814815
6	Game	5
7	Video	2.05
8	Grand Total	3.484848485

Figure 16.9: Pivot table showing average rental prices for the three categories

Note!

This is the average rental price per title, regardless of how many copies of that title are available.

Multiple fields

You can have more than one field in each area of the pivot table. Let's go back to displaying the total number of copies by type and rental price, but this time split up the type into the various certificates.

Remove the **Average of Rental price** field by dragging it out of the **pivot table**. Add **Rental price** as the **Column Field** and **Copies** as the **Data Item**, as before.

Drag the **Certificate** field from the **PivotTable Field List** window and hover your mouse over the border between columns **A** and **B**, without releasing the button yet. Figure 16.10 shows the drag in progress. Notice the grey **I-bar**, which is highlighted in the figure. This shows where the new field will be inserted with respect to the fields that are already there. Make sure that the **I-bar** appears to the right of the **Type** row, rather than to its left, and then release the mouse button to drop the field.

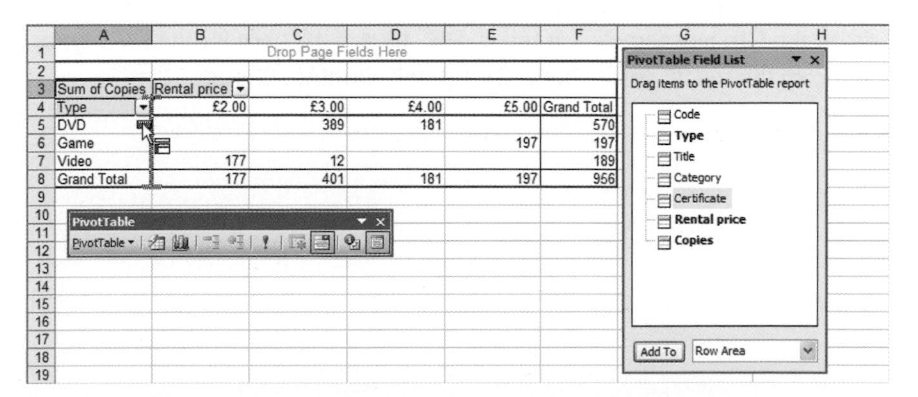

	A	B	C	D	E	F
1	Drop Page Fields Here					
2						
3	Sum of Copies	Rental price				
4	Type	£2.00	£3.00	£4.00	£5.00	Grand Total
5	DVD		389	181		570
6	Game				197	197
7	Video	177	12			189
8	Grand Total	177	401	181	197	956

Figure 16.10: Dragging the Certificate field as a second row field

The pivot table should change to look like Figure 16.11. If you still have the custom sort order set up for the certificate types then the order may be different, but this is not important.

	A	B	C	D	E	F	G
1	Drop Page Fields Here						
2							
3	Sum of Copies		Rental price				
4	Type	Certificate	£2.00	£3.00	£4.00	£5.00	Grand Total
5	DVD	12		63	51		114
6		15		77	59		136
7		18		63	35		98
8		U		61	11		72
9		PG		125	25		150
10	DVD Total			389	181		570
11	Game	12				56	56
12		15				52	52
13		18				33	33
14		PG				56	56
15	Game Total					197	197
16	Video	12	16				16
17		15	26				26
18		18	11				11
19		U	53				53
20		PG	71	12			83
21	Video Total		177	12			189
22	Grand Total		177	401	181	197	956

Figure 16.11: Pivot table showing rental prices by type, broken up by certificate

Grouping data

Suppose that what we are really interested in is the balance between the number of items for adults (18 certificate) and families (everything else). We can use grouping to find out the number of items in each of these two categories.

> **Syllabus Ref: AM4.4.1.3**
> Group/display data in a pivot table or a dynamic crosstab by a defined criterion.

Hold down the **Ctrl** key and click in the **U**, **PG**, **12** and **15** cells for the DVD type, to select them all. From the menu, select **Data**, **Group and Outline**, **Group**.

This creates a new column, as highlighted in Figure 16.12.

	A	B	C	D	E	F	G	H
1	Drop Page Fields Here							
2								
3	Sum of Copies			Rental price				
4	Type	Certificate2	Certificate	£2.00	£3.00	£4.00	£5.00	Grand Total
5	DVD	Group1	12		63	51		114
6			15		77	59		136
7			U		61	11		72
8			PG		125	25		150
9		18	18		63	35		98
10	DVD Total				389	181		570
11	Game	Group1	12				56	56
12			15				52	52
13			PG				56	56
14		18	18				33	33
15	Game Total						197	197
16	Video	Group1	12	16				16
17			15	26				26
18			U	53				53
19			PG	71	12			83
20		18	18	11				11
21	Video Total			177	12			189
22	Grand Total			177	401	181	197	956

Figure 16.12: Grouping cells in a pivot table

Select cell **B4** and enter the heading **Viewers**.

Select cell **B5** and enter the text **Family**. Notice how this also changes cells **B11** and **B16**.

Select cell **B9** and enter the text **Adult**. Again, this changes cells **B14** and **B20** to match.

Notice that a new field, called **Viewers**, has appeared in the **PivotTable Field List** window. This new field is treated in the same way as those that correspond directly with columns in our original set of data. In particular, we can create subtotals for this field.

Right-click cell **B4** and select **Field Settings** from the menu. The **PivotTable Field** dialogue appears. Change the **Subtotals** option from **None** to **Automatic**, as shown in Figure 16.13, and press **OK**.

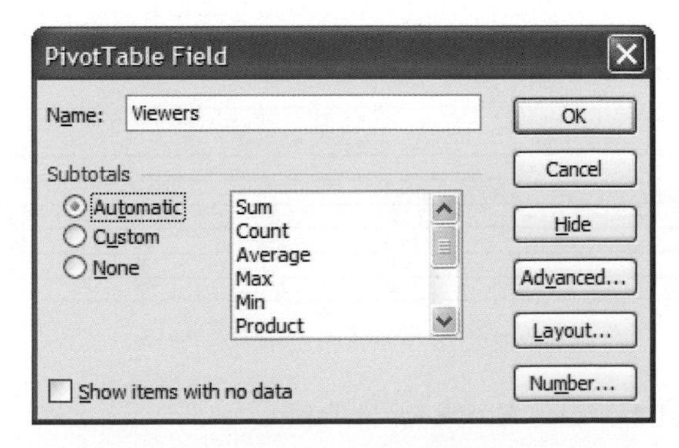

Figure 16.13: Adding a subtotal for the new group

A subtotal is added for each type of viewer – **Family** and **Adult** – as shown in Figure 16.14.

	A	B	C	D	E	F	G	H
1	Drop Page Fields Here							
2								
3	Sum of Copies			Rental price				
4	Type	Viewers	Certificate	£2.00	£3.00	£4.00	£5.00	Grand Total
5	DVD	Family	12		63	51		114
6			15		77	59		136
7			U		61	11		72
8			PG		125	25		150
9		Family Total			326	146		472
10		Adult	18		63	35		98
11		Adult Total			63	35		98
12	DVD Total				389	181		570
13	Game	Family	12				56	56
14			15				52	52
15			PG				56	56
16		Family Total					164	164
17		Adult	18				33	33
18		Adult Total					33	33
19	Game Total						197	197
20	Video	Family	12	16				16
21			15	26				26
22			U	53				53
23			PG	71	12			83
24		Family Total		166	12			178
25		Adult	18	11				11
26		Adult Total		11				11
27	Video Total			177	12			189
28	Grand Total			177	401	181	197	956

Figure 16.14: Pivot table with subtotals by viewer type

If we're only interested in the bigger picture, we can stop looking at the type-by-type (DVD, game and video) results and instead concentrate on the viewer types.

Drag the **Type** field from cell **A4** out of the pivot table.

Double-click cell **A5**. This collapses the **Family** group so that the elements that make it up (**12**, **15**, **U** and **PG**) are hidden.

Double-click cell **A6** to collapse the **Adult** group. Since there is only one **Certificate** type in **Adult**, collapsing the group just hides the subtotal.

This has created a higher-level overview, as shown in Figure 16.15. This makes it easy to compare the number of titles suitable for family viewing with those suitable only for adults. This will be useful information to have when looking at buying in more stock.

	A	B	C	D	E	F	G
1	Drop Page Fields Here						
2							
3	Sum of Copies		Rental price				
4	Viewers	Certificate	£2.00	£3.00	£4.00	£5.00	Grand Total
5	Family		166	338	146	164	814
6	Adult		11	63	35	33	142
7	Grand Total		177	401	181	197	956

Figure 16.15: Higher-level view of the data

Give this worksheet the name **Stock Pivot Table**.

Refreshing a pivot table

Syllabus Ref: AM4.4.1.2

Modify the data source and refresh the pivot table or dynamic crosstab.

Look at the **Grand Total** column: there are **814** family titles and **142** Adult titles. Let's see what happens to the pivot table if we recategorise one of the family titles as an adult one.

Switch back to the **Stock** worksheet and change the **Certificate** for the first entry (*The Bourne Identity* DVD) from **12** to **18**. This shifts it from the **Family** to the **Adult** viewer classification. Notice that there are **10** copies of this item in stock.

Change back to the **Stock Pivot Table** worksheet.

You should see that the **Grand Total** figures are unchanged. The pivot table has not automatically updated to reflect the change to its underlying data. We have to refresh it manually.

Press the **Refresh Data** button on the **PivotTable** toolbar (also available from the right-click menu). The **Grand Total** figures are updated: there are now **804** family items and **152** adult items. This reflects the **10** copies of *The Bourne Identity* that have moved classification.

Refresh Data

Drilling down

The DVD title we reclassified is now an **Adult** title that can be rented for **£4**. The pivot table tells us that there are only **45** items in total in this category. Let's find out what they are.

The term **drilling down** means examining data in stages from the most summarised form to the most detailed. In Excel, you can go from a summarised value in a pivot table and drill down to find the more detailed data on which the summarised value is based.

Double-click cell **E6**.

This creates a new datasheet containing the individual records that contribute to the drilled value (**45** in cell **E6**), as shown in Figure 16.16.

	A	B	C	D	E	F	G
1	Code	Type	Title	Category	Certificate	Rental price	Copies
2	1	DVD	Bourne Identity, The	Action	18	4	10
3	99	DVD	24 Hour Party People	Comedy	18	4	17
4	78	DVD	Kill Bill - Vol. 2	Action	18	4	10
5	34	DVD	Dawn Of The Dead	Horror	18	4	8

Figure 16.16: Drilling to details – a breakdown of the 45 DVDs that are classified 18 and can be rented for £4 each

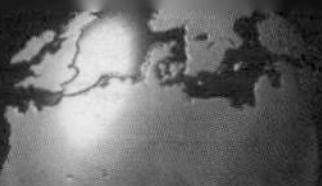

Delete the new worksheet that was created in the previous step. We don't need it any more.

Table AutoFormat

Finally, we'll apply one of Excel's colour schemes to the pivot table. You have already used this technique to format standard worksheet tables in Chapter 3.

Syllabus Ref: AM4.1.1.2 (2 of 2)

Apply automatic formatting to a cell range.

Make sure that the **Stock Pivot Table** worksheet is displayed. Click in any cell in the pivot table and, from the menu, select **Format**, **AutoFormat**. The **AutoFormat** dialogue is displayed.

Scroll down and select the **Table 8** style of **AutoFormat**, as shown in Figure 16.17. Press **OK**.

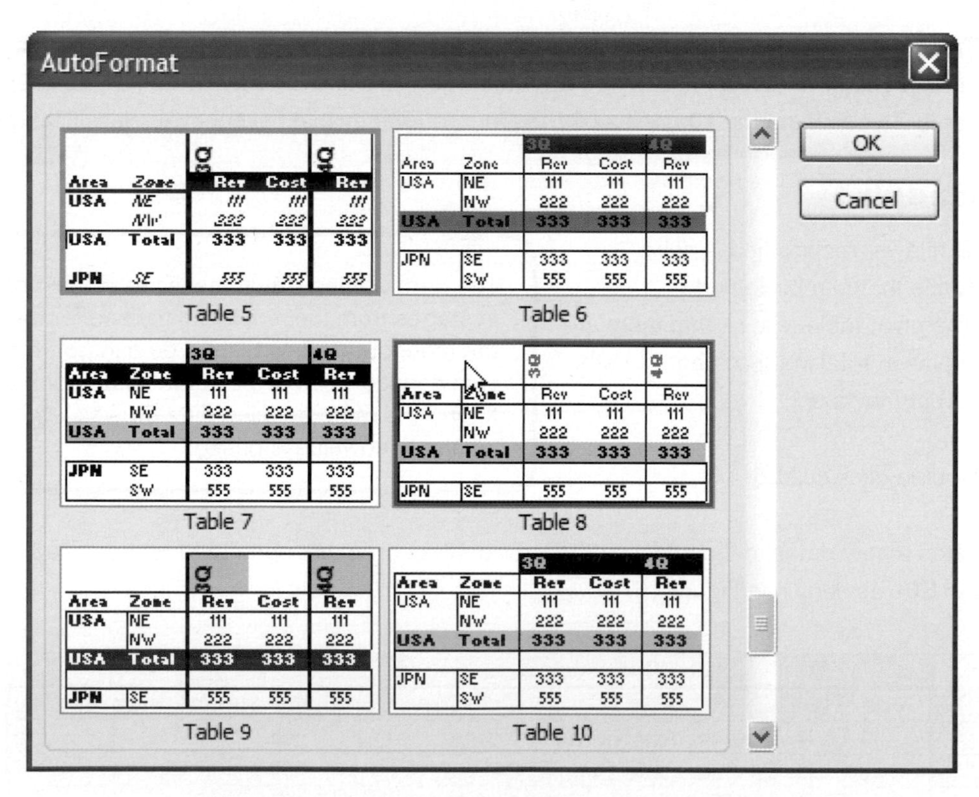

Figure 16.17: Setting the Table 8 AutoFormat for a pivot table

The reformatted pivot table looks like Figure 16.18.

	A	B	C	D	E	F	G	H
1								
2								
3	Copies		Rental price					
4	Viewers	Certificate	£2.00	£3.00	£4.00	£5.00	Grand Total	
5	Family		166	338	136	164	804	
6	Adult		11	63	45	33	152	
7	**Grand Total**		**177**	**401**	**181**	**197**	**956**	
8								
9								

Figure 16.18: Pivot table with the Table 8 AutoFormat applied

 Save the workbook.

Test yourself

1. Create a pivot table from the **Members** data, showing the total amount spent in each of the villages, as shown in Figure 16.19. Notice that you should also rename cell **E4** from **(blank)** to **Middlington**.

	A	B	C	D	E	F
1	Drop Page Fields Here					
2						
3	Sum of Total Spend	Village				
4		Blakely	Hamshaw	Pickerington	Middlington	Grand Total
5	Total	356.57	266.81	487.54	9073.13	10184.05

Figure 16.19: Pivot table showing total spend by village

2. Change the function used, so that the pivot table shows the maximum amount spent by a customer in each village instead of the total amount spent. The result should look like Figure 16.20.

	A	B	C	D	E	F
1	Drop Page Fields Here					
2						
3	Max of Total Spend	Village				
4		Blakely	Hamshaw	Pickerington	Middlington	Grand Total
5	Total	154.36	129.92	138.7	350.23	350.23

Figure 16.20: Pivot table showing the maximum spend by village

3. Add **Date Joined** as the **Row Field**. Group the dates by year and compress them so that your pivot table looks like Figure 16.21.

	A	B	C	D	E	F	G
1	Drop Page Fields Here						
2							
3	Max of Total Spend		Village				
4	Year Joined	Date Joined	Blakely	Hamshaw	Pickerington	Middlington	Grand Total
5	2000		154.36			267.76	267.76
6	2001		93.09	129.92	122.82	305.04	305.04
7	2002			39.83	18.5	226.21	226.21
8	2003			17.1	18.47	350.23	350.23
9	2004		11.9		138.7	330.31	330.31
10	Grand Total		154.36	129.92	138.7	350.23	350.23

Figure 16.21: Maximum spend by village, grouped by year of membership

4. **AutoFormat** the pivot table using the **Report 2** format. It should look like Figure 16.22.

	A	B	C	D
2				
3	Village	Year Joine	Date Joined	Max of Total Spend
4	**Blakely**			
5		2000		154.36
6		2001		93.09
7		2004		11.9
8	**Blakely Total**			**154.36**
9				
10	**Hamshaw**			
11		2001		129.92
12		2002		39.83
13		2003		17.1
14	**Hamshaw Total**			**129.92**
15				
16	**Pickerington**			
17		2001		122.82
18		2002		18.5
19		2003		18.47
20		2004		138.7
21	**Pickerington Total**			**138.7**
22				
23	**Middlington**			
24		2000		267.76
25		2001		305.04
26		2002		226.21
27		2003		350.23
28		2004		330.31
29	**Middlington Total**			**350.23**
30				
31	**Grand Total**			**350.23**

Figure 16.22: Pivot table formatted in the Report 2 style

5. How could you use your pivot table to get a list of all the members who joined from **Middlington** in **2001**? Try it.

17 Consolidating Your Knowledge

Introduction

This chapter pulls together the topics that you have already learnt, showing how you have fulfilled the criteria for some of the more general syllabus topics.

Effective communication

Syllabus Ref: AM4.1.2.1

Understand some important planning and design concepts when considering how to produce information that communicates effectively, by structuring the content to take account of different contexts and audience needs.

Spreadsheets are incredibly versatile. Sometimes they are used as simple databases, or for 'number crunching', in which case the formatting and presentation of the data might not be too important. However, you may also choose to use a spreadsheet to communicate a message, for example a trend in sales. As with any document, a spreadsheet will be able to communicate its message most effectively if some thought has been given to its structure and style in advance.

There are two fundamental things to think about when planning a spreadsheet: what is it for (the **context**) and how will people use it (the **audience needs**)?

Context

Every document is used in a context: it has a particular purpose, and it will affect and be affected by the environment in which it is used. This sounds rather philosophical, so let's look at some real-world examples.

- Suppose a small bookshop keeps records of its sales in an Access database, but exports them into Excel to hand over to their accountant. The spreadsheet that they produce needs to be easy to create (so probably won't have much formatting), and might need to have a particular structure (for example, if the accountant will need to import it into an accountancy software application).

- A company with offices in London and New York will have to take care about how they format date and currency values in the spreadsheets they produce, particularly if these spreadsheets will need to be shared.

- A hospital might have a very large workbook for recording details about the operations that have taken place. They might choose to dedicate the first worksheet to an overview that can be printed out and pinned to the staff notice board. In this case, care must be taken to ensure that this overview worksheet will fit on a single sheet of paper.

Audience Needs

It is crucial to think about whom the spreadsheet is for and how they will be using it. You cannot hope to communicate effectively in any medium unless you understand something of the other person's needs.

- What level of detail do they need? If they really only need an overview, consider using a graph (page 154) or a pivot table (page 211).

- Can you use formatting to make things easier to understand? For example, using a fixed number of decimal places can make columns of floating point numbers much easier to comprehend. Conditional formatting (page 38) might also be useful to highlight particular values.

- What can you do in advance to save the user time? Consider adding filtering (page 128), hyperlinks (page 198), subtotals (page 118), lookups (page 67) and macros (page 141) as appropriate.

Creating complex spreadsheets

Syllabus Ref: AM4.1.2.2

Understand how to produce spreadsheets that are technically complex in terms of content and analysis, as well as the understanding, skills and techniques needed to produce them.

Having worked through the exercises in this book, you have an armoury of skills for producing complex spreadsheets.

Complex content

- You can use filtering and sorting (page 128) and database functions (page 84) to manage very large worksheets.
- A knowledge of 3D functions (page 202) will allow you a greater freedom in how you structure your workbooks.
- You can use linking (page 184) to prepare complex calculations in Excel and then use them in Word and PowerPoint.
- The auditing tools (pages 24–28) allow you to create complex content with many dependencies, and still be able to understand how the cells are connected.

Complex analysis

Syllabus Ref: AM4.1.2.4

Understand what methods can be used to analyse complex data, such as to compare related totals or predict trends.

- Pivot tables (page 211) can extract summary information from large amounts of interconnected data.
- Financial functions (page 45) and scenarios (page 59) allow you to perform 'what-if' modelling..
- You can use charts and graphs (pages 154–183) to visualise your data, helping you to identify patterns and trends. You can add trend lines to graphs and use these to predict future values.
- You can use data linking (page 184) to group together totals that appear in other parts of a spreadsheet, or even in another spreadsheet file, so that they can easily be compared.
- When you have a complex equation with one or two input variables, you can use data tables page 63) to show the results across a range of input values.

Index of Syllabus Topics

AM4.1.1 Editing

AM4.1.2 Display

AM4.1.3 Protection

AM4.1.4 Security

AM4.2.1 Sorting

AM4.2.2 Querying/Filtering

AM4.2.3 Linking

AM4.2.4 Templates

AM4.2.5 Charts & Graphs

AM4.3.1 Using Functions

AM4.4.1 Pivot Tables/Dynamic Crosstabs

AM4.4.2 Scenarios/Versions

AM4.4.3 Auditing

AM4.5.1 Macros

Index